Assessing and Managing Risk

Assessing and Managing Risk

An ERM Perspective

Bruce K. Lyon and Georgi Popov

American Society of Safety Professionals, 520 N. Northwest Highway, Park Ridge, IL 60068
Copyright © 2021 by American Society of Safety Professionals
All rights reserved. Published 2021.

American Society of Safety Professionals, ASSP, and the ASSP shield are registered trademarks of the American Society of Safety Professionals.

Limits of Liability/Disclaimer of Warranty
While the publisher and authors have used their best efforts in preparing this book, they make no representations or warranties with respect to the accuracy or completeness of the contents of this book, and specifically disclaim any implied warranties of merchantability or fitness for a particular purpose. The information is provided with the understanding that the authors are not hereby engaged in rendering legal or other professional services. If legal advice or other professional assistance is required, the services of a qualified professional should be sought.

Managing Editor: Rick Blanchette, ASSP
Editor: Adept Content Solutions
Text design and composition: Adept Content Solutions
Cover design: Janet Chen, ASSP

Printed in the United States of America

29 28 27 26 25 24 23 22 21   1 2 3 4 5 6 7 8

ISBN-13: 978-0-939874-32-3 (hardcover)
ISBN-13: 978-939874-33-0 (e-book)

Library of Congress Cataloging-in-Publication Data

Names: Lyon, Bruce K., author. | Popov, Georgi (Engineer), author.
Title: Assessing and managing risk : an ERM perspective / Bruce K. Lyon and Georgi Popov.
Description: Park Ridge : American Society of Safety Professionals, 2021. | Includes index. | Summary: "Assessing and Managing Risk: An ERM Perspective provides risk professionals and students practical guidance in the fundamentals of Enterprise Risk Management (ERM) and methods for assessing, treating, and managing risk. The entire book was designed with the reader in mind, providing practical, usable information pertinent to the risk professional"-- Provided by publisher.
Identifiers: LCCN 2020046454 (print) | LCCN 2020046455 (ebook) | ISBN 9780939874323 (hardcover) | ISBN 9780939874330 (ebook)
Subjects: LCSH: Risk management. | Industrial management.
Classification: LCC HD61 .L965 2021 (print) | LCC HD61 (ebook) | DDC 658.15/5--dc23
LC record available at https://lccn.loc.gov/2020046454
LC ebook record available at https://lccn.loc.gov/2020046455

Contents

Preface		*vii*
Acknowledgments		*xi*
Chapter 1	**On the Concept of Risk**	1
Chapter 2	**Historical Perspective**	29
Chapter 3	**Managing Risk**	37
Chapter 4	**Planning the Risk Assessment**	59
Chapter 5	**Selecting Risk Assessment and Management Methods**	83
Chapter 6	**Managing Information and Decision Models**	101
Chapter 7	**Identifying Risk**	113
Chapter 8	**Analyzing Risk**	131
Chapter 9	**Evaluating Risk**	153
Chapter 10	**Treating Risk**	167
Chapter 11	**Monitoring and Reporting Risk**	193
Chapter 12	**Communicating Risk**	211
Chapter 13	**Practical Applications of Risk Management Methods**	221
Answers to Chapter Questions		*271*
Index		*295*

Preface

Organizations are becoming more focused on enterprise risk management (ERM) and risk-based decision making. "Traditional" risk management is often associated with entrenched silos. Safety professionals were very often separated from financial and strategic risk decisions and thought of as part of operations. Human resources typically managed the turnover rate, hiring, benefits, and absenteeism. Lean Six Sigma function managed productivity and quality. Accounting managed financial records, business transactions, cash flows, and accounts payable. All these functions or departments had their own management structure and very rarely worked in synergy. ERM integrates safety risks with operational, financial, and strategic risks, and it encourages an understanding of their relationships and synergistic effects.

This text presents guidance in the risk management process and techniques that can be used by risk and safety practitioners to help satisfy the need for managing enterprise risk. Lyon and Popov, as chair and vice chair of the U.S. Technical Advisory Group to ISO 31000 Risk Management standards, and chair and vice chair of the ASSP TR-31010-2020 Technical Report – *Risk Management: Techniques for Safety Practitioners,* have designed this text to blend current risk management applications within the risk management process. The text also incorporates the ANSI/ASSP Z590.3, *Prevention through Design,* standard and the ANSI/ASIS/RIMS RA.1 *Risk Assessment* standard into the concepts and uses numerous case studies and examples to illustrate their application.

This first edition of *Assessing and Managing Risk: An ERM Perspective* provides practical guidance on enterprise risk management tools and prevention through design (PtD) concepts, with practical applications, for undergraduates, graduate students, and risk professionals who recognize that they are expected to have enterprise risk management capabilities.

It serves as a guide for risk and occupational safety and health professionals who need practical guidance on the use of risk assessment and management techniques within the risk management process and satisfies the needs of university professors seeking to advance their students' knowledge and capabilities in enterprise risk management. The manual also addresses six of the ABET criteria for safety science programs.

This book includes interactive exercises, links, videos, supplemental risk assessment, and risk management techniques. The first 12 chapters are based on the elements found in the risk management process and incorporate practice examples and exercises. Chapter 13 pulls all of these elements together, using several case studies and the application of various methods that can be expected in real-life situations.

Chapter 1, On the Concept of Risk, begins with describing the risk pathway and its effect of uncertainty to the organization and its objectives. Enterprise risk is further described in its four different aspects: hazard risk, operational risk (both pure risk), financial risk, and strategic risk (speculative risk). The dynamic nature of risk is also introduced.

Chapter 2, Historical Perspective of Risk, provides a brief historical overview of the origins of risk and how it has developed in terms of managing risk.

Chapter 3, Managing Risk, describes the principles, framework, and process for managing risk as prescribed by ANSI/ASSP/ISO 31000. It also describes other important risk-based standards, their applications, and how they integrate and align with the ISO 31000 process.

Chapter 4, Planning the Risk Assessment, covers elements for establishing risk criteria to be used in the risk management process, as well as the context, scope, and purpose for risk-based decision-making and overall risk management.

Chapter 5, Selecting Risk Assessment and Management Methods, describes factors to consider when selecting, modifying, and combining methods based on the application, context, and information needed for decision-making.

Chapter 6, Managing Information and Decision Models, discusses methods for gathering, analyzing, and managing information and developing and testing decision models used in the risk management process.

Chapter 7, Identifying Risk, covers the first step in risk assessment and explains the elements that should be identified to further assess risk, including the risk drivers, exposures, controls, failure modes, causes or triggers, and potential range of consequences.

Chapter 8, Analyzing Risk, describes the process of analyzing identified hazards and estimating their risk levels. This is the heart of the risk assessment process and includes analysis of the identified risk sources, risk drivers, exposures, existing controls, failure modes, causes, and range of potential consequences.

Chapter 9, Evaluating Risk, discusses the final step of risk assessment where the estimated risk is compared to the established risk criteria to determine its acceptability or need for treatment.

Chapter 10, Treating Risk, covers the important step of selecting the proper risk treatments to reduce the risk to as low as reasonably practicable (ALARP). The hierarchy of risk treatment and the various risk treatment options are discussed.

Chapter 11, Monitoring and Reporting Risk, describes the importance of continually monitoring risk as it evolves and verifying the effectiveness of risk treatments. It further discusses the importance of documenting and reporting risk to decision makers throughout the risk management process.

Chapter 12, Communicating Risk, presents an overview of the need for communication and consultation throughout the risk management process and discusses elements of effective communication and consultation to consider.

Chapter 13, Practical Applications of Risk Management Methods, demonstrates how risk management principles and methods can be put into practice and contains a number of case studies with examples of practical applications of various methods. The chapter is broken up into sections according to the risk management process steps including: Section 1—Establishing Context; Section 2—Identifying Risk; Section 3—Analyzing Risk; Section 4—Evaluating Risk; Section 5—Treating Risk; Section 6—Monitoring and Reporting Risk; and Section 7—Communicating and Consulting.

This text is designed for the risk and safety practitioner to serve as a practical guide on the fundamentals of enterprise risk management. Assessing and managing both pure risk and strategic risk are critically important to an organization's ability to achieve their goals and objectives. Managing uncertainty and ultimately risk enables decision makers to have a level of confidence in their ability to make better decisions resulting in better outcomes. Organizations and risk professionals that recognize and implement the risk management principles, framework, and process presented in this manual will have greater opportunities for success.

Acknowledgments

We are extremely grateful to all who have assisted us during the writing of this book. It is extremely difficult to include by name all who have contributed to this endeavor in some way.

First, we wish to thank the amazing staff at ASSP that have helped support our efforts in working in the field of risk. Specifically we thank:

- Lauren Bauerschmidt and Ovidiu Munteanu for their outstanding work as the ASSP Secretariat to the U.S. Technical Advisory Group for the ISO 31000 standards and the ASSP TR-31010 Technical Report;
- Tim Fisher for his clear leadership and vision in the development of standards efforts at ASSP;
- Sue Trebswether, Tina Angley, and the *Professional Safety Journal* staff for their continual excellence in the finest safety journal available;
- and Rick Blanchette, who makes the otherwise difficult process of publishing a text seem easy and is truly amazing to work with.

Special thanks to our families and friends who endured our continuous hours working on the manuscripts and case studies. And finally, we thank Hays Companies, Dr. Leigh Ann Blunt, and the University of Central Missouri for supporting our efforts in this endeavor.

CHAPTER 1
On the Concept of Risk

Introduction

"Risk" is the effect of the unknown on an organization's objectives. For those that are charged with managing risk within an organization, the degree of uncertainty is of critical importance. Uncertainty, and its effects, can be detrimental and even debilitating to an organization's ability to achieve its objectives. Risk, and its effects, can paralyze an organization; prevent the achievement of objectives; or cause an organization to alter its course to avoid and reduce certain risks. For most organizations, decisions are based in part on the degree of risk associated with the decision. Without a clear understanding of the nature and degree of associated risks, it is difficult to make an "optimal" decision—one that takes into account the degree of risk within the context of an organization's acceptable risk levels, while pursuing stated objectives.

Risk is managed within an organization to achieve its objectives. This is the primary purpose of managing risk. If objectives are not met, the organization is at risk of losing market share and value, failing to compete, downsizing, or even going out of business. Uncertainty can be a significant obstacle to the achievement of certain objectives. To succeed and grow, organizations must be able to reduce uncertainty that impedes decision-making to be in a position to successfully achieve their business objectives. This requires sound risk management.

Interactive tools and supplemental materials are available at assp.org/ermtools.

Managing the "effects of uncertainty on objectives," defined as "risk" by ANSI/ASSP/ISO 31000-2018 (ISO 31000) as covered in this manual, requires a structured and coordinated process. This process encompasses (1) communication and consultation, (2) context, (3) risk identification, (4) risk analysis, (5) risk evaluation, (6) risk treatment, (7) monitoring and review, and (8) recording and reporting. These process elements must be integrated into the organization's management system and must be fully engaged to be effective.

This manual is intended to provide instructive guidance to risk management professionals in selecting, customizing, and applying fundamental techniques and concepts for managing risk. It is organized according to the ISO 31000 risk management process and contains risk assessment and management techniques as well as practical examples for each element of the risk management process. The manual's 13 chapters are represented in Figure 1.1.

Figure 1.1
Book Chapters.

The Concept of Risk

Risks are derived from "risk sources" that exists or are created in an activity being conducted, associated hazards, energies, or conditions. A risk source is an "element that alone or in combination has the potential to give rise to risk" (ANSI/ASSP Z690.1-2011). Risk sources can be influenced by factors or conditions that elevate its potential called "risk drivers." For a risk source to have an impact, it must have an exposure—people, property, intellectual property, financial holdings, market share, reputation, or other things of value. When the risk source and its drivers become exposed to these things of value, a triggering event can lead to an incident or event which results in a consequence or multiple consequences. This is known as a risk pathway and is illustrated in Figure 1.2.

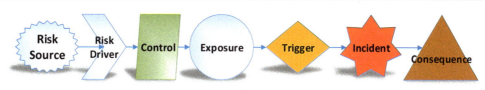

Figure 1.2
Risk Pathway.

Risks can be categorized into two types: pure risk and speculative risk. Pure risks (sometimes called absolute risks) are those risks that when taken can only result in negative outcomes (R-) such as losses from hazards and operations. Pure risks are typically insurable and are the primary focus of safety professionals and risk managers charged with assessing, reducing, and managing risk to a level that is considered acceptable to the organization. Speculative risks (sometimes referred to as opportunity risks) on the other hand are risks that are taken to achieve a gain or reward and can have a positive and/or negative outcome (R+/-). Speculative risks are generally not insurable. For speculative risk, it is necessary to take on a degree of risk that affords a higher potential return or opportunity while balancing the potential risk for loss. C-suite executives and business leaders are generally responsible for making these decisions, which involves risk-based input from stakeholders, resulting in risk-based decision-making or "risk management in practice."

> **Example:** An organization that manufacturers a product decides to expand its operations to include the transportation and distribution of their products to gain more control over on-time delivery, increase customer satisfaction, and increase market share—the opportunity. As a result, the pure risk side of the decision introduces risks from over-the-road trucking incidents resulting in driver fatalities and injuries, workers compensation and liability claims costs, and vehicle maintenance and damage costs.

Organizations must balance both the negative (pure) risks as well as the opportunities and positive (speculative) risks as they pursue their business objectives. This process is referred to as enterprise risk management (ERM). Enterprise risk management is a strategic business discipline that supports the achievement of an organization's objectives by addressing the full spectrum of its risks and managing the combined impacts of those risks as an interrelated risk portfolio (RIMS 2011). Organizations seek to manage risk exposures across all parts of their businesses so that, at any given time, they incur just enough of the right kinds of risk—no more, no less—to effectively pursue strategic goals (COSO 2012). Risk professionals are trained to look at operational and hazard risks associated with operational activities that produce negative consequences, as well as strategic and financial risks facing an organization.

The sources of risk exist within all things, conditions, and actions. There is a degree of inherent risk that comes with various activities, environments, conditions, and ventures. When managing risk, it is important to recognize the sources from which risks are derived.

ISO 31000 defines risk as the "effect of uncertainty on objectives" (ANSI/ASSP/ISO 31000-2018). Risk's effect of uncertainty, however, has different risk sources. The American Institute for Chartered Property Casualty Underwriters, known as The Institutes, defines and categorizes these risk sources in four groups or "risk quadrants" (The Institutes 2017). The risk quadrants are known as (1) operational risk, (2) hazard risk, (3) financial risk, and (4) strategic risk.

Operational risks and hazard risks are considered "pure" or absolute risks which are those that can only result in loss or negative outcomes. Financial and strategic risks represent "speculative" risks which have the possibility of a positive outcome, negative outcome, or both. Figure 1.3 represents the four quadrants of risk.

In The Institutes' course materials for the Associate in Risk Management (ARM) certification, a risk management designation program (Elliott 2017), the "quadrants of risk" are described as follows:

- Hazard Risk—Risks that are derived from property, liability, or personnel loss exposures and are generally insurable.
- Operational Risk—Risks that are derived from people or a failure in processes, systems, or controls including information technology (IT) related exposures. Both hazard and operational risks are closely aligned and interrelated and are often managed as such.
- Financial Risk—Risks derived from the effect of market forces or financial assets or liabilities and include market risk, credit risk, liquidity risk, and price risk.

Figure 1.3
The Quadrants of Risk.

- Strategic Risk—Risks derived from trends in the economy and society, including changes in economic, political, and competitive environments, as well as from demographic shifts.

Of course, risk sources have the potential of creating more than one category of risk and can occupy more than one quadrant of risk. These risk sources can affect other quadrants of risks within an organization known as a "cascading effect" (Lyon, Popov 2017). An illustration of the cascading effect of risk is presented in Figure 1.4.

> **Example:** In the cascading example illustrated in Figure 1.4, a product release of a refrigerate gas initially effects the operational aspect of the organization as a loss of product and temporary business interruption risk—an "operational risk." However, if the product is hazardous, such as ammonia, the operational risk turns into a safety, health, and environmental risk or "hazard risk" to local workers and nearby communities. And depending upon the scale and severity of the operational and hazard risks, the event may lead to significant financial loss—a financial risk—and possibly damage the organization's reputation—a "strategic risk."

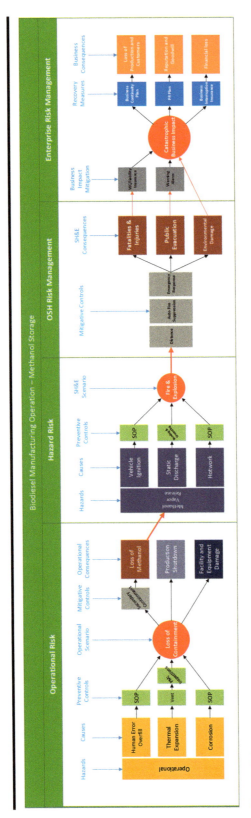

Figure 1.4
Cascading Effect of Risk.

It is recognized that organizations define types of risk differently and that each organization must define their risk categories to align with their objectives and processes. For the purpose of this manual, the authors refer to "operational risks" to include operational-related exposures and hazard risks—or insurable risks.

The Dynamic Nature of Risk

Risk is dynamic and continuously changing with conditions, risk drivers, risk treatments, and other variables. Risk should be viewed as a continuum that requires continuous monitoring and management. Its dynamic nature begins with new conditions and developments that cause new risks to emerge. As emerging risks are detected and recognized, they are monitored for their potential to become a concern for the organization. As conditions, risk drivers, and other variables occur, emerging risks become an inherent risk, leading to risk assessment, treatment, and management. This continuous and dynamic process of risk is expressed in Figure 1.5 as the Risk Continuum.

A continuum is defined as a coherent whole characterized as a collection, sequence, or progression of values or elements varying by minute degrees (Merriam-Webster n.d.)

> **Example:** An example of a continuum might be the state of water within a range of temperatures from freezing to boiling. When below 32-degrees Fahrenheit water becomes frozen—a solid. At room temperature water is a liquid. When temperature and atmospheric pressure cause the water to boil, it becomes a gas.

Within the context of the risk management process, risk is considered dynamic—ever changing—and can be viewed as a continuum. Therefore, the management of risk must extend beyond the initial or current risks, and include unknown and emerging risks, new or developing risks, previously treated risks, residual risks, secondary risks created by risk treatments, and future risk levels as shown in Figures 1.5 and 1.6.

Emerging Risk

Emerging risks can be characterized as new, developing risks that have been anticipated, detected, and apparent, and/or existing risks that are changing and increasing in new or unfamiliar conditions. These emerging risks present effects of uncertainty on objectives due to new threats, hazards, changes in frequency of occurrence, or changes in consequences or their severity or, in the case of speculative risks, new opportunities and potential gains. These can develop as a result of new

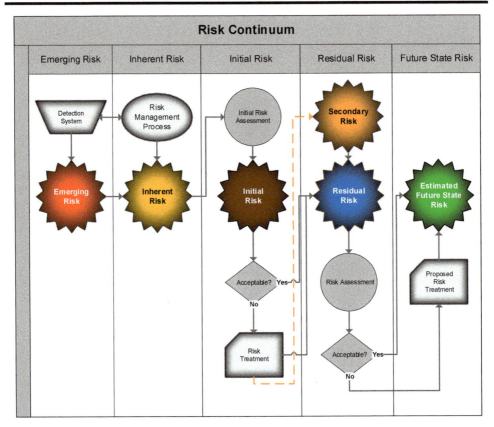

Figure 1.5
The Risk Continuum.

processes, technologies, or types of work. They may also develop from changes in the organization, or from social, public, or political changes.

Emerging risks can come from recognized risks that previously were not considered a threat (pure risks) or an opportunity (speculative risks), that have emerged to become a potential threat to an organization's objectives. Therefore, an organization should have methods and procedures for scanning, early detection, and analysis of emerging risks as part of the risk management process.

Inherent Risk

With acquisitions, new ventures, projects, existing systems or activity, there are inherent risks that are associated with or part of the system whether known or unknown. These inherent risks are derived from risk sources that are embedded in the system, external risk drivers, and potential exposures to the risk sources. Inherent risk is defined "as the risk to an entity apart from any action to alter either

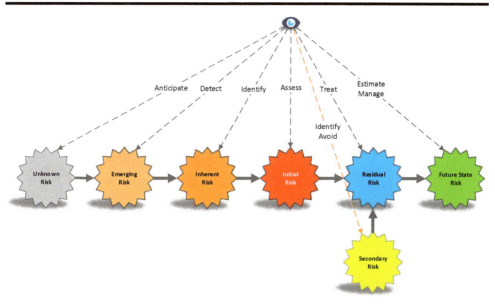

Figure 1.6
The Development of Risk from the Risk Observer's View.

the likelihood or impact of the risk" (The Institutes 2017). Inherent risk can be described as the risk that resides and is already existing in the system before any risk management is applied.

Initial Risk

Initial risk, sometimes referred to as current risk or current state risk, is the risk level determined by the initial risk assessment. It is defined by the military standard, MIL-STD-882E, as "the first assessment of the potential risk of an identified hazard. Initial risk establishes a fixed baseline for the hazard" (MIL-STD-882E 2012). It is in fact a "baseline" risk level measured for the first time by a risk assessment. Initial risk refers to the present risk level estimated from a risk assessment that takes into consideration any existing controls and their effects.

Residual Risk

It is not possible to totally eliminate risk. There will always be some level of remaining risk, even after treatment. "Residual risk" (remaining risk) is the degree of risk that remains after applying the risk treatment recommended from the risk assessment. Residual risk can also include risks that are unidentified, knowingly retained, shared, or transferred. The following definitions from risk-based consensus standards provide an understanding of residual risk's meaning:

- "the risk remaining after risk reduction measures have been taken" (ANSI/ASSP Z590.3-2011, R2016);
- "risk remaining after risk treatment." Note 1: Residual risk can contain unidentified risk. Note 2: Residual risk can also be known as "retained risk." (ANSI/ASSP Z690.1-2011/ISO Guide 73);
- "risk retention includes the acceptance of residual risks" (ANSI/ASSP Z690.1-2011/ISO Guide 73);
- "risk remaining after protective measures have been taken" (ANSI B11.TR3-2000);
- "the risk remaining after risk reduction measures (protective measures) are taken" (ANSI B11.0-2015);
- "remaining risk after risk treatment" Note: Residual risk may include risk retained by informed decision, untreatable risk, and/or unidentified risks. (ANSI/ASIS/RIMS RA.1- 2015).

The concept of residual risk is critical in managing risks both internally and externally. Risk, and its management, are dynamic and continue beyond the initial risk treatment, similar to the "plan-do-check-act" (PDCA) continual improvement process. Risk will always be present in some form and degree and requires risk management throughout its life cycle.

As inherent risks are assessed, initial risk levels from identified risks are estimated in the risk analysis. Following the analysis, a risk evaluation is performed using the established risk criteria to determine whether the initial risk levels estimated from the risk analysis are acceptable or if the initial risk requires treatment or reduction leading to residual risk.

Risk Treatment

Risk treatment strategies and their estimated risk reduction factors are considered in the treatment of risk. The selected risk reduction factors are calculated to determine "future state risk level" or the projected residual risk level. Estimating the level of risk before and after treatment allows a risk reduction percentage to be determined. This risk reduction percentage (RR%) provides the basis for determining which risk treatment option provides the most effective means of risk reduction to achieve an acceptable level. Prioritization of risk treatment should be based on an organization's risk tolerance and estimated residual risk levels. Such resources should be devoted to risks that pose the greatest concern or have the highest criticality.

Selected risk treatment efforts, for various reasons, may not always produce the expected risk reductions as indicated by ISO 31000. Therefore, it is important that implemented risk treatments and their resulting residual risks be monitored, verified, and reviewed to determine their effectiveness. These efforts will also serve to direct future risk management efforts.

Risk treatments can introduce unintended consequences that create new risks, increase existing risks, or reduce effectiveness of other controls. This potential effect must be considered in the selection of risk treatments and monitored after implementation. The residual risk must be estimated and evaluated through follow-up risk assessments. Decision makers and stakeholders should understand the nature and extent of the residual risk after risk treatment. The residual risk should be documented and subjected to monitoring, review and, where appropriate, further treatment (ANSI/ASSP/ISO 31000-2018).

Secondary Risk

As previously mentioned, some risk treatments can cause unintended or unexpected new risks. The potential for creating unwanted side effects must be considered when selecting risk treatments and included in the monitoring and reviewing process to detect and correct any additional risks created.

A secondary risk can be described as a risk that arises as the result of implementing a risk treatment or control measure. For example, if the risk treatment were not implemented, the secondary risk would not exist. Potential secondary risks should be assessed when considering the various risk treatment strategies and options. Unwanted consequences from risk treatments such as effects on existing controls, effects on existing risks, or creation of new risks should be considered, anticipated, and identified during the design of risk treatment and following implementation to verify performance. In cases where the severity of a secondary risk(s) is significant, it may be determined that the risk treatment be substituted with a better alternative.

Future State Risk

The future state risk is the projected risk level with proposed risk treatments implemented. Future state risk level is a projected or future residual risk level based on the application of prescribed risk controls. Future state risk is typically used to show a risk reduction percentage (RR%) of the proposed controls and their future state risk level in comparison to the current state or initial risk level. The RR% calculation is made using the formula:

$$RR\% = \frac{(Initial\ Risk\ Level - Future\ State\ Risk\ Level)}{Initial\ Risk\ Level}$$

The actual risk level that will be achieved will be estimated after the added risk treatments are in place and evaluated for their effectiveness.

Interdependencies and Synergistic Effects

The concept of enterprise risk management (ERM) is based on an integrated and holistic risk management approach addressing risk interdependencies and synergistic effects. As previously mentioned, risks are interdependent, meaning that they affect or are affected by other risks within an organization. Key interdependencies are shared among the four risk quadrants and their sub-risk categories. Individual risks can be amplified or reduced by other existing factors or conditions.

Synergistic and additive effects of risk exposures can pose greater risks than the sum of individual hazards and risks. For example, regulatory fines related to occupational safety and health (OSH) risks may be considered acceptable from a monetary perspective, but the negative publicly from reported citations may not be acceptable from an ERM perspective due to the additional strategic risk of reputational damage. Synergistic and/or additive risks may be misunderstood or underestimated by an organization. Understanding and managing risk interactions requires breaking down the managerial silos common within organizations and communicating the potential whole-risk effects of an event (COSO 2012).

Poorly managed hazard risks and their results can lead to the temporary shutdown of operations. Incidents that cause injuries and damage will also cause downtime and loss from incident investigations, repairs of any damaged equipment, financial loss from lost product or materials, failure to fulfil orders, and ultimately increases in insurance premiums.

Organizations use different systems and methodologies to manage various types of risk. For instance, the occupational safety and health (OSH) function may utilize risk assessment and risk management methodologies that are not familiar to business managers, while OSH managers may not be fully familiar with business risk assessment and risk management practices and tools. A fully integrated approach to managing risk is required.

Integration

Enterprise risk management (ERM) requires an integrated approach within an organization. Many larger companies have a chief risk officer (CRO) who's duties are aligned primarily to financial or internal audit functions. In some cases, the risk management function is not as closely aligned with operational and hazard risk domains. Truly integrated risk management organizations align their approach to manage operational risks, financial risks, hazard risks, and strategic risks as they relate to their organizational objectives.

ERM requires the integration of risk management strategies, as not all risks are measured equally. Under the familiar silo approach to risk identification, assessment, and management, OSH functions are frequently limited to compliance rather than effective implementation truly affecting worker and community health, environmental quality, or personnel safety. Any opportunity to align OSH projects with business objectives are often ignored or overlooked.

Organizations must have an iterative method of managing their operations and business to achieve their objectives. This method of managing is referred to as a management system. As defined by the ANSI/ASSP/ISO 45001-2018, *Occupational Health and Safety Management Systems—Requirements with Guidance for Use* standard, a management system is a set of interrelated or interacting elements of an organization designed to establish policies and objectives and processes to achieve those objectives. The scope of a management system may be narrowly focused on a single discipline, or may it include the whole of the organization and include the organization's structure, roles and responsibilities, and planning and operation (ANSI/ASSP/ISO 45001-2018). In essence, a management system represents an organization's principles, framework, and processes for conducting business—a "framework for managing."

Standards such as ISO 31000 are designed to be integrated into and contribute to an organization's existing management system. In the introduction, ISO 31000 states that "managing risk is part of governance and leadership and is fundamental to how the organization is managed at all levels. It contributes to the improvement of management systems." (ANSI/ASSP/ISO 31000-2018). Also noted among the standard's eight principles is the acknowledgement that total integration of risk management across the entire organization is crucial to success, placing an emphasis on integrating risk management into all organizational activities, processes, and decision-making.

It is important for those responsible for risk management activities to understand that every individual within the organization is managing risks, to some degree, on a daily basis. Therefore, risk management should be integrated into every aspect of the organization's management system to drive continuous improvements.

The management system model is built upon a plan-do-check-act (PDCA) template of continual improvement as shown in Figure 1.7. Originally developed by Walter Shewhart in the 1930s, and later made popular by W. Edwards Deming, the PDCA model is an iterative, systematic approach that enables an organization to control and continually improve a system, process, or product. The PDCA model, which is an endless cycle, provides a simple and effective four-step process for problem solving and managing change by testing and refining ideas before fully implementing them (Best and Neuhauser 2006).

14 | Assessing and Managing Risk: An ERM Perspective

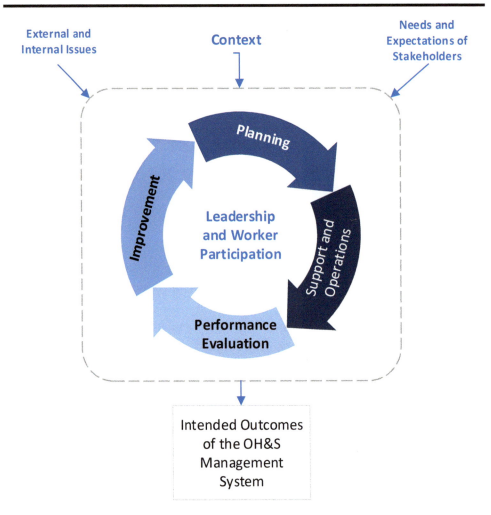

Figure 1.7
Safety Management System Plan-Do-Check-Act Model, Adapted from ANSI/ASSP/ISO 45001-2018.

Occupational Health and Safety Management Systems

Among the various standards and guidelines for occupational health and safety management systems available, there are two specific consensus standards of importance regarding risk management—ANSI/ASSP Z10.0-2019 (Z10) and ANSI/ASSP/ISO 45001-2018 (ISO 45001). Z10.0 was first established in 2005, revised in 2012 and 2017, and revised again in 2019, while ISO 45001 was established in 2018. A key component in both standards is the requirement that a risk assessment process be established. Both standards provide a structured, systematic approach that enables an organization to control its OSH risks and continually improve performance.

Z10.0 defines an occupational health and safety management system as "a set of interdependent elements that establish and/or support processes of the occupational health and safety (OHS) policy and objectives as well as mechanisms to achieve those objectives and continually improve OHS" (ANSI/ASSP Z10.0-2019). ISO 45001's definition of a OHSMS, which is similar to Z10.0, says a management system is a "set of interrelated or interacting elements of an organization to establish policies and objectives and processes to achieve those objectives" and that an OHSMS is a "management system or part of a management system used to achieve the OH&S policy" (ANSI/ASSP/ISO 45001-2018). Both standards direct organizations to manage their occupational safety and health risks and operational risks as they do other elements in their business to achieve their objectives.

The Z10.0 standard contains key requirements for managing risk through "risk assessment," the "use of hierarchy of controls," "designing in safety," "procurement," and "management of change." It includes sections 6.2, Assessment and Prioritization; 8.3, Risk Assessment; 8.4, Hierarchy of Controls; 8.5, Design Review and Management of Change; 8.6, Procurement; 8.7 Contractors; 8.9 Emergency Preparedness; and Appendix E8.3, Risk Assessment. ISO 45001 contains similar requirements for risk management in sections 6.1.2, Hazard identification and risk assessment of risks and opportunities; 8.1.2, Eliminating hazards and reducing OH&S risks; 8.1.3, Management of change; 8.1.4, Procurement; and 8.2, Emergency preparedness and response.

It should be recognized that there is an important distinction in how risk is viewed and defined by these OHSMS standards and by ISO 31000. Management system standards such as Z10.0 and ISO 45001 view risk (OH&S risk) and opportunity (OH&S opportunity) as two separate things and assume that risk can only produce negative outcomes or losses. ISO 45001 defines risk as the "effect of uncertainty" (ANSI/ASSP/ISO 45001-2018) while ISO 31000 defines risk as the "effect of uncertainty *on objectives*" (ANSI/ASSP/ISO 31000-2018). The primary difference is that ISO 31000 takes an ERM approach, recognizing that risks can create outcomes that can be negative, positive, or both.

Risk-Based Decision-Making

Risk-based decision making (RBDM) is a process that organizes information about possible unwanted outcomes into an orderly structure that helps facilitate decision-making and more informed management choices (Macesker et al. 2001). RBDM is in essence the practice of risk management in the decision-making process. It provides a consistent, systematic, structured means of making informed decisions using risk-related information in a timely fashion. Its purpose is to reduce the uncertainty of the effects and outcomes of the selected decision.

The model for making risk-based decisions can and should be applied to any important decision, especially those where uncertainty exists within an organization. RBDM takes into consideration several key questions about risk relating to the decision to be made which are: (1) what can go wrong; (2) how severe is the potential outcome; (3) how likely is it to occur; (4) is the risk acceptable or unacceptable; and (5) does the risk require reduction.

For further reading on RBDM, the US Coast Guard's "Risk-Based Decision-Making Guidelines" (US Coast Guard 2005), and ABS Consulting's book *Principles of Risk-Based Decision Making* (ABS Consulting 2001) should be considered.

The process steps, shown in Figure 1.8, are a structured sequence of risk management actions that identify and acquire information that is needed for making a specific decision. From beginning to end, the process requires effective, timely, and accurate communication among decision makers and stakeholders.

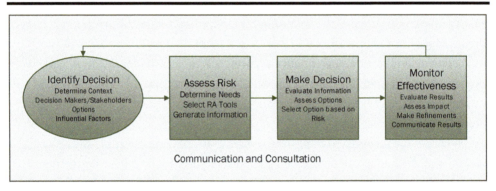

Figure 1.8
Risk-based Decision-Making Model Process.

The steps are described in the following:

1. *Identify the Decision Perimeters*—The context for a selected decision is first determined and defined. This will include the subject matter, stakeholders involved, potential options or choices to the decision makers, the uncertainty surrounding the decision, and any influential factors that need to be considered.
2. *Assess Risk*—The information needed to reduce uncertainty and make the decision is determined. Specific data and information needed is identified. A review of available risk assessment tools is made, and the tools that will acquire needed information are selected. A number of risk assessment techniques are available from various sources including ISO 31010, *Risk Assessment Techniques,*

ANSI/ASSP Z590.3, *Prevention through Design,* this manual, and other risk assessment textbooks. The selected risk assessment methods are performed by competent risk assessors, which generate the risk-based information.

3. *Make Decision*—The risk-based information is evaluated in the context of the decision to be made. Available options are assessed as to their risk-reduction potential and other benefits as well as the costs. Use of the hierarchy of controls and the "as low as reasonably practicable" (ALARP) principle are applied to the selection process. The option with the lowest risk level, greatest benefit, and lowest cost is selected and implemented.
4. *Monitor Effectiveness*—Monitoring of the decision's implementation and effects is performed and recorded. An impact analysis such as a Business Impact Analysis or other method can be used to determine and document the decision's impact. The results of the decision and impact analysis are compared to the expected outcomes to determine if the decision was successful or if adjustments are needed. Throughout the decision-making and implementation process, it is important that adequate input and feedback from stakeholders is acquired. Communication of the results and actions taken should be also provided to stakeholders.

The concept of risk-based decision-making should be integrated into an organization's risk management process. Its tenets are interwoven throughout this manual as a means of more effectively communicating and incorporating risk-based information into decision-making.

Understanding Uncertainty

In the context of risk, uncertainty is a state of not knowing or understanding completely a situation. It is a full or partial deficiency of information or understanding related to an event, its consequences, or likelihood. Uncertainty can develop from several different aspects including:

1. epistemic uncertainty—a condition where there is a lack of relevant knowledge of the system;
2. aleatoric uncertainty—a condition where a random, unpredictable nature exists surrounding the system;
3. linguistic uncertainty—a vagueness or ambiguity inherent in spoken languages; and
4. decision uncertainty—uncertainty associated with value systems, professional judgement, company values, and societal norms (ANSI/ASSP/ISO 31010-2019).

The relationship between risk, the types of uncertainty, and the objective is shown in Figure 1.9.

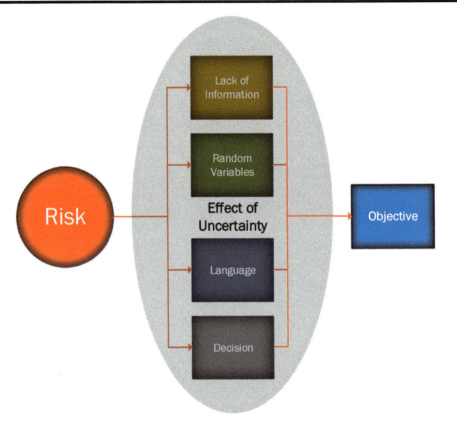

Figure 1.9
Relationship between Risk, Uncertainty, and Objective.

Uncertainty has an effect on the perspective and quality of information used in making decisions and influences the behavior of the decision makers. The level or degree of uncertainty can be difficult to measure and communicate within an organization, especially if key risk indicators are not identified. Therefore, some organizations have little or no knowledge of the degree of certainty (or uncertainty) in the risks associated with their operations.

The "Knowable" Unknowns

For the risk professional, the lack of sufficient knowledge and understanding about something or some situation is the primary reason for assessing the risk. The knowable unknowns or epistemic uncertainty result from incomplete or insufficient understanding of the hazards and risks and potential risk scenarios where the most likely outcome is unknown (Spiegelhalter and Riesch 2011). Risk assessment is used to acquire risk-based information and increased knowledge of the situation or system.

To increase the level of certainty, information that leads to knowledge and understanding of the system in respect to the quantities, qualities, inputs and outputs, and potential limits and extremes must be gathered and studied. Information about the likelihood or statistical probabilities of events, types of consequences that can result, the magnitude and severity of a consequence, and the exposed populations, property, or environment must all be considered. When there are vital pieces of information missing in these areas, suspected inaccuracies, lack of precision in measurements, and insufficient historical data for calculating probabilities, uncertainty increases. By acquiring these data, uncertainty can be reduced, though not eliminated. Epistemic uncertainty, the knowable unknowns, can be reduced through a thorough risk analysis and assessment of the system.

The "Unknowable" Unknowns

Uncertainty that comes from an unpredictable process such as flipping a coin and predicting either heads or tails is known as aleatory uncertainty. It results from random variables that cannot be predicted with any certainty and is literally unknowable. Unlike epistemic uncertainty, aleatoric uncertainty cannot be reduced, only identified and somewhat quantified. Where uncertainty is intrinsic to the nature of the risk, it may not be possible to reduce risk by further study; however, it can be represented by a statistical range of possible values (Gluckman and Bardsley 2016) such as the following examples:

- Volcanic eruptions—inherently random with multiple influencing factors, making prediction of future eruptions subject to statistical uncertainty.
- Earthquakes—while measurement of the strain in the rock is possible, the irregular movement of tectonic plates makes it impossible to accurately predict an earthquake, only forecast of general probabilities.
- Human sensitivities and reactions—sensitivities and effects of different levels of exposure to a chemical or a medicine can be estimated based on average responses within a population; however, individual variations (outliers who are very sensitive to lower exposures, or insensitive to higher ones) make it necessary to express the probable effect as a range. (Gluckman and Bardsley 2016).

The unpredictable nature of aleatory uncertainty related risks means that it is not possible to know the outcome with complete certainty (Spiegelhalter and Riesch 2011). Although complete certainty is not possible, understanding of the types of risks and uncertainties through risk assessment improves the inputs for decision-making and therefore better decisions.

Black Swans and Complex Risks

Prior to 1697, Western Europeans believed that all swans were white. The assumption was based on the fact that throughout Western European history only white swans were observed. When Dutch explorers traveled to Western Australia, they were amazed to see large flocks of black swans, shattering the long-held belief that all swans were white. In 2007, Nassim Nicholas Taleb introduced the black swan theory in his book *The Black Swan* (Taleb 2007). His theory refers to an event or phenomenon that is unprecedented or unexpected in human history at the time it occurs. Such "black swan events" are frequently catastrophic in their consequences (high severity) and unpredictable, because there is no previous historical data to rely upon (low frequency). A black swan event can be characterized as unpredictable meaning that there is no precedent or similar event history available, and that it is random in its nature. The frequency of events or the lack of frequency makes such black swan events almost impossible to predict. Examples of black swan events include earthquakes and tsunamis, volcanic eruptions, the September 11, 2001, terrorist attacks in the US, the global financial crisis of 2008, and the September 2019 *drone attacks* on the world's largest oil processing facility and a major oil field in *Saudi Arabia, which* sparked huge fires and halted about half of the supply or oil from the world's largest exporter of oil.

Organizations are becoming more aware that such unprecedented and unpredictable events are possible and that there should be some exploration of such uncertainties to better prepare for their consequences. Black swan events can result from a single cause, such as an asteroid strike in a populated area or an earthquake and the resulting tsunami (2004 Indian Ocean tsunami); however, they are more commonly triggered by a less severe event such as spilling a drink on the control panel that cascades into a catastrophic event (Three Mile Island nuclear accident).

Black swan events arise from a combination of interconnected risk factors known as "cumulative risk." Cumulative risk can develop into complex risk factors and result in a series of cascading impacts. Each risk factor alone is unlikely to result in a major disaster, but when combined with other risk factors they can cause a catastrophic event such as the Fukushima nuclear accident. This event was initiated by the Tōhoku earthquake, which then caused a 45-foot-high tsunami that struck the nuclear power plant 50 minutes later, topping the seawall, flooding the basements, and disabling the emergency power generators. Without power, the circulating pumps could not cool the reactors' cores, causing overheating, three nuclear meltdowns, several hydrogen explosions, and the release of radioactive contamination (Lipscy, Kushida, and Incerti 2013. Black swans and cascading effects can reveal vulnerabilities in systems that were not known or considered before the event.

Reducing Uncertainty

Like risk, a certain amount of uncertainty will always exist. Organizations take speculative (financial and strategic) risks such as expansions into markets or acquisitions to achieve their objectives, while avoiding pure (hazard and operational) risks to protect the organization from harm. Some fundamental strategies that can help reduce uncertainty in decision-making are presented in the following Table 1.1.

Table 1.1. Strategies for Reducing Uncertainty in Decision-Making.

Strategy	Description
Reduce the size of the decision	Break it into smaller steps, reducing potential impact from a single decision
Understand the options	Knowledge is power and the antidote to the unknown.
Defer the decision	Postpone making the decision until it is better understood.
Focus on one decision	Keep the focus on a single decision rather than combining risks from multiple decisions. Other risks and decisions that may impact the decision should be factored into the decision-making process.
Understand the credible worst case	Determine what the worst-case scenario could be that is credible and define the potential outcomes.
Clarify potential outcomes	Estimate the consequences of the decision, both positive and negative, and the risk drivers that may influence the outcomes.
Understand the context	Know the reasons for the decision, the internal and external stakeholders, and the goals and values of the organization.
Be flexible and adaptable	Keep options open and adjust as more is learned during the decision-making process.
Remain objective and unemotional	Remove emotions and maintain a calm, rational mind-set.

As indicated by ISO 31010, uncertainty in risk analysis and the results can be caused by a number of elements. These include:

- variability in the system,
- unverified or unreliable sources of information,
- ambiguity in the data,
- improper method of analysis for complexity of the system,
- overweighted reliance on subjective expert opinion or judgement,
- lack of relevant data,
- data obtained is not a reliable basis from which to forecast the future, and
- uncertainties or approximations in the assumptions that are made.

Where it is not possible to reduce uncertainty, it may be possible to better understand its nature and the potential implications. Some of the methods that can be used to gain an understanding of uncertainty include sensitivity analysis, scenario analysis, and Monte Carlo simulation described in Table 1.2.

It is important to remember that, like risk, uncertainty can never be eliminated, but it can be reduced and managed to an acceptable level. Decisions are rarely made with absolute certainty. Complete and absolute knowledge of the alternatives is not possible or practical.

Uncertainty can be reduced through effective communication of risk-based information. Communication and consultation are a major component in the risk management process. As stated in ISO 31000:

> [T]he purpose of communication and consultation is to assist relevant stakeholders in understanding risk, the basis on which decisions are made and the reasons why particular actions are required. Communication seeks to promote awareness and understanding of risk, whereas consultation involves obtaining feedback and information to support decision-making. (ANSI/ASSP/ISO 31000- 2018)

Ultimately, communication and consultation should provide sufficient information to facilitate risk oversight and reasoned decision-making.

Risk-related Terms

With any discipline, an understanding of critical terms and their definitions is required. ISO Guide 73, ISO 31000, ANSI Z590.3 and ANSI RA.1 are several references that can be reviewed. Some of the key terms important to this manual are presented and described here.

Risk—the effect of uncertainty on the achievement of strategic, tactical, and operational objectives (ANSI/ASIS/RIMS RA.1-2015). Effect of uncertainty on objectives (ANSI/ASSP/ISO 31000-2018). In addition, the standard includes notes to further explain aspects of the definition at follows. Note 1: An effect is a deviation from the expected. It

Table 1.2. Methods for Reducing Uncertainty.

Method	Description
Sensitivity Analysis	A systematic method used to understand how risk estimates and risk-based decisions are dependent on variability and uncertainty in contributing risk factors (ANSI/ASIS/RIMS RA.1- 2015). It is used in determining the variation in output of a model by testing different input values. The assessor compares the outcomes that are produced from an analytical approach using different input values. The level of uncertainty associated with each variation is evaluated and ranked accordingly. ISO 31010 suggests that sensitivity analysis be used to help test, verify, and validate results.
Scenario Analysis	Used to analyze possible future outcomes by considering alternative scenarios to determine risk levels and types of consequences. Possible scenarios are identified through imagination or extrapolation from the present, and different risks are considered assuming each of these scenarios might occur. In general terms, it consists of defining a plausible scenario and working through what might happen given various possible future developments (ANSI/ASSP/ISO 31010-2019).
Monte Carlo Simulation	Used to establish the aggregate variation in a system resulting from variations in the system for a number of inputs, where each input has a defined distribution and the inputs are related to the output via defined relationships. Calculates the probability of outcomes by running multiple simulations using random variables. The analysis can be used for a specific model where the interactions of the various inputs can be mathematically defined. The inputs can be based upon a variety of distribution types according to the nature of the uncertainty they are intended to represent (ANSI/ASSP/ISO 31010-2019).

can be positive (sometimes expressed as opportunities), negative (sometimes expressed as threats), or both. Note 2: Objectives can have different aspects and categories and can be applied at different levels. Note 3: Risk is often characterized by reference to potential events, their consequences, and their likelihood (ANSI/ASSP/ISO 31000-2018). An estimate of the probability of a hazard-related incident or exposure occurring and the severity of harm or damage that could result (ANSI/ASSP Z590.3-2016).

Risk Source—an element which alone or in combination has the intrinsic potential to give rise to risk (ANSI/ASSP/ISO 31000-2018). A risk source is defined as "a factor with the potential to create uncertainty in achieving objectives. Note: A risk source may include tangible or intangible factors alone or in combination" (ANSI/ASIS/RIMS RA.1-2015). Risk sources include hazard risks, operational risks, financial risks, and strategic risks. Hazard risks and operational risks are considered pure risks, meaning that they only produce negative effects, while financial and strategic risks are considered "speculative" with the potential to produce effects that are negative, positive, or both.

Risk Driver—factor that has a major influence on risk (ANSI/ASSP/ISO 31010-2019). A risk driver is defined as an "event, individual(s), process, or trends having impact on the objectives of the organization" (ANSI/ASIS/RIMS RA.1-2015).

Risk Exposure—something of value that comes in direct contact, proximity, or path of a risk. Assets (people, property, business objectives, etc.) that are exposed to a risk have an increased likelihood of an occurrence, while assets that are not exposed have a very low likelihood of the occurrence.

Risk Trigger—a direct cause, condition, or action that causes the risk exposure to result in an event or incident.

Event—occurrence or change of a particular set of circumstances (ANSI/ASSP/ISO 31000- 2018). Change occurring in an interval of time with the potential to alter outcomes (ANSI/ASIS/RIMS RA.1-2015). An unwanted or unexpected incident that results from a risk exposure to impact the asset.

Consequence—outcome of an event affecting objectives (ANSI/ASSP Z690.1-2011).

Risk Pathway—the pathway risk travels beginning with its source, driving influences, exposure, trigger, and event to the resulting consequence (Lyon, Popov 2018) as illustrated in Figure 1.2. Risk arises from its source (hazards, operations, strategic, or financial), is influenced by certain drivers or factors that increase risk, becomes exposed to things of value, and is released by a trigger event to create an incident that results in one or more consequences.

Risk Management—coordinated activities to direct and control an organization with regard to risk (ANSI/ASSP/ISO 31000-2018). RIMS defines risk management as "a strategic business discipline that supports the achievement of an organization's objectives by addressing the full spectrum of its risks and managing the combined impact of those risks as an interrelated risk portfolio" (ANSI/ASIS/RIMS RA.1-2015). ISO 31000 states that risk management must be based on defined principles, framework, and process as outlined in the standard so that risks are managed consistently and effectively.

Risk Assessment—overall process of risk identification, risk analysis, and risk evaluation (ISO Guide 73/ANSI/ASSP Z690.1-2011). Risk assessment is the identification, analysis, and evaluation of uncertainties to objectives and outcomes (ANSI/ASIS/RIMS RA.1-2015). The PtD standard defines risk assessment as "a process that commences with hazard identification and analysis, through which the probable severity of harm or damage is established, followed by an estimate of the probability of the incident or exposure occurring, and concluding with a statement of risk" (ANSI/ASSP Z590.3-2011, R2016). Risk assessment attempts to answer the following fundamental questions:

- What can happen and why (by risk identification)?
- What are the consequences?
- What is the probability of their future occurrence?
- Are there any factors that mitigate the consequence of the risk or that reduce the probability of the risk?

Risk Identification—the process for determining what risks are anticipated, their characteristics, time dependencies, frequencies, duration period, and possible outcomes (ANSI/ASIS/RIMS RA.1-2015). Risk identification involves the identification of threats, opportunities, criticalities, weaknesses, and strengths, as well as identifying sources of risk and potential events and their causes and impacts.

Risk Analysis—the process used to characterize and understand the nature of risk and to define the level of risk (ANSI/ASIS/RIMS RA.1-2015).

Risk Evaluation—the process of comparing the results of risk analysis with risk criteria to determine whether the risk and/or its magnitude is acceptable or tolerable (ISO Guide 73/ANSI/ASSP Z690.1-2011).

Risk Avoidance—informed decision not to be involved in, or to withdraw from, an activity in order not to be exposed to a particular risk (ISO Guide 73/ANSI/ASSP Z690.1-2011).

Risk Treatment—process used to modify risk (ISO Guide 73/ANSI/ASSP Z690.1-2011).

Control—measures that maintains and/or modifies risk (ANSI/ASSP/ISO 31000-2018).

Hierarchy of Controls—a systematic approach to avoiding, eliminating, controlling, and reducing risks, considering steps in a ranked and sequential order, beginning with avoidance, elimination, and substitution. Residual risks are controlled using engineering controls, warning systems, administrative controls, and personal protective equipment (ANSI/ASSP Z590.3-2011, R2016).

Hierarchy of Risk Treatment (HoRT)—A ranking of risk treatment strategies and options used to evaluate and select treatments according to their perceived effectiveness, reliability, advantages, and benefits as well as their costs, secondary risks, and other possible negative factors. The HoRT model includes additional design level treatments including minimization and simplification as well as two levels of engineering treatments (passive and active).

Residual Risk—the risk remaining after risk reduction measures have been taken (ANSI/ASSP Z590.3-2011, R2016).

Acceptable Risk—that risk for which the probability of an incident or exposure occurring and the severity of harm or damage that may result are as low as reasonably practicable (ALARP) in the setting being considered (ANSI/ASSP Z590.3-2011, R2016).

Uncertainty—state, even partial, of deficiency of information related to, understanding or knowledge of, an event, its consequence, or likelihood (ISO Guide 73/ANSI/ASSP Z690.1-2011).

Summary

Globally, organizations are becoming more risk-focused and are integrating risk management into their management systems. OSH risk professionals will be expected to have sufficient knowledge and skills in operational risk management tools. In particular, risk professionals will be expected to understand and apply the concept of selecting risk treatments according to the hierarchy of controls model to achieve an acceptable risk level. Risk avoidance and reduction will be incorporated into new designs and re-designs and throughout a system's life span. Knowledge and skill in these concepts, and an understanding of occupational risk management systems such as ISO 45001 and ANSI/ASSP Z10.0, will be required by organizations.

Review Questions

1. Explain what motivates an organization to manage its risks. List several reasons why risk should be managed.
2. Determine whether risk is static or dynamic and explain why.
3. Explain how emerging risks are different from inherent risks, and how initial risks are different from residual risks.
4. Identify and describe the four risk quadrants.
5. Describe the risk-based decision-making process.
6. Identify and describe the four different types of uncertainty.
7. Explain what is meant by "black swan events."
8. Provide four ways uncertainty might be reduced.

References

ABS Consulting, Inc. 2001. *Principles of Risk-Based Decision Making.* Rockville, MD: Government Institutes.

ANSI/ASIS/RIMS RA.1-2015. 2015. *Risk Assessment.* Alexandria, VA: ASIS International and The Risk and Insurance Management Society, Inc.

ANSI/ASSP Z10.0-2019. 2019. *Occupational Health and Safety Management Systems.* Park Ridge, IL: American Society of Safety Professionals.

ANSI/ASSP Z590.3-2011 (R2016). 2016. *Prevention through Design: Guidelines for Addressing Occupational Hazards and Risks in Design and Redesign Processes.* Park Ridge, IL: American Society of Safety Professionals.

ANSI/ASSP Z690.1-2011. 2011. *Vocabulary for Risk Management.* Park Ridge, IL: American Society of Safety Professionals.

ANSI/ASSP/ISO 31000-2018. 2018. *Risk Management Principles and Guidelines.* Park Ridge, IL: American Society of Safety Professionals.

ANSI/ASSP/ISO 31010-2019. 2019. *Risk Management – Risk Assessment Techniques.* Park Ridge, IL: American Society of Safety Professionals.

ANSI/ASSP/ISO 45001-2018. 2018. *Occupational Health and Safety Management Systems – Requirements with Guidance for Use.* Park Ridge, IL: American Society of Safety Professionals.

ANSI/B11.0-2015. 2015. *Safety of Machinery.* Houston, TX: B11 Standards.

ANSI B11.TR3-2000. 2000. *Risk Assessment and Risk Reduction – A Guide to Estimate, Evaluate and Reduce Risks Associated with Machine Tools.* McLean, VA: B11 Standards.

Best, M., and D. Neuhauser. 2006. "Walter A Shewhart, 1924, and the Hawthorne factory." *Quality and Safety in Healthcare.* Volume 15(2): 142–143. doi: 10.1136/qshc.2006.018093.

COSO. 2012. *Risk Assessment in Practice.* Durham, NC: The Committee of Sponsoring Organizations of the Treadway Commission (COSO).

Elliott, Michael W. 2017. *Risk Management Principles and Practices,* 2nd ed. Malvern, PA: The Institutes.

Gluckman, P., and A. Bardsley. 2016. "Making decisions in the face of uncertainty: Understanding risk." Office of the Prime Minister's Chief Science Advisor. Auckland, New Zealand. www.pmcsa.org.nz/wp-content/uploads/PMCSA-Risk-Series-Paper-1_final_2.pdf.

Lipscy, P., K. Kushida, and T. Incerti. 2013. "The Fukushima Disaster and Japan's Nuclear Plant Vulnerability in Comparative Perspective." Environmental Science & Technology. 47 (12): 6082–88.

Lyon, Bruce K., and Georgi Popov. 2017. "Communicating & Managing Risk: The Key Result of Risk Assessment." *Professional Safety,* November 2017, 35–44.

Lyon, Bruce K., and Georgi Popov. 2018. *Risk Management Tools for Safety Professionals.* Park Ridge, IL: American Society of Safety Professionals.

Macesker, B., J. Myers, V. Guthrie, D. Walker, and S. Schoolcraft. 2001. "Quick-reference Guide to Risk-based Decision Making (RBDM): A Step-by-step Example of the RBDM Process in the Field." https://www.hsdl.org/?abstract&did=449633.

www.merriam-webster.com/dictionary/continuum.

MIL-STD-882E. 2012. *Department of Defense Standard Practice: System Safety*. Washington, DC: Department of Defense.

The Risk Management Society (RIMS). 2011. "Why Strategic Risk Management?" https://www.rims.org/docs/default-source/default-document-library/faq-on-srm-and-erm-final-april-20-2011.pdf?sfvrsn=c58085ec_4.

Spiegelhalter, D.J., and H. Riesch. 2011. "Don't know, can't know: embracing deeper uncertainties when analyzing risks." *Philosophical Transactions of the Royal Society, Mathematical Physical and Engineering Sciences,* 369 (1956), 4730–4750. doi:10.1098/rsta.2011.0163.

Taleb, N.N. 2007. *The Black Swan: The Impact of the Highly Improbable.* New York, NY: Random House.

US Coast Guard. 2005. *Risk-Based Decision Making Guidelines.* Washington, DC: US Department of Homeland Security.

CHAPTER 2
Historical Perspective

Introduction
Today, the terms *hazard* and *risk* are used frequently in organizations, governing bodies, societies, and associations, but many may wonder about the origins of these terms and the implications that their roots may have for our understanding of risk management. Where did these terms come from? What are the etymological roots of the words *hazard* and *risk*? How do their origins affect modern-day concepts in risk management? This chapter will briefly explore the origins of common hazard and risk terminology, their similarities and differences, and their current definitions.

Origins of *Hazard* and *Risk*
According to Merriam-Webster, *hazard* was a game of chance played with dice (www.merriam-webster.com/dictionary/hazard.) The English word *hazard* is thought to come from the medieval French game *hasard*, a dicing game of chance, which was borrowed from the Arabic word *az-zahr*, (or *al-zahr*). While the origins of the Arabic word for dice are unclear, it may have been borrowed from Spanish *azar* or from Italian *zara*, "a game at dice called hazar." Further, the word *chance* is derived from the French word *cheance* or *cheoir* meaning "to fall" as related to the "fall of the dice" in the game of *hazard* (Weekley 1921).

The term *risk* can be traced back to the ancient Greek word ριζα, which translates to "root" in English and later is used in Latin for "cliff." Dictionaries state that the Latin word for *cliff* comes from a Greek navigation term *rhizikon*, or *rhiza*, which was a metaphor for "difficulty to avoid in the sea" (Skjong 2005). The word *risk* appears in the mid-seventeenth century possibly from the French word

---
Interactive tools and supplemental materials are available at assp.org/ermtools.

risque (noun), *risquer* (verb), which was derived from Italian *risco* "danger" and *rischiare* "run into danger." These origins are shown in Figure 2.1.

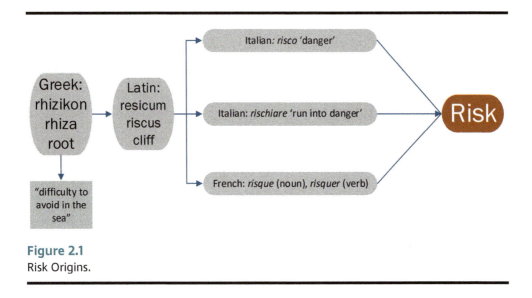

Figure 2.1
Risk Origins.

In the sixteenth century, the term *risk* was also given a beneficial meaning. In 1507, the German term *rysigo* was used as a technical term for business, meaning "to dare, to undertake, enterprise, hope for economic success" (Skjong 2005).

The Age of Exploration

In the era known as the Age of Exploration, which began in the early fifteenth century and lasted through the seventeenth century, the Dutch and English were sending ships around the world. It was a highly profitable, but risky, business. The ships and the cargo required some form of insurance. To be able to insure the ships and cargo, a group of underwriters started gathering at the Lloyd's coffee shop in London. The insurance required forecasting the risk of loss, as well as the likelihood of a gain from the journey. Hence, the risk should not be considered only in negative terms. The underwrites had to decide whether the cost was worth the risk. At that time, they had to consider variables that might affect the level of risk such as the design and age of the ship, the experience of the crew and the captain, the destination of the trip, the time of the year, the probability of storms, the length of the trip, reports of pirates, and the nature of the cargo. There were no computers at that time, and one can imagine that the process of underwriting was more like gambling game—not to mention that they were only "gambling" on one type of risk—shipping.

Around that same time in Siena, Italy, the Monte de Paschi bank was ensuring crops (Bankpedia n.d.). The bank had the advantage of serving many geographical regions, therefore, it was able to balance risk in one region against the losses in another. Losses in one region would almost certainly be offset by profits in another region. This could be considered an early form of risk diversification and taking advantage of the law of large numbers concept. It would have required some form of likelihood and consequence analysis and solving mathematical equations.

In fact, the study of risk has always been a mathematical exercise. Most of the early studies described games of chance. Unfortunately, the Hindu-Arabic numerals were not widely used at that time. In Peter Bernstein's book, *Against the Gods: The remarkable story of risk,* he writes that even in 1500 very few people could use Arabic numerals. Instead of numbers, the ancient Greeks used the Greek alphabet. Later, the Romans had the abacus, and it largely defined what they could do with numbers. Imagine using an abacus (shown in Figure 2.2) today to estimate risk and perform statistical calculations.

It wasn't until 1202 that the book *Liber Abaci,* translated to the "Book of the Abacus" was published by Leonardo Pisano. *Liber Abaci* by Leonardo Pisano, nicknamed Fibonacci, was one of the most important books on mathematics in the Middle Ages. It introduced Hindu-Arabic numerals and mathematical methods to the Europeans. It also introduced the number 0, allowing for more advanced mathematical calculations in tens, thousands, hundreds of thousands, and even negative numbers.

One can only imagine what it was like to estimate risk using Greek letters or Roman numerals or any combination of letters and numerals. Bernstein presents a very good example of the difficulties associated with Roman numerals. For instance, III II may be interpreted as 32, 302, or 3020. It is obvious that calculations based on Roman numerals are almost impossible. Therefore, the use of Hindu-Arabic numerals beginning in the 1500s contributed to the advancement of risk assessment and risk management even though the tools to estimate uncertainty still didn't exist.

Probability Theory

Risk assessment requires some form of "chance" estimate and prediction of consequences. For most of history the concept of chance (now considered "probability") was shrouded in mythology. Then, in the seventeenth century, the theory of probability was first introduced in "games of chance." Probability was used to calculate the "odds of winning," and the mathematicians at time were able to make "predictions" using numbers. The development of probability theory allowed the transition from risk being considered an "act of God" to the belief that the risks could be understood, assessed, and controlled. Blaise Pascal and Pierre de

Fermat invented probability theory in 1654 to solve a gambling problem related to expected outcomes. The probability theory became the basis for the modern-day risk assessment.

The earliest mathematical definition of risk is found in the 1662 book *Logic, or the Art of Thinking*. This book states: "Therefore, our fear of an evil ought to be proportional, not only to its *magnitude,* but also to its *probability* [emphasis added]" (Arnauld [1662] 1850). In Part IV, Chapter XVI, it states, "The rules [probabilities from previous chapters] which are employed in *judging of past events* may easily be *applied to those which are future* [emphasis added]" (Arnauld [1662] 1850). We can argue that Pascal and Arnauld laid the foundation of predictive analytics and probabilistic risk assessments. Furthermore, we can assume that some of the modern risk assessment tools like risk matrix, cumulative effects, and cumulative frequencies are based on Pascal's triangle.

Law of Large Numbers

One of the significant developments in the risk management field was the development of the law of large numbers. It was first stated by Gerolamo Cardano (1501–1576), an Italian mathematician, that the accuracies of empirical statistics tend to improve with the number of trials (Mlodinow 2008). However, he could not prove it mathematically. It wasn't referred to as a law of large numbers until Jacob Bernoulli was able to provide adequately rigorous mathematical proof, which was published in his *Ars Conjectandi* (*The Art of Conjecturing*) in 1713 (Bernoulli 2005). Later, in 1837, S.D. Poisson, one of the greatest French statisticians, also described it under the name *la loi des grands nombres* (Poisson 1837), or "the law of large numbers" in English. One can assume that the underwriters of Lloyd's and other insurers had used the law of large numbers concept even before it was mathematically proven. Ancient Chinese traders were also aware of similar concepts. They redistributed goods among different ships in order minimize the losses.

After the Great Fire of London in 1666, a law that allowed new organizations to pay owners for losses was introduced. This law could be considered the foundation for modern-day property insurance. The first insurance company, "The Insurance Office," was established in 1667 and it was in a small office behind London's Royal Exchange.

In the United States, Benjamin Franklin was one of the early advocates of mutual insurance. In 1751, Franklin and his Union Fire Company met with other Philadelphia fire-fighting companies to discuss the formation of a fire insurance company (PBS 2002). In 1752, the first successful fire insurance company in the colonies was established. It set insurance standards by refusing to insure houses that were considered a fire hazard.

Central Limit Theorem

Another important milestone in the history of risk and insurance was the publication of the standard version of the central limit theorem, which was first proved by the French mathematician Pierre-Simon Laplace in 1810 (Routledge n.d.). The central limit theorem simply states that the distribution of sample means approximates a normal distribution as the sample size gets larger (assuming that all samples are identical in size), regardless of population distribution shape (Ganti 2019). It is still used in risk management and insurance to explain pooling of losses as an insurance mechanism. The central limit theorem is related to the law of large numbers which was first mathematically proven by Jacob Bernoulli in 1713.

Risk and the Modern World

In his book *Against the Gods: The Remarkable Story of Risk,* Peter Bernstein suggests that the actual dividing line between what we call ancient times and modern times is the management of risk. Some historians believe that the earliest concept of managing risk arose during the Renaissance. However, in his article "Risk Management: History, Definition, and Critique," Georges Dionne states that the modern terms for managing risk arose after World War II (Dionne). Risk management as a discipline mostly began as a study of using insurance to manage risk. Years later, from around 1950s to the 1970s, risk managers began to realize that it was too expensive to manage *every* risk with insurance. Modern risk management practices consider prevention as an important part of managing risk.

In 1952, Harry Markowitz published an important paper titled "Portfolio selection." In his paper he emphasizes that financial and strategic type risks offer the potential of positive returns, as well as potential losses. Therefore, the concept of risks should not be limited to only negative outcomes. Markowitz also presented the notion of diversification of investment, a strategy of diversifying risks to avoid putting all your eggs in one basket. In a diversified investment, some assets will fall in value while some others will increase their value balancing out the returns to an acceptable level. It was not a novel concept, but he was able to express the expected returns vs. variance of returns mathematically (Markowitz 1952).

In fact, modern risk management practices include the concept of Enterprise Risk Management (ERM). ERM is the process of integrated risk management that places a greater importance on cooperation among departments or functions to manage the organization's full range of risks. It is a relatively new concept, which can be traced back to the early 1970s when Gustav Hamilton of Sweden's government holding company, *Statsforetag,* proposed the "risk management circle" to describe the interaction of all elements in the risk management process: assessment, control, financing, and communication (Hamilton 1996).

ERM offers several benefits like alignment of risk appetite and corporate strategy; linking of growth, risk, and returns; and managing enterprise-wide risks. An important part of ERM is that it helps organizations recognize and act upon opportunities and manages deployment of resources effectively.

The Committee of Sponsoring Organizations of the Treadway Commission (COSO 2019) is a joint initiative of five private sector organizations and provides thought leadership through the development of frameworks and guidance on enterprise risk management, internal control, and fraud deterrence (COSO 2019). COSO published the first ERM standard in 2004.

The International Organization for Standardization (ISO) 31000 *Risk Management – Guidelines* is an international risk management standard and was first published in November 2009. The accompanying ISO 31010, *Risk Assessment Techniques,* standard published soon after, in December 2009. The latest version of 31000 *Risk Management – Guidelines* was published in 2018 followed and was by ISO 31010- *Risk Assessment Techniques* in 2019. Both of these standards have been adopted in the US, published as ANSI/ASSP/ISO 31000 and ANSI/ASSP/ISO 31010. Figure 2.2 illustrates the major milestones in the development of risk concepts.

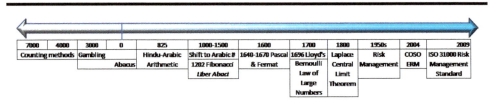

Figure 2.2
Risk Timeline.

Summary

The concept of risk has developed throughout history, and our understanding of risk continues to evolve. With the ever-increasing complexity of the world, and with newly emerging risks continually occurring, the importance of assessing and managing risk is becoming recognized by organizations. Risk professionals should be prepared for the future by understanding the past and anticipating the needs for risk management.

Review Questions

1. Describe the origins of the word *hazard* and the word *risk*.
2. Explain when and why insurance began being used.

3. What is probability theory?
4. What is the law of large numbers?
5. What is the central limit theorem?
6. Describe how modern risk management practices lead to enterprise risk management.

References

ANSI/ASSP/ISO 31000-2018. 2018. *Risk Management Principles and Guidelines*. Park Ridge, IL: American Society of Safety Professionals, 2018.

ANSI/ASSP/ISO/IEC 31010-2019. 2019. *Risk Management – Risk Assessment Techniques*. Park Ridge, IL: American Society of Safety Professionals.

Arnauld, Anthony. (1662) 1805. Logic, or the Art of Thinking. Translated by Thomas Spencer Baynes. Edinburgh: Sutherland and Knox. Text can be found at https://archive.org/details/artofthinking00arnauoft/page/n1.

Bernstein, Peter. 1998. *Against the Gods: The remarkable story of risk*. Hoboken, NJ: Wiley.

Bankpedia.com. n.d. "Accessed June 27, 2019. www.bankpedia.org/index.php/en/114-english/m/23475-monte-dei-paschi-di-siena-eng.

Bernoulli, Jakob. 2005. *Ars Conjectandi: Usum and Applicationem Praecedentis Doctrinae in Civilibus, Moralibus & Oeconomicis* (*The Art of Conjecturing: The Use and Application of the Previous Doctrine to Civil, Moral and Economic Affairs*). Translated by Oscar Sheynin. Text can be found at http://www.sheynin.de/download/bernoulli.pdf.

COSO. 2019. The Committee of Sponsoring Organizations of the Treadway Commission, from: www.coso.org/Pages/default.aspx (accessed June 27, 2019).

Dionne, Georges. 2013. "Risk Management: History, Definition and Critique." SSRN: https://ssrn.com/abstract=2231635.

Ganti, Akhilesh. 2019. "Central Limit Theorem (CLT)." Accessed June 27, 2019. www.investopedia.com/terms/c/central_limit_theorem.asp.

Hamilton, G. 1996. *Risk Management 2000*. Lund, Sweden: Studentliteratur.

Markowitz, Harry. 1952. "Portfolio Selection." *The Journal of Finance,* Vol. 7, No. 1. (March 1952), pp. 77–91. www.math.ust.hk/~maykwok/courses/ma362/07F/markowitz_JF.pdf.

Mlodinow, L. 2008. *The Drunkard's Walk*. New York, NY: Random House.

PBS. 2002. "Insurance Ben-efactor." www.pbs.org/benfranklin/l3_citizen_insurance.html.

Poisson, S.D. 1837. *Probabilité des jugements en matière criminelle et en matière civile, précédées des règles générales du calcul des probabilities*. Paris: Bachelier.

Routledge, Richard. n.d. "Central limit theorem." Accessed October 16, 2020. www.britannica.com/science/central-limit-theorem accessed June 27, 2019).

Skjong, Rolf. 2005. "Etymology of Risk." www.research.dnv.com/skj/Papers/etymology-of-risk.pdf.

Weekley, Ernest. 1921. *An Etymological Dictionary of Modern English*. London: J. Murray.

CHAPTER 3
Managing Risk

Introduction

Managing risk and its effects on objectives requires a structured, coordinated risk management process based on the principles and framework outlined in ISO 31000. The risk management process includes:

- communication and consultation
- scope, context, and criteria
- risk assessment (risk identification, risk analysis, and risk evaluation)
- risk treatment
- monitoring and review
- recording and reporting

To be effective, the risk management process must have management leadership and commitment and be fully integrated into the organization's management system. Such integration of the risk management process enables an organization to anticipate, detect, qualify, quantify, assess, treat, monitor, and communicate risks so that the organization can function at an optimum level. In addition, effective implementation is necessary at both a corporate and strategic level to support continual improvement of an organization's business activities. Ultimately, the objectives for managing risk (Figure 3.1) are to reduce uncertainty, improve decision-making, enable the organization to achieve its business objectives, and protect people and assets.

In countries outside of the United States, formal risk assessments have become more common largely due to the fact that these countries have national standards

---

Interactive tools and supplemental materials are available at assp.org/ermtools.

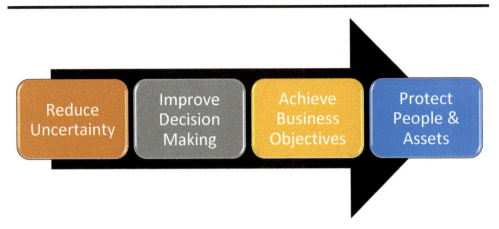

Figure 3.1
Objectives of Managing Risks.

requiring risk assessments in the workplace. For example, in the United Kingdom, the Health and Safety Executive (HSE) has legally required all employers with five or more employees to perform risk assessments since 1999. Similar requirements are found in other countries such as Australia and New Zealand (Popov, Lyon, Hollcroft 2016). However, as the needs and demands from external stakeholders, regulations, and standards change, it is expected that more organizations will be required to have in practice a formal risk assessment and management process. This is reflected in the recent establishment of several key standards.

ISO 31000 Risk Management Series

The International Organization for Standardization (ISO) introduced its series of three fundamental consensus standards for the practice of managing risk in 2009. The three standards were adopted by the American National Standards Institute (ANSI) in 2011 and included:

- ISO guide 73:2009/ANSI/ASSP Z690.1-2011, *Vocabulary for Risk Management*;
- ISO 31000:2009/ANSI/ASSP Z690.2-2011, *Risk Management Principles and Guidelines*;
- IEC/ISO 31010:2009/ANSI/ASSP Z690.3-2011, *Risk Assessment Techniques*.

In 2018, ISO 31000 was revised to reflect the evolution of risk management from a separate, at times departmentalized, activity to an integrated management competency. Language from the 2009 version that was overly technical or required a detailed understanding of risk management was rewritten to make the 2018 revised standard more understandable and accessible for users. The 2018 standard was adopted by ANSI as ANSI/ASSP/ISO 31000-2018 (ISO 31000). As listed in the

Foreword of the revised standard, the primary changes from the original edition are as follows:

- review of the principles of risk management, which are the key criteria for its success;
- highlighting of the leadership by top management and the integration of risk management, starting with the governance of the organization;
- greater emphasis on the iterative nature of risk management, noting that new experiences, knowledge, and analysis can lead to a revision of process elements, actions, and controls at each stage of the process; and
- streamlining of the content with greater focus on sustaining an open systems model to fit multiple needs and contexts (ANSI/ASSP/ISO 31000-2018).

The current ISO 31000 standard establishes that the core purpose of risk management is "value creation and protection." This is an important distinction from the previous edition, which listed "creates value" as one of eleven principles for managing risk. Working toward this goal, the standard now includes eight principles for improving an organization's risk management framework and process. These principles are designed to help organizations improve performance, encourage innovation, and support the achievement of objectives. The eight risk management principles in the revised standard are:

1. Integrating risk management into an organization's activities and decision-making;
2. Taking a structured and comprehensive approach
3. Customizing for an organization's needs and objectives;
4. Including stakeholder perspectives;
5. Being dynamic and responsive to organizational changes;
6. Using the best available information;
7. Taking human and culture factors into account; and
8. Learning and adapting for continual improvement.

The effectiveness of risk management depends largely on its integration into the governance of the organization, including decision-making, and requires support from stakeholders and especially top management. The standard provides guidance for organizations to develop a framework to assist in integrating risk management into significant activities and functions. Risk management must be an active component in governance, strategy and planning, management, reporting processes, policies, values, and culture. The framework is intended to be adapted to each organization's particular needs and structure. At the center of the framework is leadership and commitment. The components of the framework encompass integration, design, implementation, evaluation, and improvement. The organization should evaluate its existing practices to determine if there are gaps which should be addressed within the framework.

The risk management process outlined in ISO 31000 Section 6 presents a continual improvement type process. At the core of this process is risk assessment, the sequential steps of risk identification, risk analysis, and risk evaluation to determine whether the risk is acceptable or if it requires risk treatment (ANSI/ASSP/ISO 31000-2018; Lyon, Popov 2018). In addition to these core steps, two key functions should happen continually throughout the risk management process: (1) communication and consultation, and (2) monitoring and review. These key functions help to ensure risks are properly and effectively communicated, lessons learned are shared, risks will be appropriately treated, existing controls are effective, and the organization is resilient and ready for change.

ISO 31000 emphasizes that risk management is an iterative process that requires leadership from management and involvement across the organization. Top management is accountable for managing risk while oversight bodies at all functional levels of the organization are accountable for overseeing risk management. Risk management is an iterative process requiring stakeholders to communicate and consult with each other throughout the process. Although the risk management process is depicted as sequential, the standard explicitly states that the process is iterative in practice by decision makers and affected stakeholders. This emphasizes the importance of managing risk when decisions are being made, rather than as an after-thought or as an additional step after decisions have already been made.

Among other changes made in the revised standard is the graphic depiction of the relationship between the principles, framework, and process of risk management as shown in Figure 3.2.

ISO 31000 Principles, Framework, and Process

Uncertainty is created by internal and external factors that can also prevent the achievement of certain business objectives within an organization. This effect on an organization's objectives is referred to as "risk." ISO 31000 provides the following principles, framework, and process for managing risk.

Principles

An organization's core principles form the culture, structure, and actions within an organization. Merriam-Webster defines the word "principle" as:

> a comprehensive and fundamental law, doctrine, or assumption; a rule or code of conduct; habitual devotion to right principles a man of principle; the laws or facts of nature underlying the working of an artificial device. (Merriam-Webster n.d.)

Managing Risk | 41

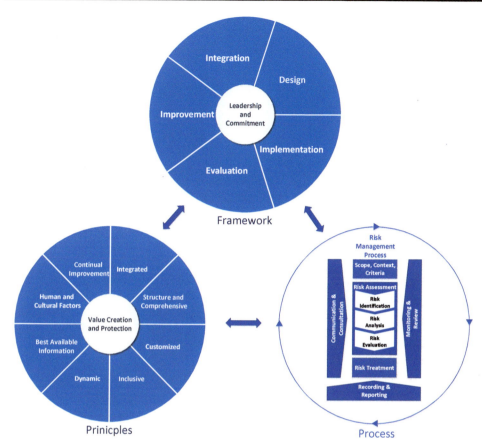

Figure 3.2
Relationship between the Principles, Framework, and Process of Risk Management, Adapted from ANSI/ASSP/ISO 31000-2018.

ISO 31000 states that the principles are the foundation for managing risk and should be considered when establishing an organization's risk management framework and processes (ANSI/ASSP/ISO 31000-2018). The standard's core principle is "the creation and protection of value," which is supported by eight risk management principles. These principles, along with the framework and process, provide guidance on the characteristics of effective and efficient risk management and are designed to enable an organization in creating and protecting value through the management of risk. The supporting principles are shown in Figure 3.3.

1. Integrated—Risk management should be integrated into an organization's management systems, activities, and decision-making.
2. Structured and comprehensive—A structured and comprehensive approach to risk management should be taken to produce consistent, iterative, and comparable results.

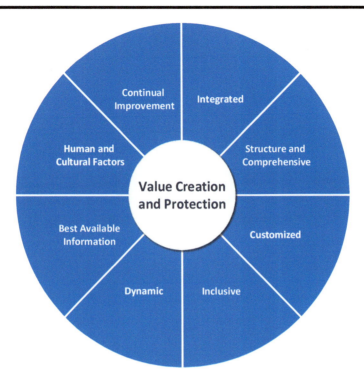

Figure 3.3
Principles of Risk Management, Adapted from ANSI/ASSP/ISO 31000-2018.

3. Customized—A customized risk management framework and process should be incorporated that is proportionate to the organization's external and internal needs and objectives.
4. Inclusive—Stakeholder participation throughout the framework and process should be leveraged to gain knowledge, views, and perceptions, and to improve overall awareness.
5. Dynamic—To effectively manage risk, an organization should be able to anticipate, detect, acknowledge, and respond to changes in existing risks and new and emerging risks within an organization's external and internal changes.
6. Best available information—Risk-based information that is clear and concise should be made available to affected stakeholders in a timely fashion to allow optimal decisions to be made.
7. Human and cultural factors—The risk management framework and process should consider how human behavior and an organization's culture influence all aspects of an organization including risk and its management.
8. Continual improvement—The risk management framework and process should be structured to continually learn, adapt, and improve.

Framework

According to the risk management principles previously described, a structural framework is designed by an organization for managing risk. As outlined in ISO 31000, a risk management framework provides organizational structure for the integration of risk management into important activities and functions. This framework, supported by management and stakeholders, should be designed to enable organizational leadership, process design, implementation and monitoring, evaluation, and continual improvement of the risk management process as illustrated in Figure 3.4. To be effective, the framework should be customized to an organization's needs and objectives as well as integrated into its day-to-day governance and decision-making process.

As with any organizational system, risk management practices and processes should be monitored and evaluated to identify and eliminate gaps and make improvements within the framework. The framework elements are further described in the following sections.

1. Leadership and Commitment—As illustrated in management system standards such as ISO 45001 and ANSI/ASSP Z10.0, a management system requires

Figure 3.4
Framework of Risk Management, Adapted from ANSI/ASSP/ISO 31000-2018.

management leadership and commitment to be successful. In the authors' opinion, it is the most critical element of a framework—without which the remaining elements are ineffective. Genuine commitment and leadership must be demonstrated through consistent actions and decision-making as part of the risk management framework. Specifically, management leadership and commitment are demonstrated within an organization through the following actions:

   a. policy statement that establishes a risk management approach, plan, or course of action that is effectively communicated to stakeholders;

   b. establishment of defined policies for risk management which are aligned with the organization's culture;

   c. customized framework and process specific to the organization;

   d. determination of risk criteria, acceptable risk levels, key risk indicators, and key performance indicators;

   e. alignment of risk management objectives with the organization's objectives;

   f. consideration of regulatory, legal, and voluntary obligations;

   g. assignment of authority, responsibilities, and accountabilities within the organization;

   h. allocation of necessary resources for risk management;

   i. effective communication with the organization and its stakeholder in the value of risk management;

   j. systematic monitoring and assessment of progress in the achievement of risk management objectives.

   Management is ultimately responsible for managing risk and should be accountable for overseeing risk management efforts when establishing and pursuing the organization's objectives. Customized systems within an organization must be implemented, operated, and monitored by management that are appropriate in the context of the organization's objectives. The framework should enable and promote risk-based information to be effectively communicated among affected stakeholders.

2. Integration—Integration is not only a risk management principle; it is also an element of the framework. ISO 31000 places emphasis on the importance of integrating risk management into an organization's culture, management

system, relationships, and decision-making. Risks continually change and require a dynamic and iterative risk management approach that is integrated into all parts of an organization, its decision-making process, and in the treatment of risk. Every person and every component of the organization are responsible for managing risk within their control. As part of the decision-making process, management should consciously consider the potential risks of any decision made to determine whether the risks are acceptable. An effective integration requires an understanding of organizational structures, goals, context, as well as its governance to achieve its objectives. The role that integration plays is highlighted by ISO 31000 in the following statements:

> *Management structures translate governance direction into the strategy and associated objectives required to achieve desired levels of sustainable performance and long-term viability. Determining risk management accountability and oversight roles within an organization are integral parts of the organization's governance. (ANSI/ASSP/ISO 31000-2018)*

3. Design—Organizations vary in their makeup, culture, environment, and objectives. Therefore, the risk management framework must be designed to fit the needs of the organization, its stakeholders, and overall objectives. In order to properly design and construct the framework, an understanding of the organization's external and internal context is needed. External context may include:
   - social, cultural, political, legal, regulatory, financial, technological, economic, and environmental factors affecting the organization
   - outside factors and trends affecting the organization's objectives
   - stakeholders' relationships, perceptions, values, needs, and expectations
   - contractual relationships
   - complexity of networks

Internal context may include the organization's own structure, overall vision, mission and objectives, culture, management system, as well as the perceptions and values of internal stakeholders. Examining the organization's internal context may include, but is not limited to:

- vision, mission, and values
- governance, organizational structure, roles, and accountabilities
- strategy, objectives, and policies
- the organization's culture
- standards, guidelines, and models adopted by the organization;
- capabilities, understood in terms of resources and knowledge (*e.g.,* capital, time, people, intellectual property, processes, systems, and technologies)

- data, information systems, and information flows
- relationships with internal stakeholders, considering their perceptions and values
- contractual relationships and commitments
- interdependencies and interconnections

Upon establishing an understanding of the context, leadership is able to clearly define and communicate its risk management policy. The organization's policy should include its philosophy and reasoning, the linkage to objectives, responsibilities and accountabilities, commitment of resources, measurement of performance, communication with stakeholders, and commitment to continual improvement. As part of the policy, management must define and communicate risk management roles, responsibilities, and authorities for all levels of the organization. Proper education, training, and resources should accompany assignments to personnel to enable the successful performance of their risk management tasks. Management should ensure that risk-based information and feedback are exchanged with internal and external stakeholders as appropriate on a timely basis. Communication throughout the implementation process is crucial.

A monitoring and evaluation process should be established to provide objective and meaningful data of the process's performance. Measurement of key performance indicators (KPIs) and key risk indicators (KRIs) should be made and compared to the initial baseline, with the results communicated to stakeholders.

Process

The risk management process involves the systematic application of policies, protocols, and practices of activities in an organization and involves (1) communication and consultation; (2) scope, context, and criteria; (3) identifying risk; (4) analyzing risk; (5) evaluating risk; (6) treating risk; (7) monitoring and reviewing; and (8) reporting and recording as shown in Figure 3.5.

Risk Assessment

At the core of the risk management process is risk assessment, which involves three sequential steps: (1) risk identification, (2) analysis, and (3) evaluation. Risk assessment can be considered the mechanism that operates the risk management process, since risks must be assessed before they can be managed.

There are several important consensus standards and technical reports that address the risk assessment process. These include:

- ANSI/ASSP/ISO 31010-2019, *Risk Management – Risk Assessment Techniques*
- ANSI/ASIS/RIMS RA.1-2015, *Risk Assessment*

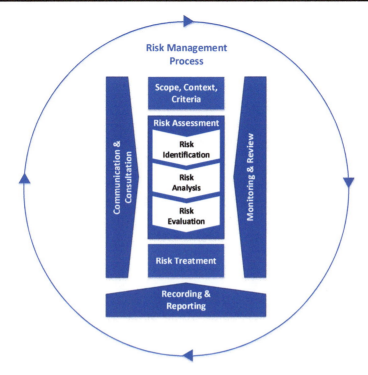

Figure 3.5
Process of Risk Management, Adapted from ANSI/ASSP/ISO 31000-2018.

- ANSI/ASSP Z590.3-2011(R2016), *Prevention through Design: Guidelines for Addressing Occupational Hazards and Risks in Design and Redesign Processes*
- ASSP TR-31010-2020, *Technical Report: Risk Management – Techniques for Safety Practitioners*

ISO 31010, *Risk Management—Risk Assessment Techniques*

Established in 2009, the ISO/IEC 31010-2019 (adopted in the US as ANSI/ASSP/ISO 31010-2019) risk assessment standard was revised to encompass the application of techniques for the entire risk management process— establishing context, risk identification, risk analysis, risk evaluation, risk treatment, monitoring and review, recording and reporting, and communication and consulting.

The revised standard provides guidance on the use, implementation, and selection of techniques for assessing and managing risk in a wide range of situations. An extensive annex is included which contains brief descriptions of 42 techniques for specific risk management elements. Selected techniques and their process steps are covered in this manual.

ANSI/ASIS/RIMS RA.1, *Risk Assessment*

ANSI RA.1 was established in 2015 as a guidance document for organizations in the integration and implementation of risk assessment in a sustainable process. RA.1 is a standard on conducting risk assessments and is complementary to ISO 31000 and ISO 31010. It is designed to be used with risk-based management system standards which require a defined, repeatable, and documented process.

RA.1 follows similar principles, framework, and process to ISO 31000 and ISO 31010 with sections on managing the risk assessment process, performing risk assessments, and confirming the competence of risk assessors. In addition, RA.1 contains seven unique annexes including: risk assessment methods, data collection, and sampling; root cause analysis; background screening and security clearances; contents of the risk assessment report; confidentiality and document protection; examples of risk treatment procedures that enhance resilience of the organization; and business impact analysis.

ANSI/ASSP Z590.3, *Prevention through Design*

ANSI/ASSP Z590.3 *Prevention through Design: Design Guidelines for Addressing Occupational Hazards and Risks in Design and Redesign Processes,* was established in 2011 and reaffirmed in 2016. It is the first standard to address risk reduction by performing risk assessments in the design and redesign phases and throughout the life cycle of a system or product.

The standard provides a framework for implementing risk assessment concepts within the progressive phases of a system's life span including conception, design, redesign, construction, manufacture, use, maintenance, decommission, and disposal. This life cycle approach to assessing risk is further discussed in the following sections.

ASSP TR-31010, *Technical Report: Risk Management—Techniques for Safety Practitioners*

In 2020, a technical report was developed by ASSP to bridge the gaps between the ISO 31010 2009 and 2019 versions and to provide additional support information to safety practitioners on risk management concepts and techniques. In the report are 50 techniques that can be used in various stages of the risk management and risk assessment process. It also includes six addendums on concepts concerning risk, treatment, monitoring, and measuring.

The Concept of Prevention through Design

Prevention through design (also known as *safety in design* or *safety through design*) is defined by ANSI/ASSP Z590.3 (Z590.3) as "addressing occupational safety and health needs in the design and redesign process to prevent or minimize the work-related hazards and risks associated with the construction, manufacture, use, maintenance, retrofitting, and disposal of facilities, processes, materials, and equipment" (ANSI/ASSP Z590.3-2011 [R2016]). Prevention through design (PtD) is a concept that assesses and manages risk throughout the life cycle of a system.

The PtD concept is considered the most effective and long-lasting way to avoid and/or reduce risk in an operation. By avoiding and reducing hazard-risk sources through design, the resulting inherent risks are reduced. For this reason, prevention through design should be integrated into the risk management process concepts and techniques. It is important to consider managing risk from the beginning stages of design throughout the system's life span to decommission and disposal rather than just in the operational phase.

While the previously discussed standards view risk from an enterprise standpoint, Z590.3 is a safety standard. Z590.3 is written to address occupational safety and health risks from conceptual design to decommission—the entire life cycle of a system. ISO 31000 and ANSI RA.1 apply a much broader perspective and are designed to address all types of risks including those that have negative and/or positive consequences with the ultimate purpose of reducing uncertainly to achieve objectives. ISO 31000 encompasses the overall risk management process while Z590.3, *Prevention through Design,* operates within a more focused occupational safety and health (OSH) context.

Z590.3's primary goals are to (1) achieve acceptable risk levels; (2) prevent or reduce risks that produce, injuries, illnesses, and property damage; and (3) reduce the need for retrofitting to address hazards and risks not addressed in the design or redesign phases. PtD, like other safety management concepts, uses a hierarchy of controls model for selection of risk reduction measures shown in Figure 3.6. The hierarchy of controls model provides a systematic way of thinking—considering steps in a ranked and sequential order—to choose the most effective means of eliminating or reducing hazards and their associated risks. The PtD hierarchy of controls model requires the user to begin with (1) avoidance of the risk, (2) elimination of existing risk, (3) substitution with lower hazard-risk, (4) reduction of hazard through engineering controls, (5) warning of existing hazards, (6) administrative controls, and, as a last resort, (7) the use of personal protective equipment. As promoted in PtD, it is best (from a risk level as well as overall costs) to avoid a hazard through design, rather than allow it to exist and try to manage it. (Popov, Lyon, and Hollcroft 2016)

Prevention through design requires the application of risk assessment and risk management in all stages of a system's life cycle and can be applied in any occupational setting. Z590.3 identifies four major stages of a system's life cycle which are:

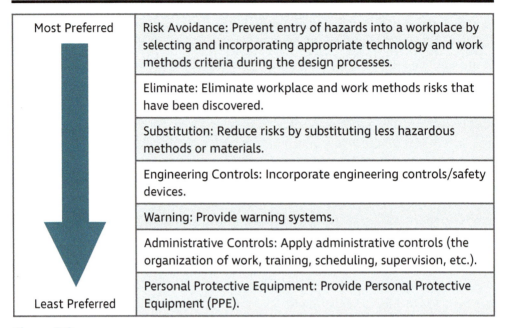

Figure 3.6
Risk Reduction Hierarchy of Controls, Adapted from ANSI/ASSP Z590.3-2011(R2016).

1. Pre-operational stage—conceptual, initial planning, design, specification, prototyping, and construction phases which offer the greatest degree of control and lowest costs.
2. Operational stage—production, maintenance, redesign, modification, addition, and other activities related to the operational phase of a system. Hazards and risk are identified and evaluated with control measures taken through redesign initiatives or work method changes before incidents occur.
3. Post-incident stage—following incidents such as injuries, illnesses, fatalities, property damage, equipment failure, product failure, non-injury incidents, and other unwanted events. Investigations and analysis of causal factors to determine appropriate interventions to reduce recurrence or control similar exposures to an acceptable risk level.
4. Post-operational stage—end of life, decommission, reuse, demolition, and/or disposal of a system. Hazards and risk are identified/anticipated and evaluated with control measures taken through redesign initiatives or work method changes before incidents occur.

Integrating Prevention through Design

Similar to ISO 31000, the ANSI Z590.3 standard requires that PtD concepts be integrated into management policies, responsibilities, and practices. Management should define and implement a process to incorporate risk reduction into the design and redesign processes that includes the following:

- Anticipating/identifying hazard-risks in the conceptual stage so that hazards can be avoided, eliminated, or substituted with less hazardous components.
- A consistent hazard analysis and risk assessment approach to address identified hazards.
- Hazards and their risks should be reduced using the risk reduction hierarchy of controls approach to achieve acceptable risk levels.
- The risk assessment process includes knowledgeable, skilled stakeholders close to the hazards and risks.
- The process monitored by stakeholders for effectiveness and continual improvement.
- Systems for recording and reporting results during design reviews are used.

The standard advises organizations to integrate their "hazard analysis and risk assessment process" into various levels of the organization and include key stakeholders such as designers, engineers, architects, procurement, production, operations, maintenance, quality, human resources, safety and health, legal, and decision makers. It promotes a collaborative approach to planning, conceptualizing, designing, and redesigning and recommends that responsibilities be defined in preventing and reducing risk when:

1. new facilities, processes, equipment, technologies, and materials are planned, designed, acquired, or installed;
2. changes or additions are planned for existing facilities, processes, equipment, technologies, or materials;
3. during incident investigations and selection of corrective actions; and
4. when demolition, decommissioning, or reusing/rebuilding operations are planned.

The level of risk an organization is willing to take—the acceptable risk level—should be established and communicated to stakeholders and integrated into the conceptual design and redesign phases. Such a defined acceptable risk level should be the basis for an organization's overall occupational safety and health goals and objectives. For hazards that cannot be totally avoided or eliminated during design, the organization should establish "acceptable risk targets" that inform decision makers in the design and selection of risk reduction options.

The design process should incorporate appropriate input from affected stakeholders including designers and engineering, procurement, quality, legal, risk management, safety and health, maintenance, supervisors, operations personnel, and others. The organization should verify that personnel knowledgeable, skilled, and experienced in performing risk assessments are utilized in the design process. Communication plans should include design safety specifications, use of risk assessment, and risk-based decision-making as part of the prevention through design process.

Supplier Relationships

Similar to the ANSI B11.0, *Safety of Machinery,* standard, the PtD standard includes sections on supplier and vendor relationships. Measures for affected contractors, suppliers, and vendors involved in new designs, equipment, and construction, changes in processes, materials and technology should be considered and included in the organization's policies and practices. This is critical since many catastrophic incidents have been caused by outside contractors and suppliers that were not properly managed by the organization. Requirements that should be considered by the organization include:

- mutual agreement with suppliers, engineers, and contractors on the expectations related to their management of risk through designs, methods, technologies, and materials;
- written safety and health performance specifications in procurement documents, purchase orders, and contracts;
- use of risk assessment and treatment to achieve an acceptable risk level;
- inspections and test protocols during factory acceptance, site acceptance, and/or commissioning;
- visits to suppliers to verify safety specifications are met prior to purchase/delivery; and
- procedures for ongoing testing and maintenance of systems.

Design Reviews

Anticipating, identifying, assessing, and controlling risks during the design and redesign phase provides the greatest opportunity for avoiding and reducing risk. Reviews and assessments of plans and conceptual designs are performed to incorporate safety into designs and avoid or reduce hazards and their risks. These are often referred to as "design safety reviews." The PtD standard includes guidance on this important management tool for integrating safety into the design process.,

To integrate safety into a new system design, a design review is performed early in the conceptual design or redesign phase. The design review process requires established policies, practices, roles, and responsibilities for conducting such design reviews on an iterative basis. The PtD standard provides guidance to organizations in the establishment of a design review process to include the following:

- Designated design safety review leader to manage the process and coordinate the review.
- Design review team consisting of qualified and trained stakeholders designated to perform design safety reviews.
- Policy outlining how, when, and to what degree design safety reviews will be performed including the risk assessment methods used.
- Appropriate safety requirements and specifications incorporated into the design process.
- Designers held accountable for adhering to established safety specifications in the design, unless the deviation has been reviewed, approved, and documented by management as meeting acceptable risk levels.
- Procedures requiring a written certification signed by the lead design professional verifying that the design safety review has been completed.

Addendum E of ANSI Z590.3 provides further information on the design safety review process.

Decision makers that understand the value of designing out risks before they are introduced into their organizations will have a great opportunity for success. Through the application of prevention through design, organizations can avoid or manage risks much more effectively and efficiently.

Hazard Analysis and Risk Assessment

Similar to the ISO 31000 and 31010 standards, the PtD Z590.3 standard addresses the fundamental steps in risk assessment—risk identification, analysis, and evaluation. However, there are several important distinctions in Z590.3. ISO 31000 and 31010 address management of risk in a much broader sense. While the ISO standards apply to all types of risk (hazard-risk, operational risk, financial risk, and strategic risk), Z590.3 is focused on the assessment and control of hazard-derived risks.

The PtD process involves a "hazard analysis and risk assessment" methodology which closely aligns with the ISO 31000 risk management process model represented in Figure 3.7. Note that "Communication and consultation" (6.2) and "Monitoring and review" (6.6) in ISO 31000 are connected to and involved with all elements of the risk management process.

The following steps are outlined in the PtD standard's hazard analysis and risk assessment process:

Management Direction

The importance of management leadership and direction is emphasized in the PtD standard. Throughout the process, management must set policy and expectations

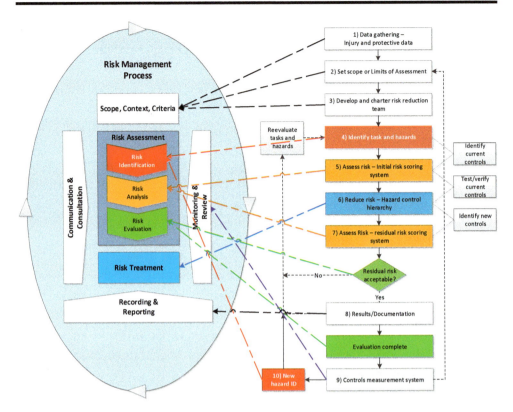

Figure 3.7
Alignment of ISO 31000 and the ANSI/ASSP Z590.3 Risk Assessment Process.

for conceptual designs and the requirement to achieve acceptable risk levels. Policy elements include (1) establishment of a risk assessment matrix and analysis parameters; (2) implementation of a risk assessment process; (3) application of risk treatment methods using the hierarchy of controls; (4) risk acceptance decision-making; and (5) communication, documentation, and follow-up, as outlined in Z590.3.

Risk Assessment Matrix

A risk assessment matrix provides a means of measuring and comparing risk by categorizing combinations of probability of occurrence and severity of outcome. Risk matrices help communicate and prioritize risk levels regarding risk treatment options with decision makers. An organization should establish a risk assessment matrix or other validated process that is suitable and agreed upon by the stakeholders to measure and compare risks.

Analysis Parameters

The context for each analysis should be well-defined prior to the analysis. It should include the parameters and scope; the process, product, project, or task to be analyzed; and the context of the analysis, boundaries and limitations, operating phase, resources, and affected stakeholders.

Hazard Identification

Hazards should be anticipated and identified, along with methods to avoid, eliminate, or reduce their presence by trained and experienced risk assessors. This requires an understanding of technologies, activities, and characteristics (equipment, technology, processes, materials, chemicals, etc.) or actions or inactions of people that could result in exposure or unwanted energy release. A systems approach, treating each hazard independently, as well as their synergistic effects should be applied with the intent of achieving acceptable risks for all. Special attention should be given to anticipating and uncovering hidden hazards or hazards that can be later created but not initially recognized.

Failure Modes

Potential failure modes resulting from credible circumstances that could result in hazardous situations shall be considered, including the reasonably foreseeable uses and misuses of facilities, materials, and equipment. Existing controls should be considered as to their effectiveness, reliability, and whether the condition of controls can cause failures or be easily defeated.

Severity Analysis

The worst credible consequences (an incident that has the potential to occur within the lifetime of the system) should be considered rather than the worst conceivable risk (an incident that could occur, but probably will not occur, within a system's lifetime). Historical data, past experience, and best engineering practices that provide objective information regarding injuries or illnesses and their severity, property or equipment values, potential business interruption, environmental damage, or market share loss can be used.

Probability Analysis

An estimate of the likelihood or probability of a hazard-risk's occurrence should be determined. Analysis may include the frequency and duration of exposure, or dose response and exposure assessments, and is typically related to an interval base such as a unit of time, activity, events, units produced, or life cycle of a facility, machine, material, process, or product.

Initial Risk

The initial risk is evaluated and determined using the selected risk assessment criteria and matrix to categorize the hazard's severity and probability risk levels. The evaluation should consider any existing controls for the hazard's occurrence or severity.

Risk Reduction and Control Methods

For risks that require further risk reduction, the hierarchy of controls model is used to select proper risk reduction measures. The PtD hierarchy model lists, in descending order of effectiveness and preference: (1) avoidance, (2) elimination, (3) substitution, (4) engineering controls, (5) warning, (6) administrative controls, and (7) personal protective equipment. Prioritizing risks for reduction and a system to track risk reduction measures for effectiveness should be included in the process.

Residual Risk

Following the risk reduction measures, a second assessment is made to determine the remaining risk, which is known as residual risk. If the residual risk is not acceptable, further risk reduction measures are applied where feasible until the risk is considered acceptable to the organization. As the standard states, "if an acceptable risk level cannot be achieved, operations shall not continue, except in unusual and emergency circumstances or as a closely monitored and limited exception circumstance with approval of the person having authority to accept the risk."

Risk Acceptance

Using the organization's defined "acceptable risk levels," decision makers will determine whether the risk is acceptable or if further action is required. In certain situations, higher risks may be tolerated temporarily until risk measures can be implemented.

Documentation

Information such as details on assessment team, dates, methods, hazards, and risks identified, measures taken to reduce risk, and other related information should be recorded by the organization conducting the assessment.

Follow Up

Effectiveness and reliability of implemented control measures should be verified to determine if the risk was adequately reduced, that no new hazards were created, or if additional measures are needed. If it is determined the risk level is not acceptable, or that unintended consequences were introduced by the control measures, the organization should take steps to reassess the risk and consider other risk reduction measures.

Assessment Methods

Methods suitable to analyze and assess the operation or system should be selected and applied by the organization. Proper training and resources to successfully apply methods should be included in the process. ISO 31010's Annex includes descriptions of 42 methods while ANSI RA.1 references 20 techniques. The PtD standard identifies eight techniques in Addendum G, and TR-31010 technical report covers 50 risk management and risk assessment techniques.

Most hazard-risk or operational risk situations can be adequately assessed using three common methods: (1) Preliminary Hazard Analysis, (2) What-if/Checklist Analysis, and (3) Failure Mode and Effects Analysis. In some cases, several techniques are used to adequately assess and communicate risks to decision makers.

Even though there are numerous methods and variations, all are based on the same fundamental process: (1) hazard-risk identification; (2) risk analysis; and (3) risk evaluation. A comparison of methods identified in ISO 31010, ANSI RA.1, ANSI/ASSP Z590.3 and ASSP TR-31010 is shown in Chapter 5, Selecting Methods.

Summary

Enterprise risk management is a complex and dynamic process that requires an integrated approach within an organization. Consensus standards in risk assessment and risk management are vitally important in providing fundamental guidance to organizations and risk professionals. An understanding of the principles, framework, and process as well as some experience in risk management techniques helps provide a foundation for risk professionals in guiding their organizations in the management of risk.

Review Questions

1. Identify the primary objectives for managing risk and explain why each objective is important to an organization.
2. List and describe the eight principles for risk management found in ISO 31000. Identify the core purpose of risk management.
3. Describe the framework for risk management found in ISO 31000.
4. Describe in order the elements within the risk management process.
5. Besides ISO 31000, list other standards for risk management and risk assessment.
6. In a paragraph, describe the prevention through design concept. Identify three unique requirements found in ANSI/ASSP Z590.3, *Prevention through Design*.

References

ANSI/ASIS/RIMS RA.1-2015. 2015. *Risk Assessment.* Alexandria, VA: ASIS International and The Risk and Insurance Management Society, Inc.

ANSI/ASSP Z10.0-2019. 2019. *Occupational Health and Safety Management Systems.* Park Ridge, IL: American Society of Safety Professionals.

ANSI/ASSP Z590.3-2011 (R2016). 2016. *Prevention through Design: Guidelines for Addressing Occupational Hazards and Risks in Design and Redesign Processes.* Park Ridge, IL: American Society of Safety Professionals.

ANSI/ASSP Z690.1-2011. 2011. *Vocabulary for Risk Management.* Park Ridge, IL: American Society of Safety Professionals.

ANSI/ASSP Z690.2-2011. 2011. *Risk Management Principles and Guidelines.* Park Ridge, IL: American Society of Safety Professionals.

ANSI/ASSP Z690.3-2011. 2011. *Risk Assessment Techniques.* Park Ridge, IL: American Society of Safety Professionals.

ANSI/ASSP/ISO 31000-2018. 2018. *Risk Management Principles and Guidelines.* Park Ridge, IL: American Society of Safety Professionals, 2018.

ANSI/ASSP/ISO 45001-2018. 2018. *Occupational Health and Safety Management Systems—Requirements with Guidance for Use.* Park Ridge, IL: American Society of Safety Professionals.

ANSI/ASSP/ISO/IEC 31010-2019. 2019. *Risk Management—Risk Assessment Techniques.* Park Ridge, IL: American Society of Safety Professionals.

ASSP TR-31010-2020. 2020. *Technical Report on Risk Assessment Techniques.* Park Ridge, IL: American Society of Safety Professionals.

Lyon, Bruce K., and Georgi Popov. 2018. *Risk Management Tools for Safety Professionals.* Park Ridge, IL: American Society of Safety Professionals.

Merriam-Webster. n.d. "Principle." Accessed October 13, 2020. www.merriam-webster.com/dictionary/principle.

Popov, Georgi, Bruce K. Lyon, and Bruce Hollcroft. 2016. *Risk Assessment: A Practical Guide to Assessing Operational Risks.* Hoboken, NJ: Wiley.

CHAPTER 4
Planning the Risk Assessment

Introduction

For any risk management effort to be successful, its context must be clearly defined, communicated, and understood by stakeholders. Planning the assessment is largely based on an established context and criteria. Without planning, the assessment will lack clear direction, boundaries, or purpose. Primary considerations in the planning process include determining the purpose of the assessment; identifying the stakeholders, the decision makers, and the decisions or actions to which the assessment relates; and the scope and limitations of the effort, timeframe, and resources needed (Lyon, Hollcroft 2012; Lyon, Popov 2018).

As described in ISO 31000, "the purpose of establishing the context is to customize the risk management process, enabling effective risk assessment and appropriate risk treatment. This involves defining the purpose and scope of the process, understanding the context, planning the approach to be taken and defining the criteria for evaluation. Establishing the context should take into account the external and internal context established as part of the risk management framework" (ANSI/ASSP/ISO 31000-2018).

A well-defined and communicated context is essential in the successful implementation of a risk management effort. Without context, and a clear purpose and scope, there is a risk of the effort drifting out of control (*i.e.*, scope creep.) Too

---

Interactive tools and supplemental materials are available at assp.org/ermtools.

many times, well-intentioned but ill-defined initiatives have evolved into something well beyond what was originally intended and agreed upon, causing misuse of resources and/or disappointed stakeholders. Establishing the context early at the beginning of the process (as shown in Figure 4.1) is essential, and its importance is reflected in key risk management consensus standards including:

- ISO 31000 (ANSI/ASSP/ISO 31000-2018), *Risk Management Guidelines,* Section 6.3, Establishing the Context.
- ISO 31010 (ANSI/ASSP/ISO/IEC 31010-2019), *Risk Management – Risk Assessment Techniques,* Section 6.1, Plan the Assessment.
- ANSI/ASSP Z590.3-2011 (R2016), *Prevention through Design: Guidelines for Addressing Occupational Hazards and Risks in Design and Redesign Processes,* begins "The Hazard Analysis and Risk Assessment Process" in section 7 with Management Direction; Selecting a Risk Assessment Matrix; and Establish the Analysis Parameters.
- ANSI/ASIS/RIMS RA.1-2015, *Risk Assessment,* Section 5.3, places context at the beginning of the risk management framework.

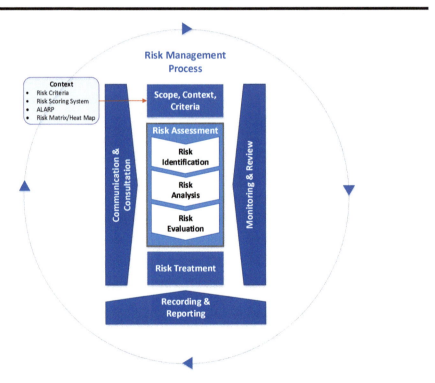

Figure 4.1
ISO 31000 Risk Management Process and Methods for Establishing Context.

According to the Business Dictionary (n.d.), *context* is defined as: (1) background, environment, framework, setting, or situation surrounding an event or occurrence; (2) words and sentences that occur before or after a word or sentence and imbue it with a particular meaning; (3) the circumstances under which a document was created, including its function, purpose, use, time, the creator, and the recipient.

From a risk management perspective, ISO Guide 73 (ANSI/ASSP Z690.1-2011) Vocabulary for Risk Management states that "establishing the context" is "defining the external and internal parameters to be taken into account when managing risk, setting the scope and risk criteria (3.3.1.3) for the risk management policy (2.1.2)." In terms of risk management, the context provides direction and meaning. It should include the initiative's: (1) purpose, (2) scope and limitations, (3) external and internal environment, (4) stakeholders and decision makers, (5) risk criteria to be used, (6) decision or action to be determined, and (7) resources and timeframe as shown in Figure 4.2.

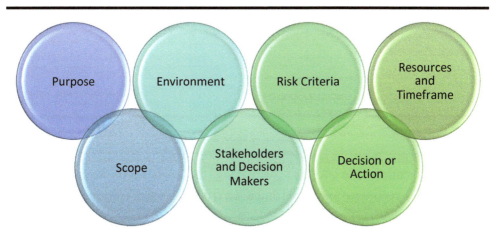

Figure 4.2
Elements within a Context.

Context and the Decision-Making Process

In the risk-based decision-making (RBDM) model introduced in Chapter 1, the process begins with identifying the decision to be made and its context. The RBDM process shown in Figure 4.3 provides the sequence of steps used in making risk-based decisions. RBDM's primary goals are to reduce uncertainty and achieve better outcomes in decision-making.

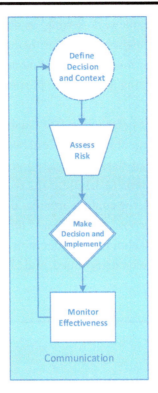

Figure 4.3
Context for Risk-based Decision-Making.

The first step in RBDM is to define the decision to be made and its context—the "decision structure" as the US Coast Guard define it. Understanding and defining the planned decision is often overlooked, but it is a critical step that requires the following:

1. Define decision. A specific description of the decision that is being planned should be developed. There are many types of decisions that can be required by organizations which can be at the strategic, tactical, or operational level. Some decisions are routine type decisions while others are unique.
2. Identify decision makers and stakeholders. Those required to be involved in the decision-making process should be identified. This includes soliciting involvement from (1) those involved in making the decision and (2) those affected by the results of the decision.
3. Identify options. The available options should be described, including their anticipated costs and benefits, as well as their expected effectiveness and reliability. Research, evidence, historical data, potential influences, and other supportive information is useful in assisting in the selection of credible alternative and options.

> **Example:** An organization may need to make several different types of decisions. These types of decisions may include the decision to:
>
> - Accept or reject a proposed action or idea
> - Determine what is to be evaluated and the responsible stakeholders
> - Select the proper option(s)
> - Prioritize actions and resources
> - Change course or direction
> - Begin or end a process

4. Identify influences. Factors that may influence the decision should be determined. Considerations such as timeframe and schedule, budgets and resources, external and internal stakeholders, environment, and other relevant factors should be identified and understood.
5. Gather information. Risk assessments, cost-/benefit analyses, and other studies should be performed, and the resulting information gathered, along with the information collected in the previous steps for the decision-making process.

Decision-making requires sound planning and the development of its decision structure or context. This is the first step of decision-making as well as the planning process for risk management.

Purpose, Scope, and Objectives

Planning for a risk management effort requires the establishment of several critical components: purpose, scope, and context. A critical part of the planning is the establishment of the purpose, parameters, limits and scope of a risk management project. Most have experienced first-hand the importance of understanding the scope and purpose of an endeavor. Much like a written contractual agreement between parties, a clear scope and purpose statement identifies and describes the specific objectives, limits and boundaries, resources, and responsibilities of each party.

Context should define the purpose and scope of the initiative, the responsibilities and accountabilities for stakeholders, the methodologies and techniques to be employed, the risk criteria, the timeframe, and the resources available. A well-defined beginning and end are critically important for setting specific boundaries for the activity with internal (resources, knowledge, culture, and values among others) and external (legal, regulatory, economy, perceptions of external stakeholders, etc.) parameters in mind. (Lyon, Popov 2018).

The purpose and scope should be defined up-front by the organization and reviewed and revised as necessary during the process. The purpose and scope should be documented and it should be clearly written and effectively communicated with affected stakeholders. Factors, both internal and external, that may influence the effort should be considered. The following includes information that is needed in the planning process:

- Type of decision(s) required;
- Business objectives affected;
- Outcomes;
- Timeframe, location, boundaries and limits, inclusions, and exclusions;
- Methods and techniques to be used;
- Resources (internal and external), materials, equipment, training, experts, etc.;
- Specific responsibilities and accountabilities; and
- Documentation and recordkeeping.

The purpose, scope and objectives statement should be used as a guide during the process to keep the effort on track. This requires a precise "Purpose, Scope, and Objectives" statement that contains "SMART" information—information that is "specific, measurable, attainable, relevant, and time sensitive." An example of a precise SMART purpose, scope, and objectives statement is provided in the following text box.

> **Example**: *Purpose, Scope, and Objectives for the Design Phase Risk Assessment of Parts Washer Station*
>
> *Purpose:* This activity is to be conducted as part of the organization's objective to practice prevention through design and manage operational risks to an acceptable level, and to follow the corporate risk assessment and risk reduction policy. The specific purpose of this design phase risk assessment is to anticipate and identify hazards in the conceptual design phase to allow designers to avoid introducing hazards and engineer the design so as to reduce risks associated with the new parts washer station. The design phase risk assessment will also provide a formal risk priority number for the new station so as to monitor, manage, and maintain risk levels associated with the workstation as low as reasonably practicable (ALARP). The risk assessment will result in helping the organization achieve its objectives related to quality of work environment, employee wellness, sustainability, governance, and regulatory compliance.
>
> *Scope:* The scope of this risk assessment will be limited to the conceptual design of the parts washer station being designed and constructed by the company's design and build department in the main manufacturing

division, sub-assembly lines (specifically the A and B lines) located in the St. Louis, Missouri, facility. The risk assessment will be conducted by a knowledgeable cross-functional team (including mechanical engineers, structural engineers, production management, maintenance, quality, operators, and OSH) trained in the risk assessment methods to be used. The effort will be facilitated by a risk assessment champion from corporate Risk Management, familiar with the operation and stakeholders. Individual responsibilities and assignments will be designated to each team member. Risk assessment methods to be used will include hazard identification using HAZID, Checklists, and Brainstorming; risk analysis using preliminary hazard analysis; and risk evaluation using the company's risk matrix and action levels. The risk assessment is expected to require two weeks to fully complete and will involve the use of the facility's conference room with white board, AV equipment, and computer setups. Documentation and recordkeeping will be maintained in the corporate Risk Register. A Risk Reduction Action Tracking spreadsheet will be used to record current and future risks, existing controls and recommended controls, assignments and responsible parties, and target dates for completion. The timeframe for the new parts washer to be installed is July 1, 2019. The assessment will begin on January 15, 2019 and end by January 30, 2019.

Objectives: The objectives of this effort are to facilitate the identification and avoidance or reduction of hazard-risks as low as reasonably practicable (ALARP) within the design of the parts washer station. This in in support of the risk management policies and practices to effectively manage and communicate risks with stakeholders. Further, this effort is to support and align with the organization's overall objective to increase market share as a Tier 1 supplier, maintain a lean process that is resilient, provide an excellent working environment for people, and be a responsible and respected corporation and member of the community.

With any risk management process, its mission and application must be clear. Is the risk management effort being applied at the strategic level, operational level, or for a specific project or activity? It is important that the established purpose and scope align with the organization's objectives. As part of the planning process, the following should be considered: (1) the objectives or decisions to be made; (2) the specific target or location and its boundaries; (3) appropriate risk management tools and techniques; (4) resources required; (5) stakeholders and responsibilities; (6) records to be kept; and (7) relationships with other projects, processes, and activities.

The context should be framed so that it aligns with and supports the organization's overall objectives. As ISO 31000 states, "objectives are the intended results to be achieved by the organization from a strategic, tactical or operational level, and can involve financial, expansion or growth, legal, safety or other types of goals" (ANSI/ASSP/ISO 31000-2018). Much like a guidance system for a missile, a clearly defined purpose, scope, and context helps ensure the target and objectives are achieved.

External and Internal Context

The basic parameters must be defined by the organization at the beginning of the risk management process. These parameters begin with considering the external environment in which the organization operates. Management must have an understanding of the external landscape, influences, interactions, and relationships that affect the organization to properly define the parameters of the risk management activity. External environmental factors can include:

- social and cultural environments
- external stakeholders' (customers, suppliers, public, etc.) perceptions, needs, objectives, and relationships
- legal and political climate
- regulatory aspects
- competitive factors
- key business drivers
- financial influences
- economic climate and outlook
- potential changes and developments
- other relevant external factors

Such factors that affect objectives and concerns of stakeholders are necessary to understand when developing the context, purpose, and scope statement, and selecting the specific risk criteria to be used.

Equally important to consider is an organization's internal context. Internal context is the organization's internal environment in which it operates to achieve its objectives (ANSI/ASSP/ISO 31000-2018). Alignment of internal elements with the context should include the following elements within the organization:

- culture, perceptions, and values
- mission, goals, and objectives
- strategy, structure, and management style
- capabilities, resources, and knowledge
- stakeholders and decision-makers
- policies, practices, and protocols

Human, organizational, and social factors should be considered since they can contribute to uncertainty and influence how techniques are selected and applied and how information is interpreted. The potential for deviation from expected or assumed behaviors should be considered when assessing risk since human factors can affect control effectiveness and reliability. Also, human factors may influence selection and use of techniques, especially where team approaches are used.

Risk Criteria

Defining the criteria to be used in risk-based decisions is an essential aspect of planning. Such criteria enable an organization to consistently compare, evaluate, and judge risks as part of the decision-making process. Criteria may include qualitative, semi-quantitative, and quantitative measures. Examples of risk criteria measures can be found in risk management standards and reference materials; however, an organization should carefully select and develop risk criteria to align with its values, goals, industry setting, and culture.

Risk criteria are the defined reference points and measurements used to evaluate and compare against the risk levels determined in the risk analysis. ANSI/ASSP/ISO 690.1-2011 defines risk criteria as "terms of reference against which the significance of a risk is evaluated." Risk criteria are used to understand the nature of risk and determine risk levels in risk analysis and are used to compare these risk levels with the organization's established criteria during risk evaluation to determine whether the risk is acceptable or in need of risk reduction treatment. Risk criteria generally include criteria or methods for:

- risk scoring
- risk acceptability
- evaluating significance of risk
- selecting risk treatment options

For hazard-risk, ANSI/ASSP Z590.3-2011 (R2016) states that an estimate of the probability/likelihood of an occurrence and the severity of harm or damage resulting from an occurrence must be calculated. This requires criteria that include two basic risk factors: likelihood and severity. Other risk factors may be necessary depending upon the context and may include:

- exposure
- frequency
- duration
- failure detectability
- control reliability
- prevention effectiveness

An organization should understand and define its criteria to evaluate the significance of risk (ANSI/ASIS/RIMS RA.1-2015). Risk criteria selection and development should reflect the values, culture, and objectives of the organization and should be considered dynamic rather than static. Risk criteria are the basis for risk-based decision-making and action taken. Specifically, it is the criteria to determine: (1) how risk is to be analyzed, (2) outputs required from the analysis, and (3) the most appropriate risk management techniques to be used (ANSI/ASSP/ISO 31010-2019).

The basis for developing risk criteria consists of determining and defining the key elements to be used including:

- Consequences—according to the established context, the nature and types of consequences to be included in the assessment such as human safety and health, environmental protection, business interruption, financial losses, legal, political, reputational damage, regulatory compliance, or other consequences are identified and defined as part of the risk criteria.
- Likelihood—somethings referred to as probability, is determined and expressed in the risk assessment based on the context, information, data, and resources available.
- Risk levels—graduated levels of risk used in the risk analysis and evaluation, and a mechanism or scoring system are determined in order to provide a consistent method of risk scoring. A risk matrix is generally selected to provide a standardized method to categorize risk levels using combinations of likelihood of an occurrence and severity of the consequence.
- Risk acceptability—the level of risk that an organization formally decides to accept is determined and defined based on the organization's culture, objectives, industry, legal and regulatory climate, as well as other factors.
- Risk treatment—decision-making guidelines for methods to avoid or reduce risk using a hierarchy of controls model and the organization's acceptable risk level.
- Combined risks—risk criteria should include how combined risks will be identified, assessed, and treated if necessary.

Risk criteria selection should be carefully considered to properly serve the organization's needs within the context, as well as provide the desired results. Caution is advised in trying to achieve "perfect" risk criteria, since this is not practical nor necessary. The risk professional should seek to select criteria that allow stakeholders to assess, measure, and achieve acceptable risk levels in a consistent, accurate, and effective manner.

Systems for Scoring Risk

A risk measurement system is needed to consistently and effectively describe, assess, and manage risks within an organization. Fundamental components of a risk scoring system include a method of scoring and the organization's stated acceptable risk level. Most risk scoring systems consist of a two-factor calculation using likelihood (L) of event occurrence and severity of consequence (S). However, more complex systems using three or four risk factors are becoming more common. The additional risk factors may include impact, frequency, failure detectability, control effectiveness, risk emergence, or other factors.

A risk scoring system provides a standardized method for estimating, measuring, and comparing risks. Such a system can be qualitative, semi-quantitative, or quantitative and is used to characterize how established risk factors combine to determine a risk level. A key purpose of a scoring system is to provide decision makers some sense of prioritization and action for reducing risks. Elements within a scoring system include (1) risk characterization, (2) risk factors, (3) risk levels, (4) risk actions, and (5) risk screening and communication.

Risk Characterization

Stakeholders should determine whether risk characterization will be qualitative, semi-quantitative, or quantitative in nature. This is largely based on the degree of complexity, available data and resources, and the detail needed. Qualitative models are based on subjective descriptions and define levels using descriptive words such as "high," "medium," and "low," which are evaluated according to qualitative criteria.

A simple qualitative risk characterization model taken from NFPA 70E is presented in Table 4.1. It is a 2 × 2 matrix with energy greater or less than the selected threshold and likelihood of improbable or possible.

Table 4.1. Simple Matrix adapted from NFPA 70E.

Likelihood of Occurrence of Harm	Severity of Harm	
	Energy ≤ (Selected Threshold)	Energy ≥ (Selected Threshold)
Improbable	Low	Low
Possible	Low	High

Table 4.2 is another example of a qualitative matrix based on the ANSI/ASSP Z10-2012 (R2017) model.

Table 4.2. Qualitative Risk Assessment (5 × 4) Matrix adapted from ANSI/ASSP Z10-2012 (R2017).

Likelihood of Occurrence or Exposure for select unit of Time or Activity	← Severity of Injury or Illness Consequence →			
	Negligible	Marginal	Critical	Catastrophic
Frequent	Medium	Serious	High	High
Probable	Medium	Serious	High	High
Occasional	Low	Medium	Serious	High
Remote	Low	Medium	Medium	Serious
Improbable	Low	Low	Low	Medium

Semi-quantitative risk models use qualitative data that is expressed by numerical values using a formula to produce a risk score. Advantages include the ability to provide more precision in definitions by including numerical ranges for severity and likelihood, and the ability to more easily compare and communicate risk levels. Semi-quantitative values are determined using qualified judgements and experience and are not based on quantitative data, which is often difficult to obtain. Tables 4.3, 4.4, and 4.5 provide an example of a semi-quantitative risk assessment matrix and its descriptions for likelihood and severity levels.

Risk Factors

Variables used to measure risk and produce a risk score are called risk factors. The primary factors are severity of consequence (S), and likelihood or probability of occurrence (L). Risk assessment codes (RACs) are used to denote risk factors using initials such as (S) for severity of consequence or (L) for likelihood of occurrence. Certain risk scoring models include additional risk factors such as exposure (E), frequency of exposure (F), time duration of exposure (T), failure detectability (D), control or prevention effectiveness (PE), vulnerability (V), or other risk measures.

Risk factors used can vary from two-dimensional formulas using severity and likelihood, to more complex three- and four-dimensional models. In the MIL-STD 882E standard, a qualitative two-factor scoring system with risk codes for severity of consequences (S) and probability (P) is presented (MIL-STD 882E, 2012). An example of a three-factor system is provided in ANSI B11.0-2015 Safety of Machinery Annex H, Sample Risk Assessment, which uses frequency (F), likelihood

Table 4.3. Semi-Quantitative Risk Assessment (5 × 4) Matrix Example.

	← Severity of Injury or Illness Consequence →			
Likelihood of Occurrence or Exposure for select unit of Time or Activity	Negligible (1)	Marginal (2)	Critical (3)	Catastrophic (4)
Frequent (5)	5	10	15	20
Probable (4)	4	8	12	16
Occasional (3)	3	6	9	12
Remote (2)	2	4	6	8
Improbable (1)	1	2	3	4

Table 4.4. Semi-Quantitative Descriptions for Likelihood of Occurrence Example.

Risk Level	Likelihood of Occurrence (L)	Description
5	Frequent	Almost certain to occur. Has occurred more than once within the last 12 months. Conditions exist for it to occur.
4	Probable	Very Likely to occur. Has occurred once within the last 12 months. Conditions often exist for it to occur.
3	Occasional	Likely to occur if conditions exist. Has occurred within the last 24 months. Conditions can exist for it to occur.
2	Moderate	May occur if conditions exist. Has occurred within the last 36 months. Conditions sometimes exist for it to occur.
1	Unlikely	Unlikely to occur. Has not occurred within last 5 years. Conditions rarely exist for it to occur.

(L), and severity (S). Risk factors and their risk assessment codes used in various three- and four-dimensional models include the following:

- Exposure (E)—measure of exposure events/units
- Frequency of Exposure (F)—number of exposure events for a unit of time

Table 4.5. Semi-Quantitative Descriptions for Severity of Consequence Example.

Risk Level	Severity of Consequence (S)	Description
4	Catastrophic	One or more fatalities; multiple serious hospitalizations; incident resulting in more than $250K.
3	Critical	Disabling injury or illness; permanent impairment; incident resulting in more than $5K.
2	Marginal	Medical treatment or restricted work; recordable incidents; incident resulting in more than $1K.
1	Low	First aid or non-treatment incidents; incident resulting in less than $1K.

- Time Duration of Exposure (T)—time period that a single exposure occurs
- Vulnerability (V)—weaknesses in a system that are factored into the risk estimation
- Detection of Failure (D)—estimate of how easily the potential failure could be detected prior to its occurrence
- Control Reliability (CR)—the reliability of a selected control into the risk estimation
- Prevention Effectiveness (PE)—control's effectiveness in preventing a failure from occurring

Multiple risk factors in a risk scoring formula can dilute the importance of severity. Keeping it simple and using only those that are necessary to properly estimate risk for the application is recommended.

Risk Factor Levels

Graduated risk levels (sometimes referred to as risk categories) for each risk factor are defined from low to high. Risk factor levels are used in calculating risk acceptability and prioritization for risk reduction. Risk levels for each factor (*i.e.*, likelihood and severity) are combined to produce a risk score used in the risk assessment. Risk score categories generally are accompanied with required action such as immediate work stoppage or required controls to reduce risk to an acceptable level. The levels (generally four to five) of risk are defined and used to create a scale for distinguishing differences in risk for the purpose of making consistent decisions regarding risk. Four-level models for a two-dimensional system

(4 × 4 matrix) require the assessor to rank risks either above or below the middle, while five-level models (5 × 5) provide a mid-level score. Models that combine four levels for one risk factor with five levels for a second risk factor (4 × 5) are also common as represented in the ANSI/ASSP Z10 standard (see Table 4.3).

Risk Scoring Mechanism

Risk scores are produced from the risk formula and are used to evaluate, rank, and prioritize risk treatment. Selecting a risk scoring system that works within an organization and is in alignment with the established context and criteria is more important than which system is selected (Main 2012).

The two-dimensional risk formula which includes severity of consequences and likelihood of occurrence is most common. Risk factors can be multiplied or added to produce the risk score as shown:

$$\textbf{Risk Score (R) = Severity (S)} \times \textbf{Likelihood (L)}$$

or

$$\textbf{Risk Score (R) = Severity (S) + Likelihood (L)}$$

Risk models can include a third factor to score risk. In applications where risk controls are analyzed, a "prevention effectiveness" (PE) factor estimating a control's reliability and effectiveness is used. When three or more risk factors are used, a risk priority number (RPN) is produced as shown in the three-dimensional risk formula:

$$\textbf{Risk Priority Number (RPN)} = S \times L \times PE$$

Four-variable scoring systems are sometimes used including factors such as frequency, exposure, vulnerability, or other factors. Three- and four-variable risk factor systems should be used with caution to avoid diluting the severity level of a particular risk if all four factors are given equal weight. For instance, when the four factors are multiplied together giving each risk factor equal weighting, severity is undervalued. With a three-factor equation, each has a weighting of 33% of the final risk score as shown below.

$$\textbf{RRN} = S \times P \times \textbf{Frequency of Exposure}$$

To provide proper weighting of severity in multiple factor equations, severity should be multiplied with the sum of the remaining risk factors as shown in the following formulas:

$$\textbf{RRN} = S \times (L + \text{Exposure})$$

or

$$\textbf{RPN} = S \times \left(\frac{L \times E}{2} \right)$$

Risk Levels

Risk levels or risk priority numbers (RPNs) are produced during the risk analysis by inputting the risk factors into the risk scoring formula. RPNs are produced from three or more risk factors, while risk scores are produced from two factors (S x L). Risk levels can be qualitative using descriptors such as unacceptable, serious, moderate, and low; semi-quantitative using numerical values from qualitative data; and quantitative using numerical values from statistical, manufacturers, or historical data. The resulting risk level or RPN is then evaluated and compared to the established risk assessment matrix to determine its ranking and necessary action.

Action Guidelines

The organization should determine what actions are to be taken for each level of risk ranging from the highest risks to the lowest. These actions should be based on the organization's risk acceptance, culture, and objectives among other factors.

Risk Screening Tools

Tools used to screen, rank, compare, and communicate risk are commonly used, such as risk matrices (examples shown in Tables 4.3 and 4.4), heat maps (as illustrated in Figure 4.4), graphs, and risk priority numbers (RPNs). They provide a means of measuring and comparing risks to help decision makers in selecting and treating risk.

When determining the risk scoring system's criteria categories, sources such as key standards mentioned in this manual, industry groups, and professional organizations should be considered in developing specific criteria needed.

Acceptable Level of Risk

A certain amount of risk will always be present requiring an organization to decide what level of risk is acceptable and where risk levels require treatment or control. Residual risks are risks that remain after treatment.

The term *acceptable risk level* can be defined as "the level of risk an organization will intentionally or knowingly accept or tolerate in its current context." The key word is "knowingly" since many times organizations "unknowingly" have risks that they would not tolerate if it were known by decision makers. Risk acceptance is determined by an organization's industry, corporate culture, societal climate, political, legal and regulatory environment, and existing technology, among other factors. It is critical that an organization put into practice a risk assessment process with defined risk criteria and acceptable risk level.

ALARP, the concept of "as low as reasonably practicable," is defined as the "level of risk which can be further lowered only by an increase in resource expenditure that are disproportionate in relation to the resulting decrease in risk" (ANSI Z590.3-2011,

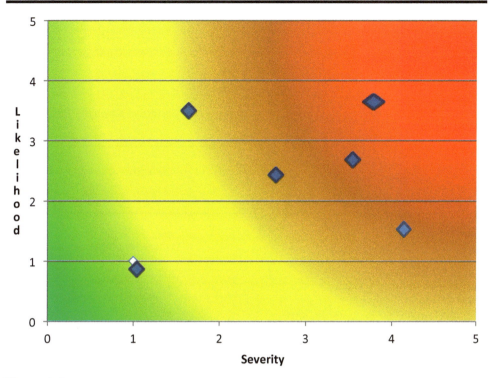

Figure 4.4
Risk Heat Map Example.

R2016). ALARP is the application of risk reduction within a positive cost-benefit analysis ratio. When a particular risk within an organization is lowered to the "point of diminishing returns," and it can no longer be effectively reduced, it is considered "as low as reasonably practicable." The ALARP concept is illustrated in Figure 4.5.

Selecting Risk Assessment Methods

The ability to properly select, customize, and combine methods to assess operational risks provides risk professionals a certain advantage and value to their organization. With the diversity and types of risks that are encountered by organizations, risk professionals must be able to determine which techniques are most appropriate for the situation's complexity and context. To be successful, the professional must be familiar with available risk assessment methods, their applications, strengths and weaknesses.

As a general rule, risk assessment techniques should be selected with the following considerations as shown in Figure 4.6. Simplicity—the simplest method that provides the risk-based information needed for the assessment should be selected. Overly complex methods should be avoided. Customize—it

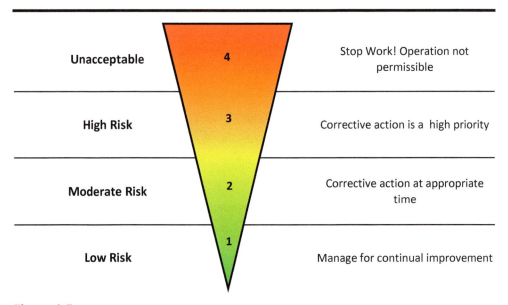

Figure 4.5
Risk Levels and Their Required Actions.

Figure 4.6
Selecting Risk Assessment Tools.

is often necessary to modify existing methods to fit the needs of the assessment. Customizing the method allows for specific elements to be included in the assessment, providing emphasis on critical elements as well as creating ownership by the assessment team. Combine—rarely is one method adequate for fully identifying, analyzing, and evaluating risk. Most efforts require the use of several methods sequentially. Chapter 5 further addresses the selection of methods.

Risk Criteria Selection

Risk criteria are determined as part of the context and include the risk type (qualitative, semi-quantitative, or quantitative), risk factors, risk levels/tiers, risk scoring system, action guidelines for risk levels, and risk screening tools. A process that can be used for selecting risk criteria is shown in Figure 4.7.

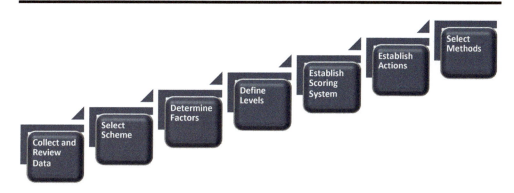

Figure 4.7
Risk Criteria Selection Process.

1. *Collect and Review Data*—To begin, the following data and information should be collected and reviewed in preparation for developing the risk criteria to be used. Internal and external data and information may include:
   - Internal Information
     - Organization's risk management philosophy, culture, policies, and objectives
     - Previous risk assessment information
     - Previous risk-based decisions and their results
     - Past safety performance records, significant incidents, incident rates, etc.
     - Existing key performance indicators (KPI) and key risk indicators (KRI)
   - External Information
     - Consensus standards
     - Industry groups, institutes, societies, and organizations
     - Government and regulatory agencies
     - Industry safety records
     - Technical publications and reference books
2. *Select Scheme*—Depending upon the scope and complexity of the initiative, and the decision to be made, the type of analysis or risk scheme in terms of qualitative, semi-quantitative, or quantitative measures is determined. For most

situations, qualitative and semi-quantitative models work well and are generally recommended. If a more precise measure is required, and the necessary data is available, a quantitative approach may be in order. In any case, proper explanation and justification for the risk measures selected should be well understood and communicated with stakeholders.

3. *Determine Factors*—Risk factor variables to be used in measuring risk are selected. In addition to the primary risk factors of severity and likelihood, other factors may be necessary. Common risk factors and their descriptions include:
   - *Severity*—magnitude of impact, harm, or consequence
   - *Likelihood*—chance for occurrence based on non-statistical data
   - *Probability*—chance of occurrence based on statistical data
   - *Exposure*—population level exposed expressed in a numerical value
   - *Frequency*—how often exposure occurs based on a rate unit (*i.e.,* 4 occurrences per hour)
   - *Duration*—the length of time exposure occurs
   - *Failure detectability*—the level of detectability of a potential failure prior to its failure
   - *Control effectiveness*—the estimated effectiveness of a given control
   - *Vulnerability*—a degree of weakness in the system
   - *Protection Factor*—a multiplier used to reflect the degree of prevention or protection from a given hazard control measure

4. *Define Levels*—For each risk factor variable, defined risk levels, categories, or tiers are established. The number of levels can range from 2 to over 10 but are more commonly 3 to 6. Two-dimensional risk models (such as S × L) feature equal levels for both risk factors (such as four levels of severity and four levels of likelihood) creating a 4 × 4 or 5 × 5 matrix model. In some cases, risk factors can have different numbers of levels (such as four levels for severity and five levels for likelihood) creating a 4 × 5 matrix. Tables 4.4 and 4.5 provide examples of defined risk levels.

5. *Establish Scoring System*—The risk scoring system to be used is selected or created to achieve the objectives of the risk assessment effort. Existing models are available from a number of consensus standards, industry practices, and other sources cited in this manual. The risk scoring system should provide a proper balance between speed and ease of use with degree of detail and discernment needed. Depending upon the number of risk factors and their levels of risk, a risk scoring formula is selected, modified, or created to produce a risk score or risk priority number (RPN). Risk factors can be multiplied or combined through addition to achieve the final result. Care should be taken not to dilute the severity.

6. *Establish Risk Actions*—Decision guidelines or action required for each risk level. Table 4.6 shows an example of decision guidelines for risk levels.
7. *Select Risk Screening and Communication Tools*—A risk assessment matrix, graph, or risk priority numbers (RPNs) used to measure, screen, compare, prioritize, as well as communicate risk within an organization.

Table 4.6. Risk Scoring Levels and Action Example.

Risk Level	Risk Score	Action
Very High	12 or greater	Operation not permissible; immediate action required
High	8 to 10	Remedial action required; high priority
Moderate	4 to 6	Remedial action suggested
Low	1 to 3	Remedial action discretionary

Risk Matrices

Risk matrices are used to communicate risk visually to stakeholders so that unacceptable risks can be reduced and managed. A risk matrix (also known as a consequence/likelihood matrix) is used to establish and display risk levels by categorizing combinations of a risk's likelihood and severity of consequence. Matrices are generally used in the risk evaluation phase of a risk assessment to compare, evaluate, and prioritize risks; and they provide stakeholders and decision makers a quick, visual comparison of risks which is useful in screening and selecting risks for further treatment. Normally, a matrix is constructed by using a horizontal axis and a vertical axis; one for severity of consequence and the other for likelihood of occurrence. The combined severity of consequences and likelihood of occurrence for each risk are plotted in the appropriate category in the matrix identifying its risk level.

A number of examples are available in standards and references. Selecting a risk matrix should include a careful review of the defined context and risk criteria to determine: (1) if a qualitative model will suffice or if a semi-quantitative or quantitative model is needed; (2) the consequences categories and number of levels; and (3) the likelihood categories. For severity of consequences, it may be appropriate to include multiple categories such as human safety and health, environmental protection or community, assets, business reputation, or others.

Summary

Planning for the assessment is a critical step in assessing and managing risk. The context of the risk management effort must include the purpose, scope, objectives, risk criteria, and risk scoring system. In addition, the organization's definition of risk levels and acceptable risk level must be determined. Resources must be used judiciously and appropriately. Time spent on planning is well spent and will help enable the risk assessment team to achieve the objectives of the effort.

Review Questions

1. List the seven elements that should be included in the "context" of a risk assessment.
2. Identify the information needed in the planning process to establish the context.
3. List five internal factors and five external factors.
4. List the four general risk criteria needed in the context.
5. Besides likelihood and severity, what are the other six factors listed in ANSI/ASSP Z590.3 that may be needed in defining the context.
6. List and describe the five elements in a risk scoring system.
7. List and describe four methods used to help establish the context.

References

ANSI/ASIS/RIMS RA.1-2015. 2015. *Risk Assessment.* Alexandria, VA: ASIS International and The Risk and Insurance Management Society, Inc.

ANSI/ASSP Z10-2012 (R2017). 2017. *Occupational Health and Safety Management Systems.* Park Ridge, IL: American Society of Safety Professionals.

ANSI/ASSP Z590.3-2011 (R2016). 2016. *Prevention through Design: Guidelines for Addressing Occupational Hazards and Risks in Design and Redesign Processes.* Park Ridge, IL: American Society of Safety Professionals.

ANSI/ASSP Z690.1-2011. 2011. *Vocabulary for Risk Management.* Park Ridge, IL: American Society of Safety Professionals.

ANSI/ASSP/ISO 31000-2018. 2018. *Risk Management Principles and Guidelines.* Park Ridge, IL: American Society of Safety Professionals.

ANSI/ASSP/ISO 31010-2019. 2019. *Risk Management – Risk Assessment Techniques.* Park Ridge, IL: American Society of Safety Professionals.

Business Dictionary. n.d. "Context." Accessed October 13, 2020. www.businessdictionary.com/definition/context.html.

Lyon, Bruce K., and Bruce Hollcroft. 2012. "Risk Assessments—Top 10 Pitfalls and Tips for Improvement." *Professional Safety,* December 2012, 28–34.

Lyon, Bruce K., and Georgi Popov. 2017. "Communicating and Managing Risk: The Key Result of Risk Assessment," *Professional Safety,* November 2017, 35–44.

Lyon, Bruce K., and Georgi Popov. 2018. *Risk Management Tools for Safety Professionals.* Park Ridge, IL: American Society of Safety Professionals.

Popov, G., Bruce K. Lyon, and Bruce Hollcroft. 2016. *Risk Assessment: A Practical Guide to Assessing Operational Risks.* Hoboken, NJ: Wiley.

Main, Bruce, W. 2012. *Risk Assessment: Challenges and Opportunities.* Ann Harbor, MI: Design Safety Engineering, Inc.

MIL-STD-882E. 2012. *Department of Defense Standard Practice: System Safety.* Washington, DC: Department of Defense.

NFPA 70E. 2018. *Standard for Electrical Safety in the Workplace.* Quincy, MA: National Fire Protection Association.

CHAPTER 5
Selecting Risk Assessment and Management Methods

Introduction
The ability to properly select, customize, and combine methods to assess and manage risks provides risk professionals a certain advantage and value to their organization. With the diversity and types of risks that are encountered by organizations, risk professionals must be able to determine which techniques are most appropriate for each situation's complexity and context. To be successful, the professional must be familiar with available risk assessment methods and their applications, strengths, and weaknesses. In this chapter, a review of risk management methodologies is provided, along with guidelines for selecting, modifying, and combining methods to successfully achieve an acceptable level of risk.

Method Selection Criteria
A critical step in assessing and managing risk is the selection of the most appropriate method or methods to employ. As described in ISO 31010, many risk management techniques were originally developed by particular industries and were used to manage particular types of risks. Some techniques are similar with variations but use different terminologies. "Over time the application of many of the techniques

---

Interactive tools and supplemental materials are available at assp.org/ermtools.

has broadened, for example extending from technical engineering applications to financial or managerial situations, or to consider positive as well as negative outcomes. New techniques have emerged, and old ones have been adapted to new circumstances. The techniques and their applications continue to evolve. There is potential for enhanced understanding of risk by using techniques outside their original application" (ANSI/ASSP/ISO/IEC 31010-2019).

With a wide array of methods available, a standardized approach to evaluating and selecting methods should be considered. This requires an understanding of the established contexts and purposes of the assessments. As ISO 31010 states, "the choice of technique and the way it is applied should be tailored to the context and use and provide information of the type and form needed by the stakeholders" (ANSI/ASSP/ISO/IEC 31010-2019). The size and degree of complexity of the targeted system, as well as the resources available, and the needed risk-based information should be considered in the selection process. The technique(s) selected may require scaling to size and modification of format to accommodate the effort.

The risk criteria established in the context will determine to a large degree the types of methods selected (see Chapter 4, Planning the Assessment). Whether a qualitative, semi-quantitative, or quantitative model is best suited for the assessment will be based on the complexity of the assessment, the established context, and the required risk-based information. A primary consideration is the form of output that will provide stakeholders the best type of information to make their decision. A summary of key elements to consider in the selection process provided by ISO 31010 includes the purpose and scope of the assessment; needs of stakeholders; legal, regulatory, and contractual requirements; operating environment and scenario; importance of the decision (*e.g.*, the consequences if a wrong decision is made); defined decision criteria and their form; time available before a decision must be made; information that is available or can be obtained; complexity of the situation; and expertise level.

Five key elements should be factored into the selection of methods including the (1) step in the risk management process being addressed, (2) the specific application, (3) the complexity of the system, (4) the criticality level, (5) output necessary to make decision, and (6) the resources available. Each of these are briefly described in the following sections.

The Risk Management Process Step

First, the point at which the effort is to be applied within the risk management process must be identified to properly select the proper method(s). Specific methods that are best applied to specific steps are available and should be selected accordingly.

The process steps are (1) communication, (2) context, (3) risk identification, (4) risk analysis, (5) risk evaluation, (6) risk treatment, (7) monitoring and reporting, and (8) recording and reporting.

Specific Application

Second, the specific target or application of the effort must be considered when selecting the method(s). Applications may range from a very broad organizational-level effort, such as a business continuity plan or a business impact analysis to a very focused, specific task-level analysis. Third, the types of hazards or exposures are considered. Are there specific or unique hazards such as occupational health risks or musculoskeletal risks associated with the target, or is there a broad range of hazards such as falls, machinery related exposures, or chemicals? Is there an industry specific exposure with a known set of exposures to consider?

Degree of Complexity

The level of complexity of the targeted application will influence the selection of the method(s). Fundamental or simple methods will be more appropriate for systems with little complexity, while more complex systems or problems generally will need more robust methods. In addition, the resources, skill levels, and time restraints will influence the selection.

Level of Criticality

The criticality level of the targeted effort or problem is an important factor to consider in selection. Normal type tasks with a known history can be assessed with more common, less sophisticated methods such as job risk assessment, preliminary hazard analysis, and similar tools. On the other hand, critical activities that are unique with a higher degree of uncertainty or have a potential for higher risk will require methods with a higher degree of rigor. Risks with a criticality potential such as fatality and serious incident (FSI) type risks must be given increased attention and proper resources to identify, analyze, evaluate, and treat the risks.

Selecting a Matrix

In ANSI/ASSP Z590.3, the second step in risk assessment process, following "management direction" is "select a risk assessment matrix." Section 7.2 outlines that "an organization shall create and obtain broad agreement on a risk assessment matrix or other validated process that is suitable to the hazards and risks with which it deals" (ANSI/ASSP Z590.3-2011 (R2016). The purpose for selecting a risk assessment matrix is to have a consistent and clear risk measurement method to determine risk within an organization.

The selected matrix should be understood by stakeholders involved in the risk management processes with clear understanding of the definitions and terms used for measuring risk such as likelihood levels, severity levels, and risk levels.

Data Output

The decision and the type of information necessary to help make the decision must be understood in the selection process. The data output from the risk management method should be geared towards informing decision makers in reducing uncertainty and facilitate decision making. Model outputs can be *qualitative* using defined levels such as high, medium, or low; *semi-quantitative* using numerical rating scales produced by a risk formula; or *quantitative* using statistical data to estimate risk values in specific units or numerical values. The degree of detail required depends upon the application, the data available, and the decision needs of the organization. In addition, the risk scoring method used in the method selected should convey the appropriate information to decision makers.

Available Resources

Resource limitations such as budgets, time frames, internal and external resources, information and data, personnel and skill levels, use of outside experts, software, and hardware all affect the selection of the method(s) to be used.

Several techniques might need to be considered and applying more than one technique can sometimes provide useful additional understanding. Different techniques can also be appropriate as more information becomes available. As risks evolve and change, additional assessments may be needed.

Risk Management Methods

There are many risk management methods available to risk professionals. Some methods are variations of a single technique, while others are specific in their use. There are also methods that are commonly used in particular industries or situations. Some methods have broad application and others are more specifically targeted in specific elements of risk management such as "identification" or "treatment." The choices can seem a little overwhelming and selecting the appropriate methodology requires some careful consideration and thought.

Guidance in defining and selecting methodologies in a risk management effort is provided in ISO 31000 in section 6.3, Establishing the Context, and in ISO 31010, Section 7, Selection of Risk Assessment Techniques. In addition, ISO 31010's Annex A provides selection guidance and descriptions of 42 risk management methods. Figure 5.1 provides an overview of methods associated with each element of the risk management process. It should be noted that many of the methods can be used in various steps of the process and are not limited to the step identified in the figure.

Selecting Risk Assessment and Management Methods | 87

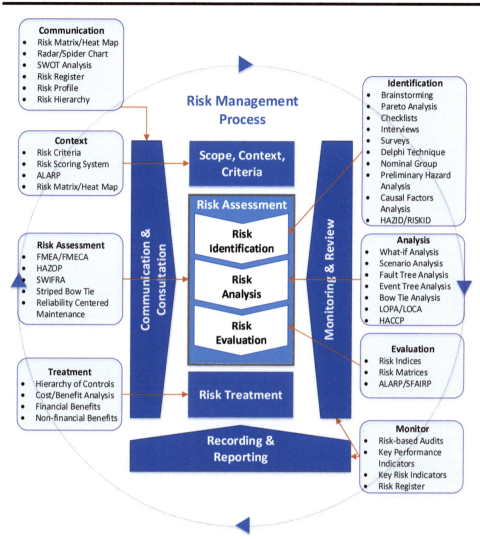

Figure 5.1
Application of Techniques in the Risk Management Process, Modified from ANSI/ASSP/ISO/IEC 31010-2019.

Other risk-related standards including ANSI Z590.3, ANSI RA.1 and technical report ASSP TR-31010 provides coverage of method selection considerations. Table 5.1 provides a comparison of risk assessment methods listed in the standards and technical report. Although there are many methods available, all are based on the same fundamental risk management process.

In these standards and technical report, 67 methods are identified. Of these, the checklist method, what-if analysis, and risk assessment matrix are listed in all four, while nine techniques are included in three of the documents (HAZOP, HACCP,

Table 5.1. Comparison of methods listed/identified in ANSI/ASSP/ISO/IEC 31010-2019, ANSI RA.1-2016, ANSI Z590.3-R2016, and ASSP TR-31010-2020.

ANSI/ASSP/ISO/IEC 31010-2019	ANSI/ASIS/RIMS RA.1-2015	ANSI Z590.3-2011 (R2016)	ASSP TR-31010-2020
		Design Safety Review	Design Safety Review
	Influence Diagram		
	Root Cause Analysis		
	Gap Analysis		
	Criticality/Consequence Analysis		
	Sensitivity Analysis		Sensitivity Analysis
	Stress Analysis		
	SWOT Analysis		SWOT Analysis
	Vulnerability/Capability Analysis		
	Risk "Frontier" Graph		
	5 Why Analysis		Multiple Why Analysis
		Management Oversight and Risk Tree (MORT)	
Brainstorming			Brainstorming
Interviews	Interviews		Structured Interviews
Delphi Technique			Delphi Technique
Checklists, Classification	Checklists	Checklists	Checklists
		Preliminary Hazard Analysis	Preliminary Hazard Analysis

Continued on next page

Selecting Risk Assessment and Management Methods | 89

ANSI/ASSP/ ISO/IEC 31010-2019	ANSI/ASIS/ RIMS RA.1-2015	ANSI Z590.3-2011 (R2016)	ASSP TR-31010-2020
Hazard & Operability Studies		Hazard & Operability Studies	Hazard & Operability Studies
Hazard Analysis & Critical Control Points (HACCP)	Critical Control Points (CCP)		Hazard Analysis & Critical Control Points (HACCP)
Toxicity Risk Assessment			Exposure Assessment
Structured What-if Analysis (SWIFT)	What If Questions	What-if Analysis What-if Checklist Analysis	Structured What-if Analysis (SWIFT)
Scenario Analysis	Scenario Analysis		Scenario Analysis
Business Impact Analysis	Business Impact Analysis		Business Impact Analysis
Nominal Group Technique			Nominal Group Technique
Failure Mode Effects (criticality) Analysis		Failure Mode & Effects Analysis	Failure Mode Effects (criticality) Analysis
Fault Tree Analysis		Fault Tree Analysis	Fault Tree Analysis
Event Tree Analysis			Event Tree Analysis
Cause Consequence Analysis			Cause Consequence Analysis
Ishikawa Analysis (Fishbone)	Ishikawa Analysis (Fishbone)		Ishikawa Analysis (Fishbone)
Layers of Protection Analysis			Layers of Protection Analysis
Decision Tree Analysis			
Human Reliability Analysis			Human Reliability Analysis

Continued on next page

ANSI/ASSP/ ISO/IEC 31010-2019	ANSI/ASIS/ RIMS RA.1-2015	ANSI Z590.3-2011 (R2016)	ASSP TR-31010-2020
Bow Tie Analysis			Bow Tie Analysis
Reliability Centered Maintenance			Reliability Centered Maintenance
Markov Analysis			Markov Analysis
Monte Carlo Simulation			Monte Carlo Simulation
Bayesian Networks			
Frequency/ Number (FN) Diagrams			
Risk Indices			Risk Indices
Consequence Likelihood Matrix	Risk Assessment Matrix	Risk Assessment Matrix	Consequence Likelihood Matrix
Cost-Benefit Analysis (CBA)	Cost-Benefit Analysis		Cost-Benefit Analysis (CBA)
Multi-Criteria Analysis (MCA)			Multi-Criteria Analysis (MCA)
ALARP/SFAIRP			ALARP
Bayes Analysis			
Causal Mapping			Causal Mapping
Cindynic Approach			Cindynic Approach
Conditional Value at Risk CVaR			
Cross Impact Analysis			Cross Impact Analysis
Game Theory			
Pareto Charts			Pareto Analysis
Privacy Impact Analysis (PIA)			
Risk Registers	Risk Registers		Risk Registers

Continued on next page

ANSI/ASSP/ ISO/IEC 31010-2019	ANSI/ASIS/ RIMS RA.1-2015	ANSI Z590.3-2011 (R2016)	ASSP TR-31010-2020
S Curves			
Surveys			Surveys
			Radar/Spider Charts
			HAZID/RISKID
			Pre-start Up Safety Review
			Management of Change
			Structured What-if Risk Assessment (SWIFRA)
			Striped Bow-tie Risk Assessment
			Quantitative Risk Analysis (QRA)
			Major Accident Risk
			Barrier Analysis
			Layers of Control Analysis (LOCA)
			Risk Hierarchy
			Risk Treatment Hierarchy
			Ergonomics Risk Assessment Tool

scenario analysis, business impact analysis, FMEA, fault tree analysis, fishbone analysis, cost-benefit analysis, and risk register.)

Each method is designed to provide a general or specific level of information for its selected application in providing decision makers proper information. In many cases, multiple methods (used in sequence or series) are required to properly address the different types of risk exposures and levels of complexities. Simpler methods that provide the rigor and sufficient information for the risk management effort should be selected over more complicated techniques. In many cases, selected methods will require some customization, and in fact customization is desirable to modify methods to improve their use and application. Table 5.2 provides a coded scale for applicability to each component of the risk management process for methods covered in ASSP TR-31010 (Table codes: Green SA = Strongly Applicable; Yellow A = Applicable; Grey N/A = Not Applicable). In Table 5.3, a list of frequently used risk management tools and their common application and complexity level is presented. Table 5.4 provides a summary checklist of selection considerations.

Table 5.2. ASSP TR-31010 Applicability of Risk Management Tools, Courtesy of the American Society of Safety Professionals.

		Risk Management Process									
				Analysis							
#	Technique	Context	Identification	Severity	Likelihood	Risk Level	Evaluation	Treatment	Monitor	Communicate	Complexity
1	Brainstorming	A	SA					A			Low
2	Structured Interviews	A	SA								Low
3	Surveys	A	SA								Low
4	Checklists		SA					A			Low
5	Multiple Why		SA								Low
6	Delphi	A	SA								Med
7	Nominal Group Technique (NGT)	A	SA								Med
8	Pareto Analysis		SA							A	Med
9	Radar/Spider Charts						A		A	SA	Med

Continued on next page

Selecting Risk Assessment and Management Methods | 93

#	Technique	Context	Identification	Analysis			Evaluation	Treatment	Monitor	Communicate	Complexity
				Severity	Likelihood	Risk Level					
10	HAZID		SA								Med
11	Preliminary Hazard Analysis (PHA)		SA	A	A	A	A	A			Med
12	Design Safety Review		SA	SA			A	SA			Med
13	Pre-Start-up Safety Review (PSSR)		SA	A				A			Low
14	Management of Change (MOC)		SA	SA				SA			Med
15	Structured What-if Technique (SWIFT)		SA	SA				A			Med
16	Structured What-if Risk Assessment (SWIFRA)		SA	SA	SA	SA	SA	SA		A	High
17	Scenario Analysis		SA	SA	A	A	A	A		A	Med
18	Bow Tie Analysis (BTA)			A	SA	SA	A	A		SA	Med
19	Striped Bow-Tie Risk Assessment (SBTRA)			SA	SA	SA	SA	SA		SA	Med
20	Fault Tree Analysis (FTA)		A		SA	A	A				Med
21	Event Tree Analysis (ETA)		A	SA	A	A					Med

Continued on next page

#	Technique	Context	Identification	Analysis - Severity	Analysis - Likelihood	Analysis - Risk Level	Evaluation	Treatment	Monitor	Communicate	Complexity
22	Failure Mode Effects Analysis (FMEA)			SA	SA	SA	SA	A			Med
23	HAZOP			SA	SA	A	A	A			High
24	HACCP			SA	SA	A	A	SA	A			High
25	Quantitative Risk Assessment (QRA)			SA	SA	SA	SA	SA	A			High
26	Major Accident Risk			SA	SA	SA	SA	SA	SA			High
27	Exposure Assessment				SA	SA	SA	SA	A			High
28	SWOT Analysis			A	A	A				SA	Med
29	Cause-Consequence Analysis		A	SA	SA	A	A				High
30	Cause and Effect Analysis (Fishbone)		SA	A							Med
31	Reliability Assessment			SA	SA	SA	SA	SA	SA			High
32	Human Reliability Analysis (HRA)			SA	SA	SA	SA	A	A			Med
33	Cross Impact Analysis				SA						Med
34	Causal Mapping		SA	A							Med
35	Barrier Analysis						A	SA			Med

Continued on next page

Selecting Risk Assessment and Management Methods | 95

#	Technique	Risk Management Process									Complexity
		Context	Identification	Analysis			Evaluation	Treatment	Monitor	Communicate	
				Severity	Likelihood	Risk Level					
36	Layers of Protection Analysis		A	SA	A	A		SA			Med
37	Layers of Control Analysis		A	SA	A	A	A	SA			Med
38	Multi-criteria Decision Analysis (MCDA)		A	SA	A	SA	A				Med
39	Cindynic Approach	SA	A	A	A	A		A			High
40	Markov Analysis		A	SA	A						High
41	Monte Carlo Simulation					A	SA	A		A	High
42	Business Impact Analysis		A	SA	A	A	A	A		A	Med
43	Cost-Benefit Analysis		A	SA	A	A	A			A	Med
44	ALARP/ALARA	SA					SA	A			Med
45	Risk Indices	SA		SA	SA	A	SA		A	A	Med
46	Consequence/Likelihood Matrix	SA	A	SA	SA	SA	SA			SA	Med
47	Risk Register								SA	SA	Med
48	Risk Hierarchy									SA	Low
49	Risk Treatment Hierarchy						A	SA			Low
50	Ergonomics Risk Assessment Tool		SA	SA	SA	SA	SA	A			Med

Table 5.3. Applicability and Complexity of Methods included in this Manual (Lyon, Popov 2018).

Tool Name	Communication	Context	Risk ID	Risk Analysis	Risk Evaluation	Risk Treatment	Complexity
Plan-Do-Check-Act Model	Yes						Simple
Risk-based Decision Making Model	Yes						Moderate
Risk Assessment Triggers	Yes						Simple
Risk Criteria Selection		Yes					Simple
Pareto Analysis		Yes					Moderate
Risk Matrices		Yes					Simple
Brainstorming			Yes				Simple
Delphi Technique			Yes				Simple
Hazard Identification Study (HAZID)			Yes	Yes			Moderate
Design Safety Review			Yes	Yes			Moderate
Preliminary Hazard Analysis			Yes	Yes			Moderate
What-if Analysis			Yes	Yes			Moderate
Failure Mode & Effects Analysis (FMEA)			Yes	Yes			Complex
Layers of Controls Analysis (LOCA)			Yes	Yes		Yes	Complex
Layers of Protection Analysis (LOPA)			Yes	Yes			Complex
Bow-Tie Analysis			Yes	Yes			Moderate
Striped Bow-Tie Risk Assessment			Yes	Yes		Yes	Complex

Continued on next page

Tool Name	Communication	Context	Risk ID	Risk Analysis	Risk Evaluation	Risk Treatment	Complexity
Risk Indices				Yes	Yes		Simple
Risk Heat Maps					Yes		Simple
ALARP					Yes		Moderate
Business Impact Analysis				Yes		Yes	Moderate
Cost-Benefit Analysis				Yes		Yes	Moderate
Financial Analysis				Yes		Yes	Complex
Non-Financial Benefits Analysis				Yes		Yes	Moderate
Risk Treatment Selection Checklist						Yes	Simple
Key Performance Indicators (KPIs) and Key Risk Indicators (KRIs)	Yes						Moderate
Risk Treatment Tracking	Yes						Moderate
Risk Register	Yes						Moderate
Risk Performance Measurement	Yes						Moderate

Customizing Methods

Even though there are numerous methods available, most methods will require at least some minor customization to fit the needs of a specific application. Each risk assessment technique or risk management method has its own applications, along with strengths and weaknesses. It is up to the user to optimize methods by making modifications that serve the purpose of the risk management application. Some methods may require additional features to enhance the information produced, such as including a risk scoring mechanism. Other methods may be too complex for the application and require removing certain features. Being flexible and adaptable when it comes to customizing methods is important. The only rule that must be followed in regard to customizing risk management methods is that the fundamental risk management principles and process be followed.

Combining Methods

Many risk management applications require multiple methods to accomplish the objective. Some situations are more complex or have a need for multiple sources of information. In these cases, a series of methods may be necessary. For instance, Figure 5.2 illustrates a series of methods used in a risk assessment.

Each situation will require consideration of the context and needed information. Some applications will require one or two methods, while other may require multiple methods used in sequence and/or in parallel. The bottom line is that risk professionals must be skilled at selecting, modifying, and combining methods to achieve the desired results and assist decision makers in their efforts.

Summary

All methods, whether unchanged, modified, or combined, should be monitored to ensure the application fits appropriately and that the intended results are being achieved. If not, the assessors must communicate their concerns and adjust as necessary. Risk and its management are dynamic in nature. The approach taken by

Table 5.4. Risk Management Tool Selection Considerations.

Process Step	Application Level	Hazard/Exposure
• Communication and Consultation • Establishing the Context • Hazard/Risk Identification • Risk Analysis • Risk Evaluation • Risk Treatment • Monitoring and Reporting	• Organizational • Regional • Plant/Location • Department • System/Process • Job • Task	• General Hazards • Energy Sources • Chemical • Machinery • Robotics • Industrial Hygiene • Environmental • Musculo-skeletal • Error-induced • Other _____
Criticality	**Output**	**Resources**
• Degree of Uncertainty • Degree of FSI Risk • Criticality or Sensitivity of Targeted Operation	• Degree of Detail Needed • Availability of Reliable Data • Decision-making Needs • Regulatory or Legal Requirements • Risk Levels or Scoring System Needs	• Budget • Timeframe • Personnel and Skill Levels • External Consultants • Software Tools

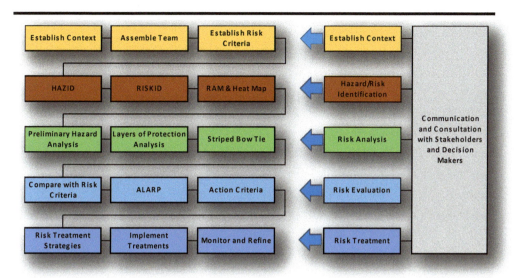

Figure 5.2
Example of Combining Methods (Lyon, Popov 2017).

risk professionals must also be dynamic, adaptable, and nimble to the needs and objectives.

Review Questions

1. Five key elements should be factored into the selection of methods. List and describe each.
2. List four standards that contain risk assessment and management methods available to the risk professional.
3. List the six factors that should be considered when selecting methods and provide two examples of each.
4. Explain why a single risk management method may not be adequate for some situations.
5. Explain why a risk management method may require modification or customization for some situations.

References

ANSI/ASIS/RIMS RA.1-2015. 2015. *Risk Assessment.* Alexandria, VA: ASIS International and The Risk and Insurance Management Society, Inc.

ANSI/ASSP Z590.3-2011 (R2016). 2016. *Prevention through Design: Guidelines for Addressing Occupational Hazards and Risks in Design and Redesign Processes.* Park Ridge, IL: American Society of Safety Professionals.

ANSI/ASSP Z690.1-2011 (R2016). 2016. *Vocabulary for Risk Management*. Park Ridge, IL: American Society of Safety Professionals.

ANSI/ASSP/ISO 31000-2018. 2018. *Risk Management Principles and Guidelines*. Park Ridge, IL: American Society of Safety Professionals.

ANSI/ASSP/ISO/IEC 31010-2019. 2019. *Risk Management – Risk Assessment Techniques*. Park Ridge, IL: American Society of Safety Professionals.

ASSP TR-31010-2020. 2020. *Technical Report: Risk Management – Techniques for Safety Practitioners*. Park Ridge, IL: American Society of Safety Professionals.

Lyon, Bruce K., and Georgi Popov. 2017. "Communicating and Managing Risk: The Key Result of Risk Assessment," *Professional Safety*, September 2017, 35–44.

Lyon, Bruce K., and Georgi Popov. 2018. *Risk Management Tools for Safety Professionals*. Park Ridge, IL: American Society of Safety Professionals.

CHAPTER 6
Managing Information and Decision Models

Introduction
Although the gathering and managing of relevant information may not be fully considered in the planning process, it is a key element in successfully managing risk. Information that is relevant and sometimes critical is necessary to inform, justify, and enable decision makers and stakeholders in the management of risk. Methods for identifying, gathering, and managing needed information in the risk management process should be determined early in the process. Such information may include data for statistical analysis models or techniques used to perform risk assessment. For more complex situations, a great amount of information will be generally be needed, while a simple assessment may only need several bits of information.

Determining what types of information are required by an organization can be derived from the established context, purpose, and scope of the risk management initiative, as well as the type of decision being made. Specific means of identifying the sources of information, how it will be collected, its storage and use, and overall management must be determined as well. Typically, the risk management team tasked with the assignment is also responsible for managing the related information, developing models for application, and providing effective risk communication to stakeholders.

Interactive tools and supplemental materials are available at assp.org/ermtools.

Gathering Information

Data and information have many sources and should be identified in an organized fashion. Some of these sources for information include internal documents and knowledgeable stakeholders; external sources such as third parties, contractors, and suppliers; public agencies and governmental sources; industry groups and professional associations; and consultants and expert opinions related to the subject matter.

Means of gathering and collecting data and information will range from simple reviews of literature, observations, and interviews, to more in-depth studies, measurements, or research of existing data. In certain cases, it may be necessary to conduct experiments and research studies to collect samples or conduct surveys to gather needed data for analysis. Data will many times represent past losses or benefits associated with the subject such as project failures or successes, causes of such failures, number of reported complaints or incidents, health impacts and financial gains or losses; and may include the output from other analytical models or techniques (ANSI/ASSP/ISO 31010-2019).

For situations where sampling data is collected and analyzed, it is important that sufficient quantities of samples be obtained to achieve statistical confidence. For sampling data used that does not require statistical analysis, it should be acknowledged and communicated as such. For data and results collected from previous efforts or assessments it should be verified that the data remains valid, applicable, and relevant to the context of the current initiative.

Analyzing Data and Information

Collected data will typically require some analysis and evaluation to understand its value and input into the planned assessment. The analysis of the collected information should provide stakeholders an understanding of similar risks and risk factors to properly assess and treat the current risks. Some of the critical elements that the risk assessment team must understand from previous experiences include:

- Types of consequences
- Severity levels and impacts
- Likelihood of past occurrences
- Trends, cycles, patterns, and frequencies of occurrences
- Circumstances and causal factors surrounding events
- Risk controls or treatments that were in place at the time of previous occurrences and the state of their effectiveness
- Escalating factors
- Limitations and uncertainties in the existing information

It is important to recognize that the collected data and information may have limitations or may not fully apply to the current situations or risks being assessed. However, information is very useful in providing indications of what events might occur and their likelihood and how they may be treated.

Developing Decision Models

Models are used to approximate a real outcome. According to the *Cambridge Dictionary* (n.d.), a model is defined as:

> something built or drawn especially to show how something much larger would look: The architect showed us a model of the planned hotel. A model is also a representation of something in words or numbers that can be used to tell what is likely to happen if particular facts are considered as true: a statistical model predicting population growth.

Models can be of a physical construction, a mathematical formula, or a software application that provides a projection.

Decision makers are required to consider and evaluate alternatives in values of probabilities and consequences, variations of risk factors, options and tradeoffs, and uncertainty in assessing risks. Decision analysis provides insight into how the defined alternatives differ from one another and provides a basis for considering new and improved alternatives (ANSI/ASIS/RIMS RA.1-2015). The evaluation of the sensitivity and reliability of a model's outcomes is a critical function of the risk professional.

Models are methods used to help simplify complex systems or situations so that they can be properly analyzed and understood. Helping to understand the meaning of data, models are used to simulate what might happen in practice under different conditions (ANSI/ASSP/ISO 31010-2019). For risk management, a model is generally used to aid the decision-making process—a decision model. ANSI RA.1 Section 5.5.7 provides guidance on decision models and their application as part of "Implementing the Risk Assessment Program."

In developing a model, it is important to understand that the process involves assumptions and judgements from qualified, knowledgeable, and objective stakeholders. ISO 31010 provides guidance on constructing a decision model which includes the following steps:

1. Define the problem.
2. Describe the purpose of the model and desired outcomes.
3. Develop a model for solving the problem.

4. Build the physical, mathematical, or software of the conceptual model.
5. Develop tools to analyze how the model behaves.
6. Process the data.
7. Review and validate outputs from the model.
8. Draw conclusions from the model and the problem.

Interconnected influencing factors, internally and externally, can have an impact on the assessment and decision-making objectives. Stakeholder influences may include societal, governmental, financial, strategic, and operational. ANSI RA.1 describes the use of influence diagrams to help identify strengths and impacts of influencing factors on objectives and risks (ANSI/ASIS/RIMS RA.1-2015). The diagram allows charting influencing factors, their connections, and impacts such as the example in figure 6.1.

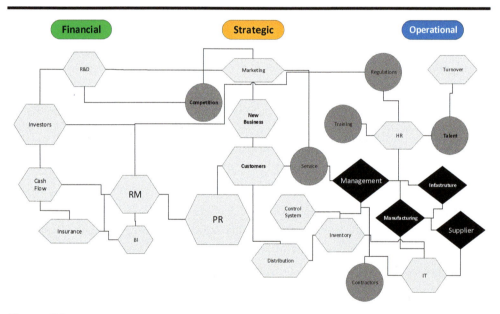

Figure 6.1
Influence Diagram Example.

These steps will likely include some assumptions, approximations, and judgements requiring the model to be tested and validated for its credibility by objective stakeholders.

Testing and Validating Models

Testing and validating the output from the selected model is critical in reducing uncertainty and improving a model's value. Such testing is needed to evaluate the model's representation of the actual situation to be assessed and decided upon. It must be applied within the context of the problem as designed with an understanding of the basic theory of the model. The parameters, mathematical representations and calculations, and input data should be evaluated for accuracy and reliability. Testing should verify that the model operates as desired without errors or miscalculations and is stable in handling small variations or changes without problems.

Validation of the model can be accomplished by several tests. Sensitivity analysis is one method used to evaluate a model's sensitivity to variations or changes in input parameters. By inputting alternative assumptions, the model then recalculates its outcomes to determine the impact of the tested variables. This can be useful in testing the stability of the model in the presence of uncertainty and understanding the relationships between inputs and outputs in the model. Errors, unexpected outputs, and inputs that create significant uncertainty in the output should be tested, corrected, or eliminated to increase reliability of the model. The model should be simplified by removing non-value adding and redundant inputs where possible. Sensitivity analysis methods include software-based scenario tools, brainstorming and "what-if" analyses, and simulation techniques used to test model sensitivity.

Using scenario analysis to stress test a model is another method used to validate a decision model. Scenario analysis is a process of analyzing plausible future events by considering alternative scenarios and outcomes that provides a basis for decision making in the context of various conditions and outcomes. This generally involves testing the model with more extreme scenarios to challenge assumptions and determine how the model will perform under such circumstances. It generally involves defining a scenario and working through what would likely happen under various conditions or combination of conditions. Scenarios can be based on past events or credible events and should be clearly defined. They are often used to explore the effects of new technology, future decisions, stakeholder needs, changes in physical environment, or changes in the macro environment (ANSI/ASSP/ISO 31010-2019). Ultimately, uncertainty is reduced in the decision-making by testing models with alternative scenarios.

A third method, Pareto analysis, can be used to evaluate a model's outputs using different alternatives and choices. Pareto analysis is a method commonly used for prioritizing possible changes by applying the theory that 80% of the effects are derived from 20% of the causes. The analysis provides an evaluation of the alternatives to identify the options (20%) that have the greatest impact (80%) to allow decision makers to focus on the most effective areas. It should be noted that a possible limitation of Pareto analysis is that small problems excluded from the analysis could grow to a significant level in the future.

All analyses and testing efforts of the model, assumptions, limitations, and theories should be adequately documented to sufficiently validate the model.

Software Models

Many software models are available and may be used to organize and analyze data. Such software models provide a relatively simple interface and application, as well as immediate output; however, as ISO 31010 cautions, these characteristics might produce invalid results that are unnoticed by the user. Some of the reasons for possible invalid results include flaws in algorithms and assumptions, errors in data input, improper data conversion, and inaccurate interpretation of outputs.

To avoid potential errors, users should test new software first with simple inputs that have known outputs to verify accuracy. In addition, testing should include increasing and decreasing input values to compare the outputs to the expected results. Evidence and documentation should be gathered to check that outputs are within the expected ranges. These simple tests can provide information on the sensitivity of a given software model to variations in data inputs.

Model Validation Methods

Sensitivity Analysis

Sensitivity analysis is a systematic method used to understand how risk estimates and risk-based decisions are dependent on variability and uncertainty in contributing risk factors (ANSI/ASIS/RIMS RA.1-2015). It is used to determine the variation in output of a risk analysis model regarding changes in the input values providing a priority ranking according to variability and uncertainty. The assessor compares the outcomes that are produced from an analytical approach using different input values. The level of uncertainty associated with each variation is evaluated and ranked accordingly.

Sensitivity analysis is used in a wide range of fields, ranging from biology and geography to economics and engineering. A financial sensitivity analysis, sometimes known as a What-if analysis or a What-if simulation exercise, is most commonly used by financial analysts to predict the outcome of a specific action when performed under certain conditions.

Financial sensitivity analysis is done within defined boundaries that are determined by the set of independent (input) variables. For example, Sensitivity Analysis can be used to study the effect of a change in interest rates on bond prices if the interest rates increased by 1%. The "What-if" question would be: "What would happen to the price of a bond if interest rates went up by 1%?" This question is answered with sensitivity analysis. (Corporate Finance Institute n.d.)

Example: An auto supply company operates an auto parts fulfilment center in the Midwest.

The company rents a warehouse for $50,000 annually. The fulfillment center sells 25,000 auto parts per year and the average price per auto part is $50. The average cost for the company to buy the auto parts is $25. The fulfillment associates are among those on the front-line fulfilling customers' orders within the fulfillment center. The fulfillment associates perform production duties like pick/pack orders, receive/stow product at elevated levels, ensure inventory accuracy, and unload/load trucks.

Unfortunately, four associates suffered back injuries and average cost per injury was $50,000 for a total of $200,000. It was an unexpected loss and that affected the bottom line of the company. The company lost $125,000 that year. The obvious solution is to reduce the cost of injuries to $0. However, that is not always possible without complete redesign of the warehouse and process automation. Management decided to perform a sensitivity analysis and evaluate all the options.

Management estimated that if they increase the average auto part price, they will sell fewer auto parts. On the other hand, if they lower the price, they will sell more auto parts, but the profit margin will be significantly reduced.

The risk manager was experienced in performing sensitivity analysis and developed an Excel file. It is easy to see that the supply company lost money last year. The risk manager can demonstrate how the values are interdependent. For instance, if the management decides to increase the auto parts price to $75 and assume that they will sell 15,000 parts instead of 25,000, the company will break even next year. The obvious preference would be to keep the price constant and reduce the cost of injuries.

The sensitivity analysis shows that at the current price per auto part, $50, even if they increase the parts sales to 29,000 the operation is still not profitable—in fact, they will lose $25,000. A sensitivity analysis example is presented in Figure 6.2.

Current Operation	
# of Auto Parts Sold	25,000
Average price per auto part	$50
Our average cost per auto part	$25
Warehouse rent	$50,000
Injuries/Illnesses Cost	$200,000 4 back injuries
Payroll	$500,000

Annual Profit/Loss	
Revenue	$1,250,000
Cost of sales	$625,000
Gross Profit	$625,000
Expenses (Rent, I&I, Pay)	$750,000
Operating Profit/Loss **(P or L)**	-$125,000

	Price		#
P or L	-$125,000	15000	17000
	$75	$0	$100,000
	$70	-$75,000	$15,000
	$50	-$375,000	-$325,000
	$45	-$450,000	-$410,000
	$35	-$600,000	-$580,000

Figure 6.2
Sensitivity Analysis Example.

Scenario Analysis

Scenario analysis is a process of analyzing possible future outcomes by considering alternative scenarios used to identify risk and explore consequences. It consists of developing a plausible scenario and analyzing what might happen given various possible future developments. Risk is then considered for each of these variables. Variables often considered include technology changes, possible future decisions, stakeholder needs, changes in regulations, demographics, or physical environment (ANSI/ASSP/ISO 31010-2019; ANSI/ASIS/RIMS RA.1-2015).

A scenario analysis requires data on current trends, changes, and ideas for future change. Scenarios can be broad and long-term or more focused, short-term situations. Although probabilities of changes cannot be predicted, scenario analysis can be used to consider consequences and anticipate how threats and opportunities might develop.

For each scenario, a "story" is developed that describes the potential path forward towards the scenario, including positive and/or negative effects. Other outputs can include an understanding of possible effects of policy or plans for various plausible futures, a list of risks that might emerge if the futures were to develop and, in some applications, a list of leading indicators for those risks.

Pareto Analysis

As previously indicated, the Pareto principle (known as the 80-20 rule) states that, for many events, roughly 80% of the effects come from 20% of the causes. It is named after Vilfredo Pareto, an Italian economist who found in 1906 that 80% of the land in Italy was owned by 20% of the population (Lavinsky 2014). Pareto analysis uses this 80-20 principle to identify and evaluate factors that contribute to the greatest frequency of events typically displayed in a diagram or chart.

Pareto analysis is considered a bottom-up approach and is applied to situations where there are varying sources or outcomes (categories of interest) to consider. It provides quantitative outputs and can be helpful in comparing and selecting causes that produce the most severe consequences, as well as selecting the most beneficial risk treatments. It is very useful in formulating a prioritized list of contributing factors based on percentages.

As a data analysis tool Pareto analysis is often presented as a bar chart (as shown in Figure 6.3) where the horizontal axis represents "categories of interest" and the vertical axis represents a "numerical factor" such as frequency, monetary value, or other performance indicator. A cumulative percentage line may be inserted/added for visualization.

Based on the scope, categories of interest or concern are identified and listed. These categories may be hazard-types, triggers or causes, job activities, failure or defect types or other things of interest. Then, for each category, a numerical value is generated from the data, such as frequency, severity, costs, or percentages related to specific categories. Information is entered into the column chart or histogram with the identified categories (1st column) and their corresponding values (2nd column) entered and sorted in descending order. The cumulative sum of the categories (3rd column) and percentages calculated for each category (4th column) as shown in table 6.1.

Table 6.1. Top 10 Injuries Causes Example.

Top 10 Injuries Causes			
Causes	# of Injuries	Cumulative Sum Injuries	Cumulative %
Overexertion	55	55	42.97
Fall to the same level	47	102	79.69
Falls to lower level	7	109	85.16
Struck by object or equipment	6	115	89.84
Other exertions or bodily reactions	4	119	92.97
Roadway incidents involving MV	3	122	95.31
Slip or trip without fall	2	124	96.88
Caught in/compressed by equipment or objects	2	126	98.44
Struck against object or equipment	1	127	99.22
Repetitive motions involving micro-tasks	1	128	100.00

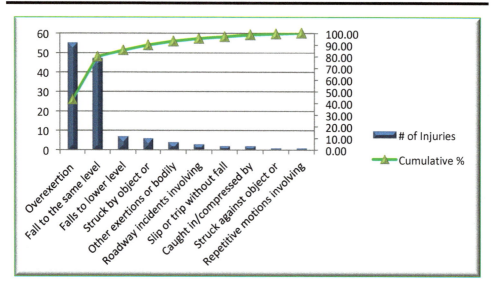

Figure 6.3
Top 10 Injuries Causes Pareto Chart Example.

From the column chart, a line graph is generated based on the cumulative percentage as shown in Figure 6.3. The Pareto line graph provides a visual of the categories and their significance, which allows prioritizing treatment making better use of available resources.

Pareto charting can also be used to identify the highest cost category. If a risk manager knows the average cost per injury, she/he can enter it as an additional column in the original Pareto table. If the cost is not known, it could be obtained from the financial department or even estimated. For simplicity, an average cost of $50,000 per injury or illness can be used. (OSHA's "$afety Pays 2019" program can help estimate the financial impact of occupational injuries and illnesses on the company's profitability available at: www.osha.gov/safetypays/ and www.osha.gov/safetypays/estimator.html.)

Using the cumulative cost of injuries, the risk manager can calculate the cumulative percentage and build a Pareto chart presented in Figure 6.4.

Summary

Gathering and managing risk-based information that will enable stakeholders in their decision making is key to risk management. This involves the gathering of data through risk assessment, analyzing the data using statistical analysis, developing decision models for data input, and testing and validating decision models. Model validation can include sensitivity analysis, scenario analysis, and Pareto analysis. The type of information required is determined by the established context, purpose, and scope of the assessment, as well as the decision being made. Means of collecting,

Table 6.2 Pareto Analysis Injuries Cost Chart Example.

Top 10 Injuries Causes				
Causes	# of Injuries	Cost of Injuries	Cumulative Cost of Injuries in $	Cumulative %
Overexertion	55	$2,750,000	$2,750,000	42.97
Fall to the same level	47	$2,350,000	$5,100,000	79.69
Falls to lower level	7	$350,000	$5,450,000	85.16
Struck by object or equipment	6	$300,000	$5,750,000	89.84
Other exertions or bodily reactions	4	$200,000	$5,950,000	92.97
Roadway incidents involving MV	3	$150,000	$6,100,000	95.31
Slip or trip without fall	2	$100,000	$6,200,000	96.88
Caught in/ compressed by equipment or objects	2	$100,000	$6,300,000	98.44
Struck against object or equipment	1	$50,000	$6,350,000	99.22
Repetitive motions involving micro-tasks	1	$50,000	$6,400,000	100.00

managing, storing, and using information should be decided early in the process. The risk management team tasked with the assignment is responsible for managing information, developing models for application, and providing effective risk communication to stakeholders.

Review Questions

1. Explain the factors or elements that must be considered in determining the types of data information needed.
2. Describe some of the sources of data that may be gathered.
3. List some of the critical elements that the risk assessment team must understand from previous experiences.

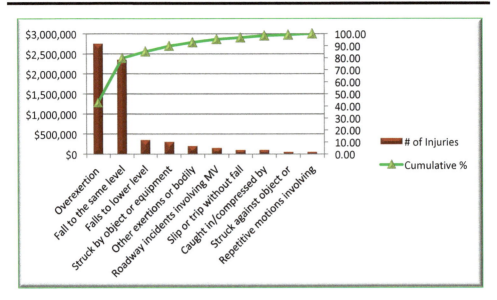

Figure 6.4
Pareto Chart Example Based on the Injuries Cost.

4. Identify the steps provided in ISO 31010 on constructing a decision-making model.
5. Identify and describe three methods used to validate decision models.

References

ANSI/ASIS/RIMS RA.1-2015. 2015. 2015. *Risk Assessment.* Alexandria, VA: ASIS International and The Risk and Insurance Management Society, Inc.

ANSI/ASSP/ISO 31000-2018. 2018. *Risk Management Principles and Guidelines.* Park Ridge, IL: American Society of Safety Professionals.

ANSI/ASSP/ISO/IEC 31010:2019. 2019. *Risk Management – Risk Assessment Techniques.* Park Ridge, IL: American Society of Safety Professionals.

ANSI/RIA R15.06-1999. 1999. *Industrial Robots and Robot Systems – Safety Requirements.* Ann Arbor, MI: Robotic Industries Association.

Cambridge Dictionary. n.d. "Model." Accessed June 5, 2020. www.dictionary.cambridge.org/us/dictionary/english/model.

Corporate Finance Institute. n.d. *What is Sensitivity Analysis? A guide to sensitivity analysis.* Accessed April 4, 2020. www.corporatefinanceinstitute.com/resources/knowledge/modeling/what-is-sensitivity-analysis/.

Lavinsky, Dave. 2014. "Pareto Principle: How to Use It to Dramatically Grow Your Business." *Forbes,* January 20, 2014. www.forbes.com/sites/davelavinsky/2014/01/20/pareto-principle-how-to-use-it-to-dramatically-grow-your-business/#7c56b2f51259_.

CHAPTER 7
Identifying Risk

Introduction

Risk assessment, the core of the risk management process, is an iterative and systematic process for identifying, analyzing, and evaluating risk so that decision makers can better understand the risk and its need for reduction and management. The risk assessment process has three distinct and sequential components: (1) risk identification; (2) risk analysis; and (3) risk evaluation as illustrated in Figure 7.3 adapted from the ISO 31000 Risk Management standard. Using a standardized approach allows an organization to consistently anticipate, discern and identify hazard/risks, measure and compare risks, formulate risk reduction measures, and prioritize treatment based on risk levels.

The first step of risk assessment, "risk identification," is most crucial since risks that are not anticipated, recognized, or identified go unmanaged. Risk identification is used to find, describe, and document risks that are of importance to the organization and that warrant further assessment. Based on an organization's defined context and scope, risks that can impact the ability to achieve stated objectives are identified, described, and recorded for further assessment.

ISO Guide 73 defines risk identification as the "process of finding, recognizing and recording risks." (ANSI/ASSP Z690.1-2011) To further clarify, risk identification is performed to identify elements, things, or situations that have a potential to affect or impact an organization's ability to achieve its objectives.

Risk identification is more than simply identifying hazards or risk sources. It involves identifying and describing the uncertainties and their effects, the related

---

Interactive tools and supplemental materials are available at assp.org/ermtools.

circumstances or concerns, any existing controls and their effectiveness, how the risk my occur, related events in the past, and the potential human and organizational factors that might apply.

ISO Guide 73 states that risk identification involves the identification of risk sources, events, their causes, and their potential consequences. A risk source can be classified as a thing or event that has the ability to create risk which, for the risk profession, translates to "hazards" and "operations." ISO defines a risk source as "element which alone or in combination has the intrinsic potential to give rise to risk" (ANSI/ASSP Z690.1-2011). From an enterprise viewpoint, risk sources can include business relations, opportunities, legal obligations, liabilities, economic shifts, technology changes, political changes and trends, natural hazards or events, human elements, management decisions, as well as exposures to hazards.

Risk Identification and Risk Management Standards

To gain a perspective of how risk is identified, a review of several key risk management standards is provided. ISO 31000 provides a larger context encompassing the management of pure risks and speculative risks. Within "risk management" is "risk assessment" of those risks which are covered in ISO 31010 and ANSI RA.1 risk assessment standards. A more specific "safety" standard is the ANSI/ASSP Z590.3-2011 (R2016), *Prevention through Design* (PtD). The PtD standard, which is focused on assessing pure risks such as hazard-based and operational-based risks, resides within the larger risk assessment sphere. This relationship is illustrated in Figure 7.1.

ISO 31000 Risk Management

The ISO 31000 risk management standard states that "the purpose of risk identification is to find, recognize and describe risks that might *help or prevent* an organization from achieving its objectives." The statement "*might help or prevent* an organization from achieving its objectives [emphasis added]" reflects the view enterprise risk management takes with risk—that risks can have positive effects (*i.e.,* opportunity or speculative risks), negative effects (*i.e.,* pure or absolute risks such as hazards and operations), or both. When identifying, assessing, and managing risk, organizations must be able to manage both pure risks and speculative risks to fully achieve their objectives.

There are many methods available for identifying risk, some of which are discussed in this chapter. Factors to be considered in the identification process as listed by ISO 31000 include:

- tangible and intangible sources of risk;
- causes, triggers, conditions, and events;

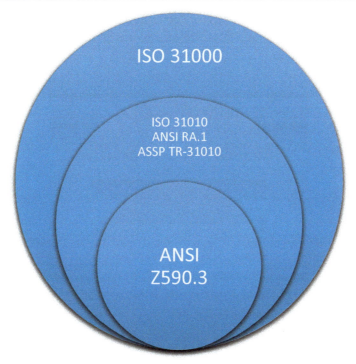

Figure 7.1
Relationship Between Risk Management Standards.

- threats and opportunities;
- vulnerabilities and capabilities;
- changes in the external and internal context;
- indicators of emerging risks;
- the nature and value of assets and resources;
- consequences and their impact on objectives;
- limitations of knowledge and reliability of information;
- timeframes and time influences;
- biases, assumptions, and beliefs of those involved.

It is recommended that organizations take account of their risks, including those that have current controls or are considered controlled. In some cases, there are multiple types of outcomes, consequences, or objectives affected by certain risks.

ANSI/ASSP/ISO/IEC 31010 Risk Management—Risk Assessment

In the ANSI/ASSP/ISO 31010-2019 standard, it states that "identifying risk enables uncertainty to be explicitly taken into account," which includes both beneficial and detrimental risks depending upon the context and scope of the effort. In Annex

B, the standard includes "techniques for eliciting views" in B.1, "techniques for identifying risk" in B.2, and methods for "determining sources, causes and drivers of risk" in B.3. In addition to those mentioned in ISO 31000, the ISO 31010 standard lists key factors that should be identified including:

- sources of risk,
- existing controls and their effectiveness,
- how certain events might occur,
- past experiences and incidents, and
- human aspects and organizational factors.

Risks should be identified as early as possible so that any unacceptable risks are known and addressed, and a mechanism for recognizing new and emerging risks should be in place. Risk identification, like the entire risk assessment, should be performed in a methodical and iterative way that is thorough and efficient.

ASSP TR-31010, Technical Report: Risk Management—Techniques for Safety Practitioners

The technical report by the American Society of Safety Professionals was developed in 2020 to compliment and align with other risk management standards. It specifically was designed to provide guidance to safety practitioners in their role of supporting the risk assessment and management process and bridge the gap between the ISO 31010 2009 and 2019 versions. In addition to covering 50 methods, many of which can be used to identify risk, the technical report contains several annexes. Annex F, the Risk Continuum, includes the various stages of risk, from new and emerging to future risks, which require detecting and identifying to be properly managed.

ANSI RA.1 Risk Assessment

The purpose of risk identification is to ascertain "the sources and nature of risk and the effect of uncertainty on achieving the organization's objectives" (ANSI/ASIS/RIMS RA.1-2015). Risk identification should include natural, unintentional, and intentional events for risks that can lead to negative outcomes as well as risks pursued as opportunities. Identification of malevolent, criminal, technical, institutional, logistical, logical, demographic, environmental, and social/political events should be considered. Risk identification should seek to answer basic questions regarding "what," "where," "when," "why," "how," and "who," so that the risk analysis and evaluation can occur.

In addition to identifying sources of risk or uncertainty, the assets at risk, their characterization and criticality to the organization, and potential consequences should also be identified. Disruption or loss of assets that are considered critical may result in unacceptable risk to an organization. The value of an asset may be measured relative to more than one consequence such as an event that causes minor harm to people but major harm to brand or reputation (ANSI/ASIS/RIMS RA.1-2015). Tangible and intangible assets may include human resources, property, process controls, financial and administrative processes, information and telecommunication systems, transportation systems, critical infrastructure, intellectual property, brand, and reputation.

Methods discussed in RA.1 include threat and opportunity analysis, vulnerability/capability analysis, and criticality and consequence (impact) analysis.

ANSI/ASSP Z590.3, Prevention through Design

The ANSI/ASSP Z590.3-2011 (R2016), *Prevention through Design: Guidelines for Addressing Occupational Hazards and Risks in Design and Redesign Processes* (PtD), standard operates within the same fundamental principles, framework, and process as ISO 31000 and ISO 31010 for assessing risk. However, being a safety standard, it has some subtle differences. First, Z590.3 focusses on hazard-risk from design to decommission (life cycle) of a system. Rather than risk assessment, Z590.3 calls the process "hazard analysis and risk assessment," and its first step in the process is "Anticipate/identify the hazards."

The word *anticipate* means to "give advance thought, discussion, or treatment." (Merriam-Webster n.d.) For the context of risk identification, "anticipate" also seems to imply that risk sources/hazards may not be known to currently exist, hidden and difficult to observe, or only occur under specific circumstances. The ability to anticipate hazards requires the assessor to have knowledge and foresight in hazard types and the operation or system being reviewed. Hazard/risk identification involves finding, anticipating, recognizing, and describing hazards that could affect the achievement of an organization's objectives including:

- existing and potential hazards—sources of risk such as operational functions, operational failure modes, actions, inactions, interactions, upsets, changes, energy sources, existing conditions, conditions created, materials, chemicals and substances, and combined elements or conditions that create synergistic effects;
- potential exposures to hazards—direct or indirect contact, proximity, duration, magnitude, frequency, exposure routes or pathways;
- possible failure modes—functions that perform outside of a defined parameter, incomplete or intermittent performance, or not as intended such as failure to start or stop, delayed start or stop, failure during operation, degraded operation, exceeded capacity, foreseeable misuse;
- cause or trigger—events or conditions that allow or cause an exposure to a risk source such as machinery, human actions or inactions, environment, materials, or methods;

- existing controls—type and function, effectiveness, reliability;
- potential consequences—general description of types of consequences and impact.

On Emerging Risks

Emerging risks can be characterized as new, developing risks that have been detected and are apparent and/or existing risks that are changing and increasing in new or unfamiliar conditions. These emerging risks present effects of uncertainty on objectives due to new threats, hazards, changes in frequency of occurrence, or changes in consequences or their severity; or in the case of speculative risks, new opportunities, and potential gains. These can develop as a result of new processes, technologies, or types of work. They may also develop from changes in the organization, or from environmental, social, public, or political changes. Emerging risks may have a low likelihood or frequency potential; however, such risks may have significant consequences such as black swan events. Risks can emerge, develop, increase, or disappear as an organization's external and internal context changes. The risk management process must be designed to anticipate, detect, identify, acknowledge, and respond to those changes and events in an appropriate and timely manner.

There are several considerations needed when identifying emerging risks. Emerging risks must be considered throughout the life-cycle—design, procurement, construction, installation, operation, maintenance, and decommission—of new technologies, products, services, or other elements. They must be viewed in a holistic way, and the potential for cascading effects must include atypical scenarios, which may require multiple or different methods for identifying or detecting such risks. Scanning and early detection of emerging risks is necessary so as to monitor their development before they become a threat. As emerging risks scenarios are identified, they are entered into the risk assessment and management process.

After the emerging risks are characterized, a formal decision is made regarding which emerging risks should be selected to be analyzed in greater depth. The outcome of the emerging risks characterization would be a decision whether the emerging risk should be "discarded," "monitored," or "assessed" as depicted in Figure 7.2.

Risk Identification

Risk identification includes more than identifying the risk source. It included the identification and description of the risk drivers; exposures; existing controls; potential failure modes, causes, or triggers; and the potential range of consequences. These can contribute towards estimating the likelihood of an occurrence or consequence and help to identify risk controls or treatments and prioritization, early warning or detection, and common causes or triggers.

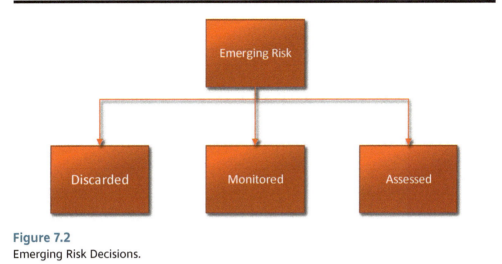

Figure 7.2
Emerging Risk Decisions.

Risk Source

A risk source is generally defined as an element either by itself or in combination that has potential to create risk and uncertainty. In other words, risk and uncertainty are derived from risk sources. For pure risk (risk that can only result in negative outcomes), the most effective means of managing the risk is at its source. If the risk source can be avoided, eliminated, or reduced to an acceptable level of risk (ALOR), it will require little if any management going forward.

Sources of risk can include events, decisions, actions, and/or conditions that alone or combined create risk. Events are occurrences or things that happen at a point in time or that have a potential to occur. An event can be something that is expected to occur but does not, or something that is not expected that does occur. Actions are an intentional act, movement, or physical activity carried out to accomplish a particular goal that can have intended and/or unintended consequences. A condition is the state of something that exists or has the potential to exist regarding its properties or characteristics. Conditions, such as hazards, can exist or have a potential to be created and present certain inherent properties or characteristics that give rise to risk. Events and consequences can have multiple causes or causal chains.

Hazards exist in many places and forms, some of which include operational functions, operational failure modes, actions, inactions, interactions, upsets, changes, energy sources, existing conditions, conditions created, materials, chemicals and substances, and combined elements or conditions that create synergistic effects. There are many references and resources for categories of hazards including the following list in Table 7.1 taken from OSHA's Publication 3061, *Job Hazard Analysis,* Appendix 2 (OSHA 2002).

Table 7.1. Hazards List taken from OSHA Publication 3071 "Job Hazard Analysis," Appendix 2.

Hazards	Hazard Descriptions
Chemical (Toxic)	A chemical that exposes a person by absorption through the skin, inhalation, or through the blood stream that causes illness, disease, or death. The amount of chemical exposure is critical in determining hazardous effects. Check Material Safety Data Sheets (SDS), and/or OSHA 1910.1000 for chemical hazard information.
Chemical (Flammable)	A chemical that, when exposed to a heat ignition source, results in combustion. Typically, the lower a chemical's flash point and boiling point, the more flammable the chemical. Check SDS for flammability information.
Chemical (Corrosive)	A chemical that, when it comes into contact with skin, metal, or other materials, damages the materials. Acids and bases are examples of corrosives.
Explosion (Chemical Reaction)	Self-explanatory.
Explosion (Over Pressurization)	Sudden and violent release of a large amount of gas/energy due to a significant pressure difference such as rupture in a boiler or compressed gas cylinder.
Electrical (Shock/Short Circuit)	Contact with exposed conductors or a device that is incorrectly or inadvertently grounded, such as when a metal ladder comes into contact with power lines. 60Hz alternating current (common house current) is very dangerous because it can stop the heart.
Electrical (Fire)	Use of electrical power that results in electrical overheating or arcing to the point of combustion or ignition of flammables or electrical component damage.
Electrical (Static/ESD)	The moving or rubbing of wool, nylon, other synthetic fibers, and even flowing liquids can generate static electricity. This creates an excess or deficiency of electrons on the surface of material that discharges (sparks) to the ground resulting in the ignition of flammables or damage to electronics or the body's nervous system.
Electrical (Loss of Power)	Safety-critical equipment failure as a result of loss of power.
Ergonomics (Strain)	Damage of tissue due to overexertion (strains and sprains) or repetitive motion.

Continued on next page

Identifying Risk | 121

Hazards	Hazard Descriptions
Ergonomics (Human Error)	A system design, procedure, or equipment that is error provocative. (A switch goes up to turn something off).
Excavation (Collapse)	Soil collapse in a trench or excavation as a result of improper or inadequate shoring. Soil type is critical in determining the hazard likelihood.
Fall (Slip, Trip)	Conditions that result in falls (impacts) from height or on traditional walking surfaces (such as slippery floors, poor housekeeping, uneven walking surfaces, exposed ledges, etc.)
Fire/Heat	Temperatures that can cause burns to the skin or damage to other organs. Fires require a heat source, fuel, and oxygen.
Mechanical/ Vibration (Chaffing/ Fatigue)	Vibration that can cause damage to nerve endings, or material fatigue that results in a safety-critical failure. (Examples are abraded slings and ropes, weakened hoses and belts.)
Mechanical Failure	Self-explanatory; typically occurs when devices exceed designed capacity or are inadequately maintained.
Mechanical	Skin, muscle, or body part exposed to crushing, caught-between, cutting, tearing, shearing items or equipment.
Noise	Noise levels (>85 dBA 8 hr TWA) that result in hearing damage or inability to communicate safety-critical information.
Radiation (Ionizing)	Alpha, Beta, Gamma, neutral particles, and X-rays that cause injury (tissue damage) by ionization of cellular components.
Radiation (Non-Ionizing)	Ultraviolet, visible light, infrared, and microwaves that cause injury to tissue by thermal or photochemical means.
Struck By (Mass Acceleration)	Accelerated mass that strikes the body causing injury or death. (Examples are falling objects and projectiles.)
Struck Against	Injury to a body part as a result of coming into contact of a surface in which action was initiated by the person. (An example is when a screwdriver slips.)
Temperature Extreme (Heat/Cold)	Temperatures that result in heat stress, exhaustion, or metabolic slowdown such as hypothermia.
Visibility	Lack of lighting or obstructed vision that results in an error or other hazard.
Weather Phenomena (Snow/Rain/Wind/Ice)	Self-explanatory.

Risk Drivers

A risk driver is a "factor that has a major influence on risk" (ANSI/ASSP/ISO 31010-2019). Risk drivers influence the status and development of risk exposures and can affect more than one risk. Because of their potential influence on multiple risk sources, risk drivers can require more attention and scrutiny.

The identification of risk requires that risk drivers with the potential for influencing the risk source(s) also be identified. Examples of risk drivers for an electrical risk source might include wet or humid conditions (influencing electrical transmission and shock), dry conditions (influencing a higher potential for static electrical buildup or electrical fire), poor management culture (lack of oversight or consistent enforcement, lack of proper resources, or lack of training and accountability), or other conditions or factors that could influence an incident. Such factors should be taken into account as part of the risk identification process.

Risk Exposures

A risk exposure is something of value that comes in direct contact, proximity, or path of a risk. These things of value consist of the organization's business objectives (profits, cash flow, growth, stability, public relations and good well, customers, regulatory and legal compliance, reputation, etc.), assets, people, property, equipment, and the local community and environment. These things of value that are exposed to a risk have an increased likelihood of an occurrence and resulting consequences, while those that are not exposed have a very low likelihood of the occurrence. It is important to identify which things of value are at risk of exposure in the identification process. Identification of the exposure routes or pathways for identified risk sources is also needed to then analyze, evaluate, and control the risk.

Existing Controls

Risk identification should include the identification and description of existing controls, and their effectiveness and reliability. As stated in ISO 31010, consideration should be given to:

- the mechanism by which the controls are intended to modify risk;
- whether the controls are in place, are capable of operating as intended, and are achieving the expected results;
- whether there are shortcomings in the design of controls or the way they are applied;
- whether there are gaps in controls;
- whether controls function independently, or if they need to function collectively to be effective;
- whether there are factors, conditions, vulnerabilities, or circumstances that can reduce or eliminate control effectiveness including common cause failures;

- whether controls themselves introduce additional risks (ANSI/ASSP/ISO 31010- 2019).

It should be noted that multiple controls can be in place for certain risks, and multiple risks can be controlled by a single control. Identification of existing controls should also describe how the control modifies the risk such as:

- prevents exposure (changes likelihood),
- mitigates or reduces impact (changes severity),
- prevents and controls (changes likelihood and severity), and
- how the burden of risk is shared between stakeholders (insurance, risk transfer, and risk financing).

Control effectiveness and reliability assumptions made during the identification process should be verified during the risk analysis. All assumptions made during risk analysis about the actual effect and reliability of controls should be validated where possible, with a particular emphasis on individual controls or combinations of controls that are assumed to have a substantial modifying effect. This should consider information gained through routine monitoring and review of controls (ANSI/ASSP/ISO 31010-2019).

Failure Modes

As part of the risk identification, potential failures of the system should be identified and described. A failure mode is described as a condition where a system fails to perform as expected or deviates from its design tolerances resulting in a potential for harm or a hazardous event. In identifying failure modes, a "what-if" approach can be used to identify potential system failures by exploring various ways something might go wrong.

> **Example:** Failure modes are conditions or states where the system fails to perform as designed or expected. Systems or equipment such as conveyors, pumps, press brakes, local exhaust ventilation, containment vessels, and forklifts have specific failure modes. These conditions or states might include:
>
> 1. pre-mature operation (*i.e.*, unexpected startup or release of energy),
> 2. failure to start operation (*i.e.*, sump pump fails to operate when water level rises beyond flood level),
> 3. failure to stop operations (*i.e.*, press brake fails to stop when interlock is activated),

> 4. failure during operation (*i.e.*, local exhaust system fails during welding operation),
> 5. degraded or deterioration of operation (*i.e.*, leak in containment vessel),
> 6. exceeded capability/capacity of operation (*i.e.*, over pressurization of vessel),
> 7. reasonably foreseeable uses and misuses of operation (*i.e.*, using forklift to raise worker to reach component).

The end result is to identify credible circumstances and potential failures that could arise and result in an undesirable incident or exposure. As ANSI Z590.3 states, each failure mode should include a description of the circumstances and events that could lead to the failure so that it can be understood.

Causes or Triggers

Causes or triggers are the circumstances, conditions, actions, or inactions that can expose a hazard or initiate a hazardous event. Hazards can be of an acute nature causing immediate harm from a single exposure, or cumulative in nature developing over time from prolonged or repeated exposure. Fundamental causes include:

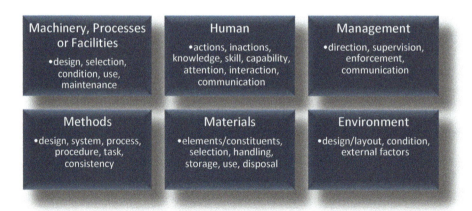

Understanding how a hazard can be caused or triggered is critical to hazard/risk identification.

Range of Consequences

Consequence is defined by ISO Guide 73 as an "outcome of an event affecting objectives" (ANSI/ASSP Z690.1-2011). For a risk source to present a risk to the organization, there must be an "objective" at risk (something of value) and a consequence. Most often, there are multiple potential consequences associated with a risk. Sometimes the risk presents only negative effects from hazards or operations, while speculative risks present positive and/or negative potential effects.

The anticipated or reasonably foreseen consequences that might result from exposure to the risk sources should be identified. The subject of its impact such as objectives, people, property, liability, reputation, environment, or other should be identified. A general description of types of consequences associated with the risk source is needed to conduct the risk assessment.

Identification Methods

Many formal and informal methods for risk identification are available including those in this manual and in ISO 31010 as illustrated in Figure 7.3. Methods will vary in application, complexity, and output. As stated before, the method should be selected according to the context and needs of the assessment. In certain cases, more than one method is needed to adequately identify risks (Lyon, Popov 2016).

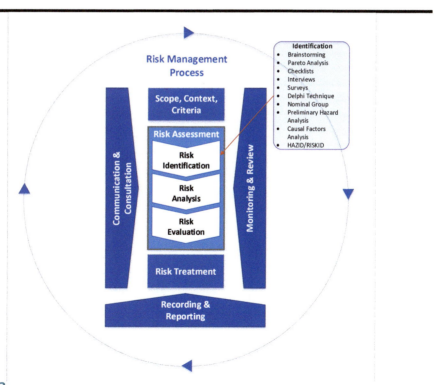

Figure 7.3
Risk Identification Methods and the ISO 31000 Risk Management Process (ANSI/ASSP/ISO 31000-2018).

For hazards and operational risks, various methods including checklists, guidewords, inspections, and audits can be used. Organizations often use checklists and structured processes to methodically identify types or categories of risks to capture difficult to observe or hidden risks. A list of identification methods is presented in table 7.2.

Methods for identifying risk include the collection of information such as document reviews, interviews, and observations. Historical reviews of available data on losses, incident investigations, and near hit reports can help identify the types of incidents, hazards, and causes at the site, the organization, or industry sector. Regulatory reviews of applicable codes, regulations, and consensus standards can

Table 7.2. Risk Identification Methods.

Identification Methods	Descriptions
Brainstorming	Team-based method used in workshops to stimulate imaginative thinking and generate ideas.
Cause and Effect Analysis	A team-based method used to identify and categorize possible causes and contributory factors so that all possible hypotheses can be considered.
Checklists	A simple form of identification that uses a listing of typical hazards or exposures often taken from industry experience, codes, or standards.
Cindynic Approach	Semi-structured interviews performed in a structured meeting or workshop to identify intangible hazards and sources of risk that can lead to different consequences.
Delphi Technique	A method used to collect informed opinions on a topic through a set of sequential questionnaires. Participants provide their opinions anonymously while receiving others' responses after each set of questions
Design Safety Review	A structured review of design plans, specifications, and safety related factors using safety specifications and performance standards to identify hazards and failure modes.
Failure Mode and Effects Analysis (FMEA)	A qualitative or semi-quantitative method that lists systematically the failure modes, their effects, existing safeguards, and any additional controls that are needed to reduce risk to an acceptable level.

Continued on next page

Identification Methods	Descriptions
Hazard Identification Study (HAZID)	A structured, qualitative method using guidewords or checklists to identify potential hazards' causes and potential consequences.
Hazard Analysis and Critical Control Points (HACCP)	A systematic, proactive, and preventive system for hazard identification and placement of controls at critical points in a process to effectively prevent hazards from occurring.
Hazard and Operability Study (HAZOP)	A more involved qualitative method used to identify both hazards and operability problems using "guide words" to prompt team members in identifying deviations that can lead to the failures.
Human Reliability Analysis	A technique used to identify the potential for human error and its causes so the probability of error can be reduced.
Job Hazard Analysis	A step-by-step listing of a job's sequential tasks, associated hazard, and prescribed safety measures
Structured Interviews	Structured or semi-structured one-on-one conversations using prepared questions to elicit views
Nominal Group Technique	Technique for eliciting consensus and ranking of ideas from a group of people in a workshop setting. Similar to the Delphi Technique, individuals identify their ideas and then vote on the list to rank the top ideas.
Preliminary Hazard Analysis	A simple inductive method of analysis whose objective is to identify the hazards and hazardous situations and events that can cause harm for a given activity, facility, or system.
Preliminary Hazard List	Used prior to a Preliminary Hazard Analysis to identify and compile a list of the most evident or worst-credible hazards associated with a system's design. A PHL is only a list of the hazards; however, it can be the basis for an analysis that becomes a PHA or other risk assessment.
Reliability Centered Maintenance	A method to identify the policies that should be implemented to manage failures so as to efficiently and effectively achieve the required safety, availability, and economy of operation for all types of equipment.

Continued on next page

Identification Methods	Descriptions
Scenario Analysis	A method used to identify possible future scenarios through imagination, brainstorming, or extrapolation from modeling. Risks are then considered, assuming each of these scenarios might occur.
Toxicity Assessment	A method used to identify and analyze environmental hazards and their possible exposure pathways to a susceptible population.
What-if Analysis	A team-based brainstorming process that uses the question "what if" to identify deviations and analyze hazards of a system or process.

be used to identify common compliance needs, hazards, and controls. Document reviews and examinations of design plans, specifications; operational manuals or instructions; procedural instructions; maintenance documents and instructions; complaints and hazard reports; perception surveys; and audits, inspections, and survey reports can be valuable information to consider. Similar operations, energy sources, site surveys, checklist surveys, interviews, and brainstorming can help identify existing, potential, and less obvious hazards in the operation.

Checklists are a quick and easy way to identify hazards; however, it is important to remember that checklists serve as a guide and should not limit the focus too narrowly as to miss hazards not on the list. Checklist findings can be summarized in other methods like HAZID or Hazard Identification Study, brainstorming sessions, or nominal group techniques for further study. Although there are many means of identifying and describing risks, a single systematic and consistent approach to their use is most important.

Conducting Risk Identification

A systematic and iterative approach to identifying risks and their related elements should always be used. Having a basic plan for conducting risk identification is recommended. The following steps for such a plan are adapted from the MIL-STD-882E standard Task 101:

- Review Context—To begin, a review of the organization's established context for risk assessment should be performed in preparation of developing a plan.
- Develop Plan—The specific purpose, methods for identification along with the team members and facilitator, resources, budget, timeline, and other elements needed for the effort should be defined as part of the plan.

- Define Responsibilities—The plan should also clearly define the roles and responsibilities, interrelationships, and lines of communication within the organization and among affected stakeholders. The plan and responsibilities should be communicated and understood by stakeholders.
- Initiate Identification Process—Following the plan, the assessment team uses the selected methods to find, identify, and document existing and potential risks, risk drivers, causes, possible consequences, and existing controls.
- Document and Track Risks—The identified risks should be documented and tracked for further analysis, evaluation, and treatment. A tracking system should include pertinent information such as:
    - the system or task assessed,
    - the risk type/description,
    - failure modes,
    - causes,
    - what is at risk,
    - exposure,
    - potential consequences,
    - and existing controls.
- Communicate Results—The documented risks and tracking system should be shared and communicated with affected stakeholders and decision makers for further steps in the risk assessment.

As RA.1 states, "some risks are continuous, and some vary with time" (ANSI/ASIS/RIMS RA.1-2015). Variables that should also be considered include duration and frequency of events, criticality of systems at risk, cascading affects that might occur from risks, and other unique characteristics important to the identified risks.

Summary

The success of a risk assessment is dependent upon proper identification of risks and the associated elements. Risk identification includes the identification and description of the risk source, associated risk drivers, causes or triggers, exposures, existing controls, and the potential consequences. The better the risk is understood, the more likely it can be analyzed, evaluated, and managed.

Review Questions

1. Explain how risk identification is more than simply identifying hazards.
2. Identify the factors to be considered in the identification process as listed by ISO 31000.
3. Described how emerging risks can be characterized and why they are important.

4. Explain what risk sources are and provide several examples.
5. Describe the difference between pure risk and speculative risk.
6. Give four examples of fundamental causes.
7. Define what a failure mode is and provide five examples.
8. As stated in ISO 31010, consideration should be given to what elements?
9. Identify and describe five methods used to identify risk.

References

ANSI/ASIS/RIMS RA.1-2015. 2015. *Risk Assessment.* Alexandria, VA: ASIS International and The Risk and Insurance Management Society, Inc.

ANSI/ASSP Z590.3-2011 (R2016). 2016. *Prevention through Design: Guidelines for Addressing Occupational Hazards and Risks in Design and Redesign Processes.* Park Ridge, IL: American Society of Safety Professionals.

ANSI/ASSP Z690.1-2011. 2011. *Vocabulary for Risk Management.* Park Ridge, IL: American Society of Safety Professionals.

ANSI/ASSP/ISO 31000-2018. 2018. *Risk Management Principles and Guidelines.* Park Ridge, IL: American Society of Safety Professionals.

ANSI/ASSP/ISO/IEC 31010-2019. 2019. *Risk Management – Risk Assessment Techniques.* Park Ridge, IL: American Society of Safety Professionals.

ASSP TR-31010-2020. 2020. *Technical Report: Risk Management – Techniques for Safety Practitioners.* Park Ridge, IL: American Society of Safety Professionals.

Lyon, Bruce K., and Georgi Popov. 2016. "The Art of Assessing Risk—Selecting, Modifying, and Combining Methods to Assess Operational Risks," *Professional Safety*, March 2016, 40–51.

MIL-STD-882E. 2012. *Department of Defense Standard Practice: System Safety.* Washington, DC: Department of Defense.

Merriam-Webster. n.d. "Anticipate." Accessed October 14, 2020. www.merriam-webster.com/dictionary/anticipate.

OSHA. 2002. *Job Hazard Analysis.* Publication 3071. Washington, DC: US Department of Labor. www.osha.gov/Publications/osha3071.pdf.

CHAPTER 8
Analyzing Risk

Introduction
Once a risk has been identified and described, it can then be analyzed for its estimated risk level. Risk analysis is considered the heart of risk assessment and is used to gain an understanding of the risk, its consequences, and likelihood of occurrence. It is used to estimate risk levels so that risks can be evaluated, prioritized, and treated according to the established risk criteria. To properly analyze risks, a standardized and iterative approach must be used throughout the risk management process.

Risk Analysis Defined
Risk analysis is defined by ISO Guide 73 as the "process to comprehend the nature of risk and to determine the level of risk." It notes that "risk analysis provides the basis for risk evaluation and decisions about risk treatment" (ANSI/ASSP Z690.1-2011). ANSI RA.1 defines *risk analysis* as the "process to characterize and understand the nature of risk and to define the level of risk." It further notes that "risk analysis assesses the likelihood and consequences of a risk to provide the basis for risk evaluation and risk treatment decision-making" (ANSI/ASIS/RIMS RA.1-2015).

From a safety or hazard-risk standpoint, the ANSI/ASSP Z590.3, Prevention through Design, standard uses the term *hazard analysis* to include both hazard identification and analysis. It defines hazard analysis as "a process that commences with the identification of a hazard or hazards and proceeds into an estimate of the severity of harm or damage that could result if the potential of an incident or

---

Interactive tools and supplemental materials are available at assp.org/ermtools.

exposure occurs" (ANSI/ASSP Z590.3-2016). It is not considered a *risk analysis* until the "estimation of likelihood" is complete. This is an important point: a risk analysis includes an estimation of severity and an estimation of likelihood which combine into a risk level.

Without risk analysis, a risk cannot be evaluated as to its acceptability or need for treatment by an organization. As indicated in Figure 8.1, risk analysis is preceded by risk identification, and followed by risk evaluation within the risk management process. It is also important to remember that all risk analyses and assessments are "estimations," albeit educated estimates, since risk deals with future uncertainty. ISO Guide 73 supports this assertion in a note that states that "risk analysis includes risk estimation" (ANSI/ASSP Z690.1-2011).

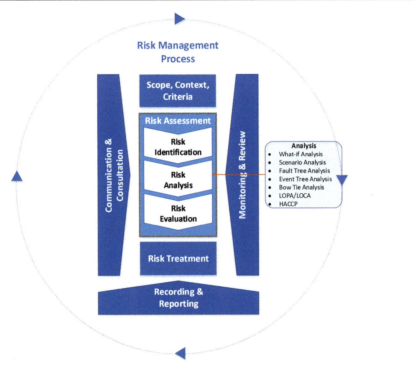

Figure 8.1
Risk Analysis and the Risk Management Process adapted from ANSI/ASSP/ISO 31010-2019.

Understanding the Nature of Risk

ISO 31000 states that "the purpose of risk analysis is to comprehend the nature of risk and its characteristics including, where appropriate, the level of risk" (ANSI/ASSP/ISO 31000-2018). It involves analysis of identified uncertainties, risk sources, consequences, likelihood, events and scenarios, and existing controls and their effectiveness and reliability as illustrated in Figure 8.2. Events and scenarios can have multiple causes and multiple consequences, as well as impact on multiple objectives. This should be kept in mind during risk analysis.

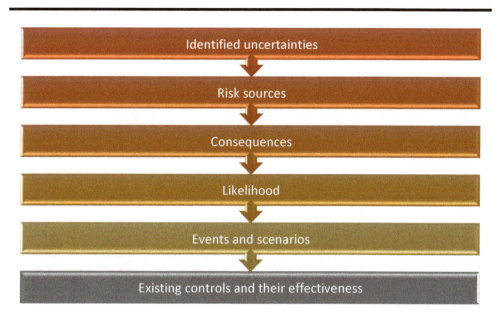

Figure 8.2
Elements within Risk Analysis.

Risk analysis is used to gain an understanding of risk. The ANSI/ASIS/RIMS RA.1 risk assessment standard outlines the analysis process as a way an organization can take information generated from the risk identification process and analyze it within the context of its operations and the established risk criteria. This involves assessing the likelihood of its occurrence and the resulting consequences should it occur to determine the level of risk it presents.

Fundamental Terms

There are some fundamental terms in risk management that are critical for the risk professional to understand and use properly. These terms are *hazard, risk, hazard analysis, risk analysis,* and *risk assessment* and are occasionally misused or used interchangeably. For instance, the term *hazard* is often used in place of *risk*. Some use the terms *hazard analysis, risk analysis,* and *risk assessment* incorrectly or to mean the same thing. It is important to recognize the differences when applying risk management principles (ASSP TR-31010-2020).

Hazard

ISO Guide 73 defines hazard as a "source of potential harm" that if left uncontrolled, can create risk (ANSI/ASSP Z690.1-2011). A hazard is considered a "source of risk." Hazards are created by equipment or machinery, technology, energy sources, substances and chemicals, materials, or by human actions or inactions. Basic workplace hazard classifications include physical and mechanical, chemical, biological, ergonomic, and psychosocial. For a hazard to create risk, there must be a series of elements that interact as shown in Figure 8.3. A hazard or "risk source" is influenced by "risk drivers" and if "exposure" to the hazard exists, a trigger or cause can result in an "event" that leads to "consequences," which in summation is "risk" (ASSP TR-31010-2020).

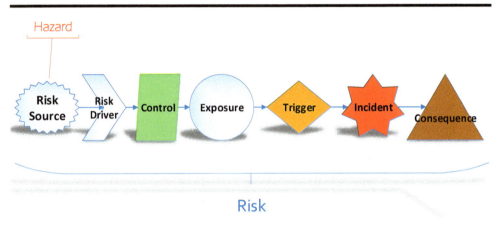

Figure 8.3
Relationship between Hazards and Risk.

Risk

Risks that are derived from risk sources such as hazards and operational aspects are considered pure risks that can only produce negative consequences. Risk sources can also include speculative risks that present opportunity such as financial and strategic aspects that can result in positive or negative outcomes. A "risk" is produced when a "risk source" influenced by "risk drivers" with "exposure" to people or assets, and effects to an organization's objective is "triggered" causing a chance for loss (pure risk) or an opportunity for gain (speculative risk). Risk (R) is estimated by combining the likelihood (L) of the event occurring and the resulting severity (S) of the consequence (ASSP TR-31010-2020).

Hazard Analysis

Hazard analysis is considered the fundamental process of determining if a hazard or failure can lead to an incident or undesired event. Hazard analysis involves analyzing the identified hazards, their existing controls, and potential exposures. As a result, the analysis produces a range of possible consequences and severity estimates. Note: A hazard analysis does not estimate risk derived from the hazard.

Risk Analysis

ISO Guide 73 defines "risk analysis" as the "process to comprehend the nature of risk and to determine the level of risk" (ANSI/ASSP Z690.1-2011). It includes the steps of a hazard analysis (identified hazards, existing controls, and potential exposures), as well as several additional steps. In a risk analysis, a consequence is selected to determine how the event could occur and estimate its severity (S), likelihood (L), and risk level (R). A risk analysis allows for the ranking and prioritizing of risks using risk level estimations. Note: A risk analysis does not determine whether risks are acceptable or if risk treatment is required (ASSP TR-31010-2020).

Risk Assessment

Risk assessment is the sequential process of identifying, analyzing, and evaluating risk. It goes beyond a risk analysis by including an "evaluation" or judgement of risk acceptability. A comparison of the "estimated risk level" with the established risk criteria is performed to determine whether the risk level is acceptable or if actions are needed to reduce the risk to an acceptable level. Figure 8.4 shows a comparison of the steps of a hazard analysis, risk analysis, and risk assessment (ASSP TR-31010-2020).

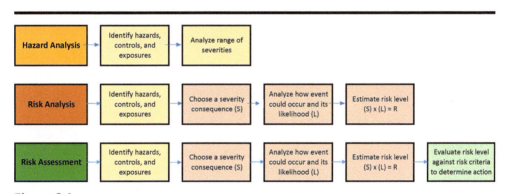

Figure 8.4
Comparison of Hazard Analysis, Risk Analysis, and Risk Assessment Steps.

Hazard Analyses Methods

A hazard analysis is the identification of hazards, existing controls, and the exposures to the hazards, and an analysis of the potential severity of consequences. It is the fundamental step in a risk assessment; however, by itself, it does not estimate risk or evaluate its acceptability. Examples of hazard analyses are presented in

Table 8.1. It should be noted that these traditional hazard analysis techniques can be modified to include risk estimations that would convert them to risk analysis methods.

Table 8.1. Hazard Analysis Methods.

Hazard Analysis Methods	Descriptions
Bow Tie Analysis	A barrier type analysis using a visual diagram to describe and analyze risk pathways of hazards, their causes, preventive controls, the hazardous event, mitigating controls and consequences. Traditionally, there is no risk estimation, however, it can be modified to include risk analysis.
Cause and Effect Analysis (Ishikawa analysis or fishbone diagram)	A team-based method of generating and sorting potential causes and contributory factors for a defined problem that is typically illustrated in a fishbone type diagram. Traditionally, there is no risk estimation; however, it can be modified to include risk analysis.
Causal Mapping	A network diagram representing the events, causes, effects, and their relationships.
Job hazard analysis	A method used to break down a job into its main steps and identify the hazards associated for each step and the controls for each hazard. It is documented in a three-column spreadsheet and used for job training and accident investigation. Traditionally, there is no risk estimation; however, it can be modified to include risk analysis.
Structured What-if Technique (SWIFT)	A team-based process that uses a structured, pre-determined list of "what-if" questions to identify deviations and analyze hazards of a system or process. Questions are developed through research of related information on the system being analyzed. Traditionally, there is no risk estimation, however, it can be modified to include risk analysis
Task hazard analysis	Similar to job hazard analysis, it is a more focused analysis of the operator's actions for a small task. The task is broken into steps with associated hazards and controls for each step.

Continued on next page

Hazard Analysis Methods	Descriptions
What-if Analysis	A team-based, brainstorming process that uses the question "what if" to identify deviations and analyze hazards of a system or process. Traditionally, there is no risk estimation; however, it can be modified to include risk analysis.
What-If/Checklist	A team-based, structured analysis that combines the creative, brainstorming aspects of the What-if with the systematic approach of the Checklist. The combination of techniques can compensate for the weaknesses of each.

Process Hazard Analysis

A process hazard analysis is a set of organized and systematic analyses of identified hazards and controls associated with a process. It provides information to assist in making decisions for improving safety and reducing operational risk associated with a process. Process hazard analyses such as "What-if" analyses are used to break down a series of actions or steps to understand process-related hazards and their causes and effects. These methods are often used to analyze potential causes and consequences of fires, explosions, releases of highly hazardous, toxic, or flammable chemicals. Process safety analysis focuses on equipment, instrumentation, utilities, human actions, and external factors that may impact the process. One additional benefit of conducting such an analysis is a more thorough understanding of the industrial process, leading to opportunities for improving process efficiency and cost reduction.

Risk assessments have been legally required of businesses in the United Kingdom since 1999 by the Health and Safety Executive. However, for businesses in the United States, there are only two standards that mandate the assessment of risk. These are the Occupational Safety and Health Administration (OSHA) Process Safety Management of Highly Hazardous Chemicals, and the Environmental Protection Agency (EPA) Risk Management Plan, both of which require process hazard analyses. Summaries of these two standards follow:

- OSHA 29 CFR 1910.119 *Process Safety Management (PSM) of Highly Hazardous Chemicals* standard, established in 1992, requires process hazard analyses for regulated industrial processes containing 10,000 pounds or more of a hazardous chemical for protecting the employees working in and around such processes. Specifically, OSHA's PSM standard addresses mandated process hazard analyses in 1910.119 (e)(1) stating that "an initial process hazard analysis (hazard evaluation)" of covered processes be conducted by the operation. What-if Hazard Analysis is one of several process hazard analysis methodologies referred to in the OSHA Process Safety Management standard and EPA Risk Management Plan Rule as an acceptable method (Popov, Lyon, Hollcroft 2016). Methods listed in OSHA 1910.119(e)(2) considered appropriate to determine and evaluate process hazards include checklists, What-if Analysis, What-if/Checklist Analysis, HAZOP, Failure Mode and Effects Analysis and Fault Tree Analysis.

- EPA 40 CFR PART 68 Chemical Accident Prevention Provisions, Risk Management Plan (RMP) Rule issued in 1994 because of the Clean Air Act Amendments of 1990 mirror's the OSHA Process Safety Management requirements for process hazard analyses in regulated facilities for the purpose of protecting the public and the environment from undesired consequences of explosions or releases.

The what-if method is also listed in ISO 31010:2019, *Risk Management – Risk Assessment Techniques,* ANSI/ASIS/RIMS RA.1-2015, *Risk Assessment,* and ANSI/ASSP Z590.3-2011 (R2016) *Prevention through Design.*

Process hazard analysis methods such as What-if Analysis can be applied at any point of the lifecycle of a system and are commonly used to identify failures or deviations and the resulting effect so that proper controls can be implemented. These methods can be applied broadly to a system or they can be more targeted to a more specific piece of equipment, procedure, or activity. Some areas where methods such as what-if can be useful include:

- Process safety management operations that contain hazardous chemical processes;
- Refrigeration systems containing ammonia such as meat packing, food processing, and cold storage;
- Non-routine activities such as equipment installations, repair, or decommission
- Business continuity threat assessments and "Tabletop drills" used to develop emergency scenarios and necessary measures for preparedness, disaster recovery, and business continuity;
- Design safety reviews of new facilities, systems, and equipment;
- Management of change procedures;
- Procurement of new technology, equipment, or materials; and
- Emerging or developing risks.

Methods such as What-if Analysis are relatively easy to apply; however, they rely heavily upon the experience and knowledge of the analysis team. To be successful, these methods require experienced facilitators and teams knowledgeable in the system being analyzed.

Traditional What-if Analysis

What-if Analysis is a qualitative hazard analysis method that uses team-based brainstorming to determine what can go wrong in a given scenario. Originally used by chemical and petrochemical industries as an easier alternative to HAZOP, "What-if" and its variations (What-if/Checklist and Structured What-if Analysis Technique or SWIFT) are commonly used in energy, manufacturing, high-tech, food processing, transportation, healthcare, and other industries.

A cross-functional team knowledgeable in the system being analyzed is used to discuss aspects in a brainstorming fashion using What-if questions to identify weaknesses, deviations, or hazards. The team should include "subject matter experts" in the system or component being analyzed and be led by an experienced facilitator. Through the process, potential hazards, their causes, effects, and controls are identified. As a result, additional controls to prevent the hazard from occurring are identified. The "What-if" questions along with resulting consequences, existing safeguards, risks levels, and recommended additional controls are recorded on a what-if spreadsheet such as the example in Figure 8.5. The steps are briefly described in the following:

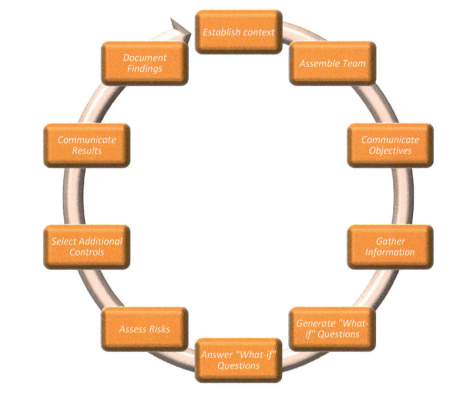

Figure 8.5
What-if Process.

Establish Context
As part of the context, a clear purpose and scope are defined including the activity or system to be analyzed, boundaries of the analysis, level of detail desired, and risk criteria to be used.

Assemble Team
A cross-functional team of trained, experienced, and knowledgeable members is selected to conduct the What-if Analysis. An experienced facilitator and scribe are also needed. Members from engineering, design, production, operations, maintenance, and safety, health, and environmental are generally included. Knowledge of design standards, regulatory codes, operational error potential, incident history, maintenance needs, and other practical experience is required.

Communicate Objectives
The purpose, scope, boundaries of the analysis, and team responsibilities should be clearly communicated to the team by the facilitator. Risk criteria and definitions to be used in the analysis should be clearly communicated to the team.

Gather Information
Applicable information regarding the system, historical information, specifications, and instructions is gathered by the facilitator, and provided to the team for review. The team should observe the activity or system if in place. Specially, reference materials such as piping and instrumentation diagrams (P&IDs), schematics, drawings, instruction manuals, maintenance and service guidelines, component specifications, and safeguarding elements should be gathered and studied by the team prior to the analysis.

Break Down into Tasks/Elements
Using information gathered, the activity or system is broken down into sequential tasks or elements for analysis.

Generate "What-if" Questions
For each task/element, the team generates What-if questions to identify potential hazards and hazard scenarios. The questioning process is applied to each task separately, investigating potential scenarios such as procedural upsets, miscommunications, operator errors, equipment failures, and software errors. An unstructured or structured brainstorming method can be used. As team members pose specific What-if questions, the scribe records each question on a flipchart or laptop projection in view of the team. Additional questions are generated during this process and are recorded by the scribe. The facilitator completes and refines the list of What-if questions for the analysis.

Answer "What-if" Questions

The team discusses and answers each What-if scenario as to the causes, resulting effects and consequences, and existing safeguards or controls.

Assess the Risks with Current Controls

An estimate of severity and likelihood can be included in the analysis. A risk level is estimated based on the severity and likelihood of occurrence. Risk levels are evaluated and compared to a predetermined criterion. If the risk levels are not acceptable, additional risk treatment is recommended based on the risk treatment strategies (Lyon and Popov 2019).

Select Additional Controls

If additional risk reduction measures are necessary. Risk reduction options are identified and selected according to the hierarchy of controls, effectiveness, and feasibility.

Communicate Results

Following the analysis, the spreadsheet is finalized, and the recommendations communicated to decision makers for further action.

Document Findings

The What-if Analysis spreadsheet can be used as an "action plan" for documentation, assigning responsibilities, and completing recommended risk reduction measures. An example of traditional What-if Hazard Analysis form is shown in Figure 8.6.

What-If Analysis						
Facility/Operation/Process:						
Date:		Team:				
A. Process						
ID #	What-If...		Causes	Consequences	Controls	Recommendations
A.1.						
A.2						
A.3						

Figure 8.6
Traditional What-if Hazard Analysis Example.

The What-if Analysis method is easy to use and involves affected stakeholders that are knowledgeable in the system. However, it is only effective if the "right" questions are asked, and the team is objective and knowledgeable. Also, as a hazard analysis method, it does not estimate risk level of the identified hazards prohibiting effective prioritization and treatment.

Risk Analysis Methods

In a risk analysis, the hazards, controls, exposures, and severities are all identified; however, specific consequences are selected for further analyses and risk estimation. Each consequence is analyzed as to how it could occur and its likelihood or probability of occurring. Risk estimates are derived from the analysis for severity level, likelihood level, and risk level. To take the risk analysis to a "risk assessment," the risk analysis and its risk estimates are evaluated and compared against the established risk criteria to determine whether each risk estimation is acceptable or if addition risk treatment is required. The established risk criteria and the risk treatment actions for each risk level are used to determine action steps. The sequential application of risk identification, analysis and evaluation are required to complete a risk assessment. It is important understand the similarities and differences of hazard analysis, risk analysis, and risk assessment. Table 8.2 provides an example list of risk analysis methods commonly used.

Table 8.2. Risk Analysis Methods.

Risk Analysis Methods	Descriptions
Business Impact Analysis	An analysis of critical functions of an organization and the resources needed to maintain them in the event of a disruption or change.
Cause and Consequence Analysis	A combination of fault and event tree analysis that allows inclusion of time delays. Both causes and consequences of an initiating event are considered.
Design Safety Review	A structured review of plans, specifications, and safety related factors during the design or redesign phase to identify and avoid or eliminate potential hazards and failure modes.
Event Tree Analysis	Models the possible outcomes from a given initiating event and the status of controls thus analyzing the frequency or probability of the various possible outcomes.

Continued on next page

Risk Analysis Methods	Descriptions
Failure Mode and Effects Analysis (FMEA)	A qualitative or semi-quantitative method that lists systematically the failure modes, their effects, existing safeguards, and any additional controls that are needed to reduce risk to an acceptable level
Fault Tree Analysis	A deductive technique which starts with an undesired event (top event), determines the ways in which it could occur, and uses a logical tree diagram. After completing the fault tree, consideration should be given to ways of reducing or eliminating potential causes/sources.
Hazard Analysis and Critical Control Points (HACCP)*	A systematic and preventive system for hazard identification and placement of controls at critical points in a process to effectively prevent hazards from occurring. Used in food safety related processes.
Hazard and Operability Study (HAZOP)*	A qualitative method used to identify hazards and operability problems using "guide words" to prompt team members in identifying deviations that can lead to the failures.
Human Reliability Analysis	A technique used to identify the potential for human error and its causes, so the probability of error can be reduced.
Layers of Protection Analysis (LOPA)	A barrier type analysis of existing physical controls and their effectiveness for controlling a hazard.
Management Oversight and Risk Tree (MORT)	Generally used following an incident or exposure, MORT is a comprehensive type analysis following a disciplined approach for identifying and analyzing weaknesses in a system's design and procedures.
Multi-Criteria Analysis	A method for comparing options that makes trade-offs explicit. Provides an alternative to cost-benefit analysis that does not need a monetary value to be allocated to all inputs.
Preliminary Hazard Analysis (PHA)	A simple method used to identify and analyze hazards and risks that can cause harm for a given activity, facility, or system.
Risk Indices	Rates the significance of risks based on ratings applied to factors which are believed to influence the magnitude of the risk.

Continued on next page

Risk Analysis Methods	Descriptions
Striped Bow Tie Risk Assessment	A modified version of Bow Tie Analysis, which incorporates the hierarchy of controls, layers of control analysis, and a risk scoring system.

*It should be noted that HAZOP, HACCP, and PHA methods could be used early in the hazard identification step or as hazard analysis methods without adding the likelihood of consequences/impact.

Analyzing and Understanding Consequences

To analyze risk, the identified consequences must be characterized and understood. Their potential impact and magnitude of the impact on the organization's objectives and assets must be identified and analyzed. Depending upon the context and complexity of the system being analyzed, consequences or outcomes may be described generally or in more detail using quantitative modelling or vulnerability analysis. Consequential cascading effects where one consequence leads to another should be considered in the analysis.

> **Example:** For instance, in bio-diesel manufacturing process methanol is a key ingredient. Methanol, a flammable liquid, is generally stored in atmospheric, aboveground storage tanks. However, physical and chemical properties of methanol are unique and are not the same as those of other bulk-stored flammable liquids. Due its corrosive nature, cathodic protection, and regulator inspection of methanol storage tanks and trim hardware is required to avoid tank failure (Methanol Institute 2016).
>
> Methanol is the risk source in this example. Risk drivers may include corrosion, lack of inspection or maintenance, and other factors influencing the rise of risk. A single trigger such as over pressurization relief valve failure can cause a release of methanol.
>
> This loss of product is an operational risk, affecting the manufacturing process. However, the operational risk cascades into a hazard risk with the exposure to people and operations at the facility due to methanol's flammable properties. This can result in fatalities, serious injuries, and property and equipment loss or damage. Depending upon the amount of methanol released the risk can cascade into a catastrophic event and result in an enterprise risk from the threat to the local community, a significant loss of business, and damage to the organization's public image as illustrated in Figure 8.8 (Lyon and Popov 2017).

Analyzing Risk | 145

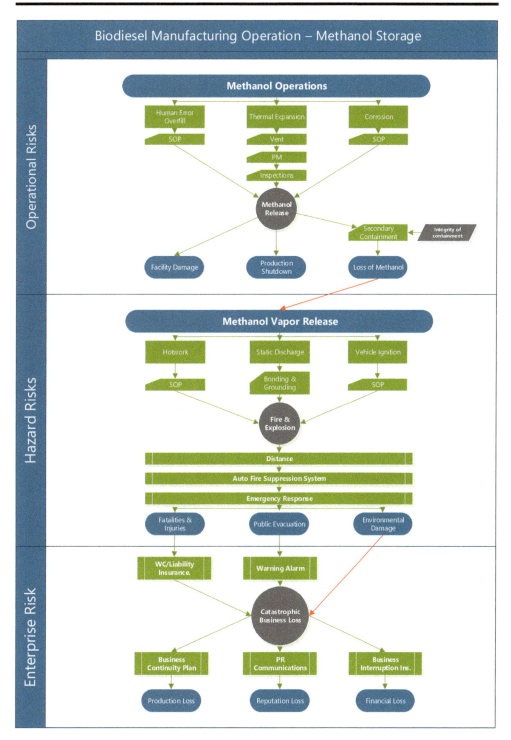

Figure 8.7
Cascading Effects of Consequences Example.

When analyzing a risk's consequences, the assessor should remember that a single risk can result in multiple consequences, some more severe than others, and some that have low severity but a potential for cascading effects. Consequences can also affect different objectives or assets of the organization. Risk estimations should first consider the most credible worst-case scenario and resulting consequences and then prioritize the remaining risks and their impacts. For example, in Figure 8.8 the Striped Bow Tie Risk Diagram illustrates a methanol release that results in multiple consequences including fire and explosion loss to the facility, injury to workers, damage to the corporate image, financial loss, and liability claims and compliance losses to the organization.

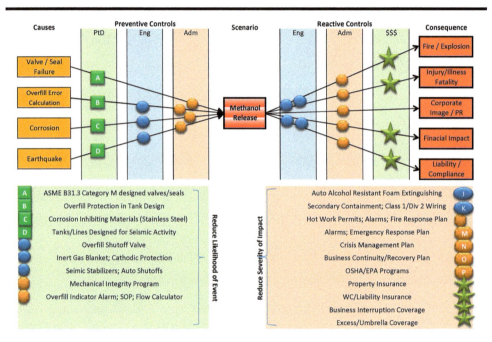

Figure 8.8
Striped Bow Tie Risk Diagram Example.

As stated in ISO 31010, the severity of consequences can be expressed quantitatively as a point value or as a distribution. A distribution may be appropriate where there is uncertainty in the consequence's severity level, or dependent upon multiple variables that may affect the severity level. A distribution of values can be in the form of a point value such as the expected value, variation, or the percentage in the tail or some other relevant part of the distribution (ANSI/ASSP/ISO 31010-2019).

Risks are dynamic in nature and their resulting impacts on objectives can also change or vary. For instance, a consequence may grow in intensity the longer it is allowed to exist such as cumulative exposures to toxic materials. In other cases, a particular consequence may result from exposures to multiple risk sources that have a synergistic effect.

Analyzing Likelihood

The second factor used in the risk analysis is likelihood. Likelihood (sometimes referred to as probability) can refer to a specific event or consequence and must be clearly defined as part of the context of the assessment. Likelihood of occurrence should consider the parameters, exposure, and duration, and can be described as a frequency, an expected probability or in qualitative terms. Qualitative descriptors such as "very high," "high," "moderate," etc. must be well-defined as to their meaning so that they are applied consistently. When using percentages to express measures of likelihood, the nature of the ratio and its justification should be clearly explained. In addition, the time period and exposed population or objective should be identified and defined in accordance with the context. It should be remembered that likelihood ratings like other risk factor ratings are informed "estimates" and that biases can sometimes influence ratings. The assessor must be aware that individual and cultural biases are possible, and that interpretation of the likelihood estimate may vary depending on the context.

Analyzing Interactions and Dependencies

As previously described, risks can have interactions and dependencies with other risks, consequences, and occurrences. As shown in Figure 8.8, a single cause can result in multiple consequences, a single consequence can result from multiple causes, or certain occurrences may influence the occurrence of other events resulting in cascading effects as shown in Figure 8.7. Causal mapping can be used to link interactions or dependencies between risks, events, causes, or consequences.

SWIFRA: Structured What-if Risk Assessment

The traditional What-if Analysis method is a hazard analysis rather than a risk analysis since it does not include an estimation of risk level. Hazard analyses, like job hazard analyses, are useful in identifying and analyzing hazards; however, they do not provide risk-based information needed for prioritizing and treating risks. By including an estimation of risk with a hazard analysis, a more complete method is formed.

To convert a hazard analysis to a risk assessment, three additional steps are needed. First, specific consequences are selected to be analyzed and evaluated.

Second, for each consequence, an estimate of its severity (S) level, likelihood of occurrence (L) level, and resulting risk level (R) are determined. Third, the estimated risk levels are then compared and evaluated with the established risk criteria to determine acceptability and required action.

An additional feature to the SWIFRA model is a "what-how-why" questioning process that includes (1) "what-if" it occurs, then (2) "how" it can occur, and (3) "why" is it possible for it to occur. These are followed by identifying the effects of the occurrence and existing controls to prevent it from occurring. Current state risk is determined considering the existing controls. If current state risk level is unacceptable, additional controls are recommended and a future state risk estimation made. A risk reduction percentage is then calculated to demonstrate the proposed controls' effectiveness to decision makers.

The purpose of the "what-how-why" approach is to find the root causes and systemic causal factors similar to a "5 why" method. Figure 8.9 provides an example of a SWIFRA worksheet.

Note* The risk evaluation, risk treatment, and risk analysis of the residual risk of SWIFRA are used during risk evaluation and risk treatment steps. The progression from risk analysis to risk evaluation and risk treatment are covered in the following chapters. Other examples of risk analyses can be found in chapter 13 of this book, as well as ISO 31010 and other references.

> **Example:** A chemical transportation company planned to acquire a vapor combustor to eliminate hazardous chemical residues in tank cars and decided to assess the plan. To begin, the organization defined the context, purpose, and scope for the vapor combustor system to be assessed, boundaries, and risk criteria to be used. A "Structured What-if Risk Assessment" method was selected for the assessment.
>
> A trained and knowledgeable assessment team, facilitator, and scribe was assembled to conduct the "What-if." The team included an outside consultant and the organization's EHS staff, selected engineering, operations, maintenance, legal, human resources, and finance personnel. The team gathered and reviewed information on the vapor combustor system, regulatory information, loss information, previous risk assessments performed, equipment specifications, limits, performance standards, maintenance needs, and operating instructions.
>
> The vapor combustor system and operational process were broken down into sequential tasks similar to a JHA for assessment including: (1) Pre-Startup and Vapor Combustor Purging, (2) Combustor Start-Up,

Analyzing Risk | 149

Structured What-if Risk Assessment (SWIFRA)

#	What if?	How?	Why?	Current Controls	L	S	Risk Level	Risk Level Acceptable (Y/N)	Additional Controls	L2	S2	Risk Level 2	% RR
1	...the operator connects to the wrong chemical during filling? **Answer:** Chlorine gas generation and possible release, possible fatalities and injuries.	The filling ports are all the same allowing mis-matching of chemicals.	Original design - not previously considered. Management not aware.	Signage/labeling; procedural training	4	3	12	N	Design unique connections for each chemical. Upgrade chemical unloading and transfer equipment with chemical portal separation, signage, locks, and fittings; update procedures and training.	2	3	6	50%
2	...the operator is exposed to Chlorine gas? **Answer: Probable death or severe injury**	Inadvertently connecting and filling wrong chemical causing Chlorine gas release. Operator at point of connection in proximity of release.	Universal ports allow mis-matching. Connecting procedure requires operator to be a point of release.	Signage/labeling; procedural training	4	3	12	N	Design unique connections for each chemical. Upgrade chemical unloading and transfer equipment with chemical portal separation, signage, locks, and fittings; update procedures and training. Provide emergency escape respiratory protection.	2	3	6	50%
3	...local population is exposed to Chlorine gas release? **Answer: Possible multiple fatalities and injuries to public and workers, business interruption**	Inadvertently connecting and filling wrong chemical generating and releasing Chlorine gas that drifts over community	Universal ports allow mis-matching. Community within 1 mile of tank farm. Task complexity or design; Communication; Experience	Signage/labeling; procedural training	4	4	16	N	In addition to above controls, add new emergency shutdown devices to complement the devices that were already in place. Upgrade monitoring, detection and warning equipment to decrease the risk of chemical releases.	2	3	6	63%

| Risk Identification | Risk Analysis | Risk Evaluation | Risk Treatment | Risk Analysis of Residual Risk |

Figure 8.9
SWIFRA Worksheet.

> (3) Combustor Shut-Down, (4) De-gas and Steam Tanks to Combustor Disconnect Tank, (5) De-pressure Tanks less than 25 psi vapor pressure, (6) Combustor Operation, and (7) Maintenance.
>
> The team developed specific "what-if" questions for each step of the vapor combustor process using a brainstorming session. For each "what-if" question, the team discussed and investigated potential scenarios, upsets, miscommunications, errors, and failures; the potential causes or triggers; the consequences; and existing controls.
>
> Then the team estimated the severity, likelihood, and risk levels for each "what-if," which were entered in the worksheet. For risk levels requiring risk reduction, the team recommended risk treatments, which were presented to management along with cost-benefit justifications. The resulting decision from the assessment was to acquire the vapor combustor with 29 recommended risk treatments to the equipment, system, and process. Example: A chemical transportation company planned to acquire a vapor combustor to eliminate hazardous chemical residues in tank cars and decided to assess the plan. To begin, the organization defined the context, purpose, and scope for the vapor combustor system to be assessed, boundaries, and risk criteria to be used. A "Structured What-if Risk Assessment" method was selected for the assessment.

The Concept of Risk Summation

An important concept in risk assessment is understanding "whole-system risk"—the combined or synergistic effects of multiple risk sources. Conventional risk assessment methods can be described as "linear" or singular in nature. For instance, many risk assessment methods used, such as failure mode and effects analysis (FMEA) or preliminary hazard analysis, are applied in a manner that analyzes hazards individually, hazard-by-hazard, rather than considering the multiple hazards as a whole. As such, a hazard-by-hazard analysis approach would only consider partial risks within the system or operation. In certain cases, the partial risks may be found to be acceptable, leading to the judgement that the system or operation is "safe." However, such conclusions may be misleading if there are combined or synergistic effects from multiple risk sources or hazards.

The potential effect of combined or whole-system risks is often greater than any single risk in a system. Risk assessors that identify and catalog individual hazards as line items may miss the potential for certain risks occurring at the same time and producing additive or synergistic effects. An example of such an effect might be found in the meat processing industry where cold temperatures combined with hand-arm vibration from pneumatic hand tools increase risk of soft-tissue damage. If such risks are analyzed individually, the true "whole-risk" may not be considered (Lyon, Hollcroft 2012). The concept of risk summation is further explained using a case study in Chapter 13.

Summary

Risk analysis is considered the heart of risk assessment and the most involved step in risk assessment. It is used to gain an understanding of the risk, its consequences, and likelihood of occurrence and to estimate risk levels so that risks can be evaluated, prioritized, and treated according to the established risk criteria. To properly analyze risks, a standardized and iterative approach must be used throughout the risk management process. One potential pitfall in risk analysis is the tendency for assessors to try to achieve perfection in their risk analysis estimations. However, it is more important and useful to ensure risk estimations are consistent, and guided by experience, knowledge, and available information.

Review Questions

1. Explain the purpose of risk analysis and the elements that are involved.
2. Describe the differences between the terms *hazard, risk, hazard analysis; risk analysis,* and *risk assessment.* List the steps in a hazard analysis, steps in a risk analysis, and steps in a risk assessment.
3. Identify and describe five methods used in hazard analysis.
4. Identify and describe five methods used in risk analysis.
5. List and describe the three elements that must be analyzed in risk analysis.
6. Describe the difference between a traditional What-if Analysis and a Structured What-if Risk Assessment.
7. Explain the concept of risk summation.

References

ANSI/ASIS/RIMS RA.1-2015. 2015. *Risk Assessment.* Alexandria, VA: ASIS International and The Risk and Insurance Management Society, Inc.

ANSI/ASSP Z590.3-2011 (R2016). 2016. *Prevention through Design: Guidelines for Addressing Occupational Hazards and Risks in Design and Redesign Processes.* Park Ridge, IL: American Society of Safety Professionals.

ANSI/ASSP Z690.1-2011. 2011. *Vocabulary for Risk Management.* Park Ridge, IL: American Society of Safety Professionals.

ANSI/ASSP/ISO 31000-2018. 2018. *Risk management – Guidelines.* Park Ridge, IL: American Society of Safety Professionals.

ANSI/ASSP/ISO 31010-2019. *Risk management – Risk assessment*. Park Ridge, IL: American Society of Safety Professionals.

ASSP TR-31010-2020. 2020. *Technical Report: Risk Management – Techniques for Safety Practitioners*. Park Ridge, IL: American Society of Safety Professionals.

Environmental Protection Agency (EPA). 1994. 40 CFR PART 68 Chemical Accident Prevention Provisions, Risk Management Plan (RMP) Rule. Washington, DC: US Environmental Protection Agency.

Lyon, Bruce K., and Bruce Hollcroft. 2012. "Risk Assessments—Top 10 Pitfalls & Tips for Improvement." *Professional Safety,* December 2012, 28–-34.

Lyon, Bruce K., and Georgi Popov. 2017. "Communicating & Managing Risk: The Key Result of Risk Assessment." *Professional Safety,* November 2017, 35–44.

Lyon, Bruce K., and Georgi Popov. 2019. "Risk Treatment Strategies: Harmonizing the Hierarchy of Controls & Inherently Safer Design Concepts." *Professional Safety,* May 2019, 34–43.

Methanol Institute. 2016. Methanol Safe Handling Technical Bulletin: Atmospheric Above Ground Tank Storage of Methanol. Washington, DC: Methanol Institute. www.methanol.org/wp-content/uploads/2016/06/AtmosphericAboveGroundTankStorageMethanol-1.pdf.

Popov, G., Bruce K. Lyon, and Bruce Hollcroft. 2016. *Risk Assessment: A Practical Guide to Assessing Operational Risks*. Hoboken, NJ: Wiley.

OSHA. 2002. *Job Hazard Analysis*. Publication 3071 Washington, DC: US Department of Labor. www.osha.gov/Publications/osha3071.pdf.

OSHA. 1992. 29 CFR 1910.119 Process Safety Management (PSM) of Highly Hazardous Chemicals. Washington, DC: US Department of Labor. https://www.osha.gov/laws-regs/regulations/standardnumber/1910/1910.119

CHAPTER 9
Evaluating Risk

Introduction

Risk evaluation is the judgment and decision-making step in the risk assessment process. It is defined as the "process of equating the results of risk analysis with risk criteria to determine whether a particular risk level is within an acceptable tolerance or presents a potential opportunity" (ANSI/ASIS/RIMS RA.1-2015). Risk evaluation is used to determine a risk's acceptability to the organization. Without a judgement as to the acceptability or tolerance of a particular risk, there would be no decision to prioritize or act upon risks.

As ISO 31000 describes, the purpose of risk evaluation is to support decisions by comparing the results of the risk analysis with the established risk criteria to determine where additional action is required. This may lead to the decision to take no action, to consider treatment options, to conduct further analysis, to maintain existing treatments, or to reconsider the objectives. Any decision made should consider the context and the consequences to stakeholders (ANSI/ASSP/ISO 31000-2018).

As stated in ISO 31010, "the outcomes from risk analysis provide an input to decisions that need to be made and actions that are taken." (ANSI/ASSP/ISO/IEC 31010-2019) The risk analysis provides the "input"—the risk estimates—to the risk evaluation phase, which than decides whether risk treatment is required or if the risk is considered acceptable to the organization. The risk evaluation decision is made by comparing the estimated risk level to the established risk criteria. In essences, risk evaluation can be considered "risk-based decision-making."

Interactive tools and supplemental materials are available at assp.org/ermtools.

The purpose of risk assessment is to create and protect value within an organization. This is accomplished by understanding those risks that are capable of affecting the organization's objectives. Understanding the nature of risks includes an understanding of its components as illustrated in Figure 9.1. These include the risk's source, its drivers or influencing factors, how a risk can materialize, what exposures and assets are at risk, causes and triggers, the resulting consequences, the severity of the risk's impacts, the likelihood of its occurrence, and its estimated risk level.

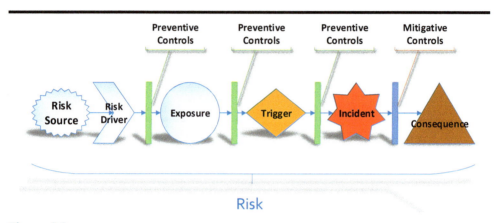

Figure 9.1
The Components of Risk.

The risk criteria and decision-making factors that are used in evaluating risk should be developed up front as part of the "context" of the risk assessment. The established risk criteria are used to make two fundamental decisions in risk evaluation which include the significance of risk and the prioritization of risks.

Significance of Risk

The estimation of a risk's significance or magnitude is derived from risk analysis and is used to determine whether the risk should be accepted or if action is required to reduce the risk to an acceptable level. This decision is based on a comparative evaluation of the risk relative to the objectives and performance thresholds of the organization. This evaluation is an important and primary input into the decision regarding the risk and how it should be treated. The significance or magnitude of risk is the first consideration in risk evaluation, and those risks that are outside of the acceptable range and are not tolerable to the organization.

There are some risks that may be acceptable for a specific period of time based on certain parameters; however, risks are dynamic and ever-changing according to the variables and require continual monitoring. Such decisions for temporary acceptance should be clearly defined and communicated, along with details for re-assessment of the risk.

Risk significance is based on the severity and likelihood of occurrence and generally expressed in a risk matrix. Other factors in determining risk significance include:

- potential worst credible consequences,
- effectiveness of existing controls,
- stakeholders' views and perceptions,
- the cost and practicability of treatments, and
- interactions between risks.

It is important that an iterative approach to evaluating risk be used. Decisions as to the significance of risk and its acceptability to the organization must be consistent.

Prioritizing Risks for Treatment

A second judgement made in risk evaluation is the prioritizing of risks for treatment. This is based on the degree of risk as it relates to the established risk criteria and action levels. As stated in ISO 31010, this type of decision is often made using expert judgement based on the understanding from an analysis of the options concerned and the risk associated with each, taking into account: trade-offs that may need to be made between competing objectives, the organization's appetite for risk, and the different attitudes and beliefs of stakeholders (ANSI/ASSP/ISO/IEC 31010-2019).

Defined risk criteria, risk levels, and corresponding actions are established in the context and can range from a simple method of two risk categories (those that require treatment and those that do not require treatment) to more complex methods that use multiple risk levels with graduated degrees of actions. For example, a simple method of dividing risks into three bands could be used where risks are (1) unacceptable, (2) marginal, or (3) acceptable. Such an approach follows the concept of ALARP— "as low as reasonably practicable," which is used to determine when the cost of further risk reduction exceeds the benefit gained from the resulting risk reduction or reaches a "point of diminishing returns."

Acceptance of risk is unique to each organization and within its context. Risk acceptance may also vary within an organization according to the project, opportunity, product or service, division or region, as well as over time. For each risk, the organization makes an informed decision as to the risk's acceptability according to several factors. A risk may be found acceptable if the organization judges the current risk level to be as low as reasonably practicable. In certain situations, a risk may be tolerated if it is beyond the control of the organization such as weather conditions or political climate. There may be other risks that have no practical treatment available, or the available treatment(s) for the risk are cost prohibitive. And a major factor in accepting risk is that its perceived opportunities outweigh the threats.

Risk-Based Decision-Making

As presented in chapter 1, risk-based decision-making (RBDM) is the practice of risk management in the decision-making process. The RBDM model presented in figure 9.2 provides a systematic approach for making decisions using risk-related information to reduce risk and uncertainty and ultimately achieve better outcomes. The decision made in the RBDM process is conducted in the risk evaluation and risk treatment phases of the risk assessment. Risk evaluation uses the established risk criteria to determine whether the risk is acceptable or if risk reduction is required and the priority level for action (Popov, Lyon, and Hollcroft 2016).

Figure 9.2
Risk-Based Decision-Making Model.

Using the risk criteria established in the context and results of the risk analysis, an evaluation of the risk is performed. The evaluation of risk involves comparing the estimated risk level with the organization's established acceptable risk level to determine if the risk is acceptable. After risk treatment, the risk is re-evaluated to determine acceptability and prioritization. Considerations in risk evaluation identified in ANSI/ASIS/RIMS RA.1-2015, Risk Assessment Standard should include:

- the objectives of project;
- both tangible and intangible effects;
- legal, regulatory, and contractual requirements;
- critical control points;
- tolerability of risks to external stakeholders or society;
- whether a risk needs treatment;
- deciding whether risk is acceptable;
- whether an activity should continue; and
- priorities for treatment.

The goal of risk-based decision-making (and risk management) is to reduce risk as much as practical. Risk-based decision-making (RBDM) is a systematic approach for making decisions using risk-related information so as to reduce risk and uncertainty and ultimately achieve better outcomes. The model for making risk-based decisions is applied to critical decisions where some uncertainty exists. RBDM takes into consideration key questions about risk concerning the decision to be made which include: (1) what can go wrong, (2) the severity of the potential outcome, (3) the likelihood of it occurring, (4) the acceptability of the risk, and (5) the need for risk reduction.

Effective risk evaluation and decision making requires adequate risk-based information concerning the risk gather through the risk identification and analysis steps. This requires a formalized risk management process that is integrated into the overall management system, led by management and communicated throughout the organization.

Risk Evaluation Methods

The process of evaluating risk usually will include the use of one or more methods or tools. There are a number of methods available for evaluating risk as shown in Figure 9.3 some of which are listed and described in Table 9.1. ISO 31010 lists several techniques that range in application, complexity, and ease of use including ALARP (as low as reasonably practicable), SFAIRP (so far as is reasonably practicable), Frequency-number (F-N) diagram, risk indices, and value at risk. No matter which methods are selected, the organization should consider modifying or customizing methods to meet their specific needs and applications.

Risk evaluations involving complexity or criticality are generally best performed by a team of qualified and knowledgeable stakeholders. Adequate information including key stakeholder input, and physical observations of the system, operation, task, or element being evaluated should be captured. Risk matrices, heat maps, opportunity and threat matrices, risk frontier graphs, and risk indices are common methods used and are briefly presented here.

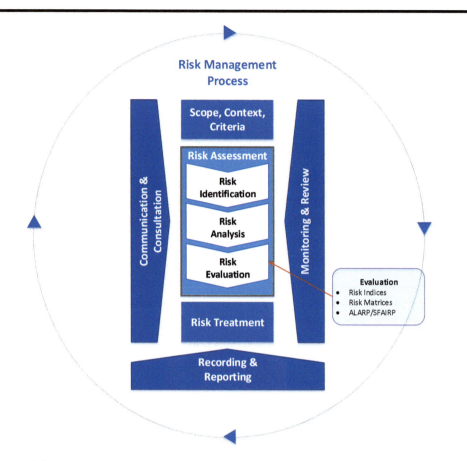

Figure 9.3
Risk Management Process and Evaluation Techniques.

Table 9.1. Methods for Evaluating Risk.

Risk Evaluation Methods	Descriptions
Consequence likelihood matrix	Compares individual risks by selecting a consequence likelihood pair and displaying them on a matrix with consequence on one axis and likelihood on the other.
F/N diagrams	Special case of quantitative consequence likelihood graph applied to consideration of tolerability of risk to human life.
Cause and Consequence Analysis	A combination of fault and event tree analysis that allows inclusion of time delays. Both causes and consequences of an initiating event are considered.

Continued on next page

Risk Evaluation Methods	Descriptions
Risk Indices	Risk indices are used in rating the significance of risks based on numerical ratings applied to factors which are believed to influence the magnitude of the risk.
Risk Heat Maps	A risk heat map is a two-dimensional map used to plot and present the results of risk assessments to visually communicate risk to decision-makers.
Risk Matrices	In addition to being used during the establishment of context and risk assessment process, a risk matrix plots and presents risks according to their severity and likelihood to assist decision making.
ALARP—As Low As Reasonably Practicable	The ALARP concept seeks to reduce residual risk as low as reasonably possible and practical considering the costs and benefits of the risk treatment(s). ALARP is used as criteria for determining risk acceptability, and in the regulation and management of safety-critical and safety-involved systems.
ALARA—As Low As Reasonably Achievable	ALARA is a safety concept based on the minimization of ionizing radiation doses and releases of radioactive materials into the environment using all "reasonable methods" to achieve an acceptable level. ALARA which is an acronym for "as low as reasonably achievable" is defined in Title 10, Section 20.1003, of the Code of Federal Regulations (10 CFR 20.1003).
SFAIRP—So Far as is reasonably practicable	Similar to ALARP, SFAIRP generally requires that safety be ensured so far as is reasonably practicable. SFAIRP is usually interpreted as a criterion by which controls are assessed to see if further treatments are possible; then, if they are possible, whether they are practicable.

Risk Matrices and Heat Maps

Many organizations use risk assessment matrices or heat maps based on defined risk criteria to visually compare risk levels within the graduated risk level categories (Lyon and Popov 2017). Risk matrices are generally constructed in two dimensional grids with one axis for severity of consequences and the other for likelihood of occurrence. Matrices can be expressed in qualitative, semi-quantitative, or quantitative terms and range from very simple (2 × 2) to complex (10 × 10 or larger).

160 | Assessing and Managing Risk: An ERM Perspective

A qualitative 5 × 4 model that has been used by many industries comes from the Military standard MIL-STD-882E presented in figure 9.4. The categories and their descriptions for severity levels (figure 9.5) and probability levels (figure 9.6) are used to plot risks in the matrix.

A risk heat map uses colors on a grid or matrix (as shown in Figure 9.7) to visually represent risk rankings to decision makers in their evaluation and treatment of risk. Such maps are generated from risk indices and risk analyses like What-if

RISK ASSESSMENT MATRIX

SEVERITY \ PROBABILITY	Catastrophic (1)	Critical (2)	Marginal (3)	Negligible (4)
Frequent (A)	High	High	Serious	Medium
Probable (B)	High	High	Serious	Medium
Occasional (C)	High	Serious	Medium	Low
Remote (D)	Serious	Medium	Medium	Low
Improbable (E)	Medium	Medium	Medium	Low
Eliminated (F)	Eliminated			

Figure 9.4
Risk Matrix from MIL-STD-882E.

SEVERITY CATEGORIES

Description	Severity Category	Mishap Result Criteria
Catastrophic	1	Could result in one or more of the following: death, permanent total disability, irreversible significant environmental impact, or monetary loss equal to or exceeding $10M.
Critical	2	Could result in one or more of the following: permanent partial disability, injuries or occupational illness that may result in hospitalization of at least three personnel, reversible significant environmental impact, or monetary loss equal to or exceeding $1M but less than $10M.
Marginal	3	Could result in one or more of the following: injury or occupational illness resulting in one or more lost work day(s), reversible moderate environmental impact, or monetary loss equal to or exceeding $100K but less than $1M.
Negligible	4	Could result in one or more of the following: injury or occupational illness not resulting in a lost work day, minimal environmental impact, or monetary loss less than $100K.

Figure 9.5
Severity Categories from MIL-STD-882E.

PROBABILITY LEVELS			
Description	Level	Specific Individual Item	Fleet or Inventory
Frequent	A	Likely to occur often in the life of an item.	Continuously experienced.
Probable	B	Will occur several times in the life of an item.	Will occur frequently.
Occasional	C	Likely to occur sometime in the life of an item.	Will occur several times.
Remote	D	Unlikely, but possible to occur in the life of an item.	Unlikely, but can reasonably be expected to occur.
Improbable	E	So unlikely, it can be assumed occurrence may not be experienced in the life of an item.	Unlikely to occur, but possible.
Eliminated	F	Incapable of occurence. This level is used when potential hazards are identified and later eliminated.	Incapable of occurence. This level is used when potential hazards are identified and later eliminated.

Figure 9.6
Probability Categories from MIL-STD-882E.

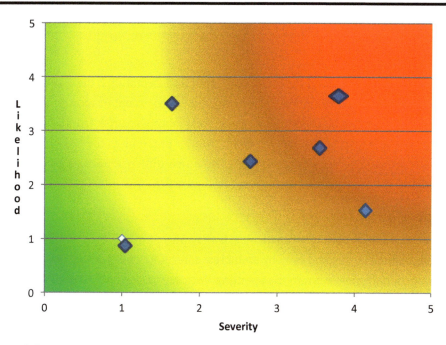

Figure 9.7
Risk Heat Map.

analyses, FMEAs, and Process Hazard Analyses. Individual risks are plotted on the heat map grid according to the colors corresponding to the level of the risk. The heat map is typically constructed as a two-dimensional matrix measuring severity of risk and the frequency or likelihood of occurrence. The number of levels can range from a simple 2 × 2 model to a more complex model. Risk criteria and risk level

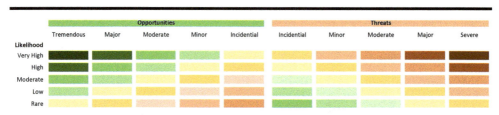

Figure 9.8
Opportunity Threat Matrix.

definitions developed by the organization should be used to characterize the heat map risk levels.

Methods such as risk matrices and heat maps provide a means of visually communicating risks in relationship to established risk criteria. For example, a risk opportunity-threat matrix is shown in Figure 9.8. This two-dimensional matrix provides a visual measure of risk opportunities levels and risk threats levels based on defined likelihood and magnitude levels. Such methods are useful in prioritizing risks for treatment or action.

Risk Frontier Graph

By considering the risk and the factors affecting its acceptability, the assessors make a determination using risk-based information to accept or treat the risk. One method that can be used to determine acceptability is a risk frontier graph. Similar to a heat map or risk matrix, a risk frontier graph plots the risk's likelihood of occurrence and severity of consequence on a two-dimensional axis graph with a "acceptable risk frontier" curve as shown in Figure 9.9.

ALARP and SFAIRP

ALARP, as low as reasonably practicable, is the concept of achieving a risk level that can be further lowered only by an increase in resource expenditure that is disproportionate in relation to the resulting decrease in risk (ANSI/ASSP/ Z590.3-2011, R2016). ALARP, originally developed in the United Kingdom's Health and Safety at Work 1974 Act, represents criteria used in risk evaluation to test a risk's acceptability level and determine whether it is reasonably feasible and practicable to reduce risk further.

The concept of ALARP establishes risk level boundaries between unacceptable, ALARP, and broadly acceptable regions. The middle category can be further divided into sub-categories where certain actions are required such as cost-benefit analysis for lower risks and required risk reduction for higher risks as illustrated in figure 9.10.

ALARP is used to assist organizations in risk evaluation and decision-making to judge whether the level of risk is acceptable or unacceptable and requires

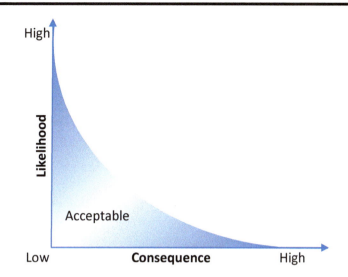

Figure 9.9
Conceptual Risk Frontier Graph Example.

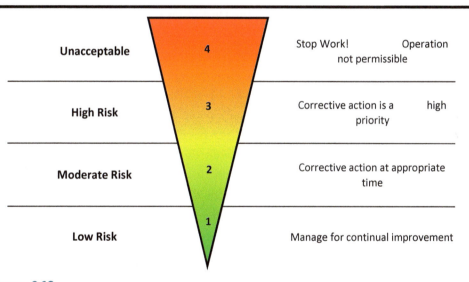

Figure 9.10
ALARP Model.

treatment. It should be applied within the context of the organization's culture, workplace environment, industry, regulatory requirements, and community setting. Depending upon the established risk criteria, the defined risk categories and their prioritized actions are used to evaluate and treat risk. A similar concept, SFAIRP or "so far as is reasonably practicable" generally refers to safety related risk, however, it makes no reference to the level of risk. SFAIRP is usually interpreted as a criterion by which controls are assessed to see if further treatments are possible; then, if they are possible, whether they are practicable (ANSI/ASSP/ISO/IEC 31010-2019).

Risk Indices

Risk indices use a combined likelihood and severity of a hazardous event or consequence anticipated from an identified hazard. They are used to rank and compare risks as part of the risk evaluation. A risk index is designed to help distinguish those risks that are unacceptable to the organization and provide a ranking of risks by risk level to prioritize treatment. They are typically developed to summarize the risk of an event or condition by using numbers or categorical values for the purpose of identifying and comparing risks. Risk indices models can be qualitative (word descriptors, letters, and colors), semi-quantitative (numerical rankings based on non-statistical data), or quantitative (numerical rankings based on statistical data) in nature and are used to describe and communicate the level of risk to stakeholders and decision makers.

An example of a risk index is the US Occupational Safety and Health Administration's (OSHA) Heat Index. The Heat Index uses an index system developed by the US National Oceanographic and Atmospheric Administration (NOAA) and combines both air temperature and relative humidity into a single value that indicates the apparent temperature in degrees Fahrenheit. This reflects how hot the weather will feel to the human body. The higher the index, the hotter the weather will feel. For each risk level, action and protective measures are recommended (OSHA 2015.) The NOAA Temperature and Humidity index is an example of "risk measures" (Figure 9.11), while the OSHA Heat Index (Figure 9.12) represents a "risk index" based on the risk measures.

Risk indices are developed using historical data and analysis tools such as fault tree analysis, event tree analysis, and general decision analysis. It is important that sufficient data are used so as to validate the index. Generally, values and scores are applied to each factor and combined using an equation to represent the relationship between them. Factors that increase the level of risk are multiplied together and divided by those that decrease the level of risk.

Value at Risk

According to ISO 31010, the value at risk (VaR) method is used widely in the financial sector as an indicator of the amount of possible loss in a portfolio of financial assets over a specific time period within a given confidence level. Losses greater than the VaR are suffered only with a specified small probability. The distribution of profit and loss is usually derived in one of three ways (ANSI/ASSP/ISO/IEC 31010-2019). These include Monte Carlo simulations used to model

NOAA's National Weather Service
Heat Index

Temperature (°F) →	80	82	84	86	88	90	92	94	96	98	100	102	104	106	108	110
Relative Humidity (%)																
40	80	81	83	85	88	91	94	97	101	105	109	114	119	124	130	136
45	80	82	84	87	89	93	96	100	104	109	114	119	124	130	137	
50	81	83	85	88	91	95	99	103	108	113	118	124	131	137		
55	81	84	86	89	93	97	101	106	112	117	124	130	137			
60	82	84	88	91	95	100	105	110	116	123	129	137				
65	82	85	89	93	98	103	108	114	121	128	136					
70	83	86	90	95	100	105	112	119	126	134						
75	84	88	92	97	103	109	116	124	132							
80	84	89	94	100	106	113	121	129								
85	85	90	96	102	110	117	126	135								
90	86	91	98	105	113	122	131									
95	86	93	100	108	117	127										
100	87	95	103	112	121	132										

Likelihood of Heat Disorders with Prolonged Exposure or Strenuous Activity

☐ Caution ☐ Extreme Caution ■ Danger ■ Extreme Danger

Figure 9.11
NOAA's Temperature and Humidity Index.

Heat Index	Risk Level	Protective Measures
Less than 91°F	Lower (Caution)	Basic heat safety and planning
91°F to 103°F	Moderate	Implement precautions and heighten awareness
103°F to 115°F	High	Additional precautions to protect workers
Greater than 115°F	Very High to Extreme	Triggers even more aggressive protective measures

Figure 9.12
OSHA's Heat Index Summary.

the drivers of variability in a portfolio and create the distribution; historical simulation models that make projections based previously observed outcomes and distributions; and analytical methods based on assumptions that underlying market factors have a multivariate normal distribution.

Summary

Risk evaluation, the third step within risk assessment, is the act of reviewing risk-based information produced from the first two steps, risk identification and analysis, to determine whether the risk is acceptable to the organization. This requires an established set of risk measurements by the organization to compare with those risks estimated by the analysis. Judgement as to whether risks are acceptable, and whether risk treatment is required, occurs in the risk evaluation step. Without proper risk evaluation by an organization, existing risks are not prioritized for treatment, and may go untreated.

Review Questions

1. What are the primary reasons for evaluating risk? Why is the risk evaluation step important?
2. Identify and explain several key elements that are required to be developed by the organization up front during the establishment of context used in risk evaluation.
3. What role does risk evaluation play in terms of decision-making and risk treatment?
4. Describe what is meant by "risk significance" and list five elements that it is based on.
5. Risk-based decision-making takes into consideration five key questions that must be answered in the process. What are these five questions?
6. List and describe five methods used in evaluating risk.
7. Describe the concept of ALARP.

References

ANSI/ASIS/RIMS RA.1-2015. 2015. *Risk Assessment.* Alexandria, VA: ASIS International and The Risk and Insurance Management Society, Inc.

ANSI/ASSP Z590.3-2011 (R2016). 2016. *Prevention through Design Guidelines for Addressing Occupational Hazards and Risks in Design and Redesign Processes.* Park Ridge, IL: American Society of Safety Professionals.

ANSI/ASSP/ISO 31000:2018. 2018. *Risk Management Principles and Guidelines.* Park Ridge, IL: American Society of Safety Professionals.

ANSI/ASSP/ISO/IEC 31010-2019. 2019. *Risk Management – Risk Assessment Techniques.* Park Ridge, IL: American Society of Safety Professionals.

Lyon, Bruce K., and Georgi Popov. 2017. "Communicating & Managing Risk: The Key Result of Risk Assessment." *Professional Safety,* November 2017, 35–44.

MIL-STD-882E. 2012. *Department of Defense Standard Practice: System Safety.* Washington, DC: Department of Defense.

OSHA. 2002. *Job Hazard Analysis.* Publication 3071 Washington, DC: U.S. Department of Labor. www.osha.gov/Publications/osha3071.pdf.

Popov, G., Bruce K. Lyon, and Bruce Hollcroft. 2016. *Risk Assessment: A Practical Guide to Assessing Operational Risks.* Hoboken, NJ: Wiley.

CHAPTER 10
Treating Risk

Introduction

To manage risk is to treat those risks that are unacceptable. Risk treatment, the process of reducing risks that are considered unacceptable, involves the selection and application of one or more options to achieve and maintain an acceptable level of risk to the organization as defined by ISO 31000. Risk treatment is arguably the most important step in the risk management process since it is designed to achieve and maintain an acceptable risk level.

Risk treatment is the output of the risk evaluation and the primary purpose of risk assessment. Following the evaluation of risk, those risks that are judged to be unacceptable require treatment to reduce their risk level. Without treating risks that have been assessed, a risk assessment is of no value and in fact may constitute negligence by the organization. When specific risks have been identified and assessed as being unacceptable, it is incumbent upon the organization to take action to treat those risks in an appropriate and timely manner.

As stated by ISO 31000, the purpose of risk treatment is to select and implement strategies that manage risk in an iterative process. The process includes formulating and selecting options, planning, and implementing risk treatments, assessing their effectiveness, determining the acceptability of residual risks, and implementing additional risk treatments as needed (ANSI/ASSP/ISO 31000-2018).

Interactive tools and supplemental materials are available at assp.org/ermtools.

Treating and Controlling Risk

When an organization judges a level of risk to be unacceptable, it must make decisions to treat the risk to modify its level. Such treatment of risk involves the careful selection and application of risk treatment strategies that will modify and reduce the risk to an acceptable level. These strategies can include avoidance, reduction, transfer, retention, or pursuing certain opportunities depending upon the type of risk.

Risk treatment is defined as the "process to modify risk" (ISO Guide 73/ANSI/ASSP Z690.1-2011) and may include different or multiple strategies. The term "risk control" is often used in the insurance industry and occupational safety and health (OSH) profession. *Control* is defined by ISO 31000 as a "measure that maintains and/or modifies risk." Controls include any process, policy, device, practice, or other conditions or actions that maintain and/or modify risk (ANSI/ASSP/ISO 31000-2018). A "process" may include multiple steps working together to modify risk, while a "practice" could be a single measure. "Policy" is generally referred to as an administrative measure while "devices" are hardware-type engineering controls or warning and awareness controls. There are many forms of risk treatment; some are more effective and reliable than others (ASSP TR-31010-2020).

Figure 10.1
Risk Treatment Options.

Risk treatment options can be applied in many ways and are not necessarily mutually exclusive or appropriate in all circumstances as indicated by ISO 31000 and ASSP TR-31010. In many situations, more than one treatment strategy is required to adequately reduce and control the risk to an acceptable level. Risk treatment strategies available to an organization's risk management include avoidance of risk, pursuing of risk, eliminating risk, reducing risk, transferring risk, sharing risk, and retaining risk as illustrated in Figure 10.1 (ASSP TR-31010- 2020).

Avoid Risk

The most effective means of managing risks that are derived from hazards and operations, is to avoid the risk entirely. An organization may make an informed decision to not engage in a particular activity that presents a risk that is considered unacceptable. In a new facility, a design safety review can be used to identify and avoid new hazards from being introduced into the design. Avoiding risk may not always be possible; however, it should be the first consideration regarding pure risks.

> **Examples of Avoiding Risk**
>
> - A pharmaceutical company may determine that a new experimental drug presents potential risks that are too great for the expected benefits and decide not to pursue the endeavor.
> - A financial organization considering the purchase of a business may discover through due diligence and risk assessment that there are potential unacceptable risks and liabilities associated with the business, resulting in a decision not to acquire the firm.
> - An organization designs a new facility and its equipment to be at the same level with easy access for production, service, and maintenance work to avoid falls from heights.
> - To avoid the risk of damage and business interruption caused by hurricanes, an organization decides to locate their new distribution center in central Kansas.

Pursue Risk

For speculative type risks that result from financial and strategic type ventures, it may be advantageous to pursue a risk for expected gains and benefits. Organizations are continuously looking for ways to create and protect value to achieve their business objectives. Through proper cost-benefit analysis and assessment of the risks, an organization may choose to pursue an opportunity such as an acquisition, an expansion into a new market, or a financial investment to advance their financial or strategic position.

> **Example of Pursuing Risk**
>
> - An international insurance firm decides to expand their market to areas in Asia by acquiring an existing Asian firm, balancing the increased market share opportunities with the political and cultural risks.
> - An organization decides to make a "significant" investment in the Research and Development of robotics to increase their capacity, performance, and quality.

Eliminate Risk

For existing risks that are judged to be unacceptable, the most effective and immediate risk treatment is removal or elimination of the risk source. It is important to recognize that such controls may introduce other risk sources that require assessment, treatment, and management.

> **Examples of Eliminating Risk**
>
> - Realizing that elevated work presents a potential for falls and a significant risk of fatalities and serious injuries, a manufacturing company decides to eliminate elevated work by removing elevated work platforms making all work at surface level through redesign of the facility.
> - An assembly operation with costly musculoskeletal injuries resulting from manual material handling decides to eliminate these exposures by installing an automated system that eliminates excessive manual material handling.
> - An organization eliminates all sharp edges on their workstations by rounding corners and rolling over edges.
> - A manufacturer eliminates the exposure to a hazardous chemical process in the facility by redesigning it as an enclosed system and relocating it outside of the workplace.

Reduce Risk

Pure risk can be reduced by reducing the risk source's likelihood of occurrence or by reducing the severity of its consequences through risk control measures. Risk reduction measures are used to minimize or reduce the likelihood and severity of an unwanted risk as shown in Figure 10.2. Risk reduction is defined as making risk smaller by reducing its severity of impact, reducing the chance for it to occur, or reducing the exposure.

ISO Guide 73 notes that "risk treatments that deal with negative consequences are sometimes referred to as risk mitigation, risk elimination, risk prevention, and risk reduction" (ISO Guide 73/ANSI/ASSP Z690.1-2011). It is important to understand these terms and their proper applications.

1. **Risk Prevention**

    Prevention is the act of keeping something from occurring that would otherwise cause risk or harm (reducing the likelihood of occurrence). Risk prevention is taken to reduce or eliminate the probability of specific undesirable events from

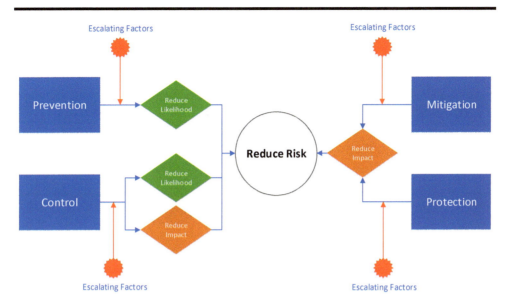

Figure 10.2
Risk Reduction Options and Their Effects.

happening. Examples of risk prevention include pressure relief valves to prevent over-pressurization or level indicators to detect levels in aboveground storage tanks to reduce probability of overfilling.

2. **Risk Mitigation**

   Mitigation is the act of reducing the severity of something, making a condition or consequence less severe (reducing the severity of consequences). Mitigation is a reactionary measure used to reduce the impact on things at risk after the event occurs. Examples of risk mitigation include berms and containment dikes around tanks, evacuations, shelter-in-place, and emergency response plans.

3. **Risk Protection**

   Protection is the act of shielding, covering, or keeping an asset from harm. Like mitigation, protection is a measure designed to limit the severity of harm or impact rather than prevent the event from occurring (reducing the severity of consequences). Examples of protection might include automatic fire suppression systems and sprinkler systems, fall protection systems, and protective shielding of computer systems and other high value assets.

4. **Risk Control**

   Control is to manage risk by reducing the likelihood of occurrence and/or severity of its impact. A risk control is a measure that modifies risk and may include processes, policies, devices, practices, or other actions.

5. Escalation Factor

Escalation factors are control decay mechanisms or conditions that can lead to increased risk by defeating or reducing the effectiveness of preventive, protective, or mitigative controls. Controls are seldom 100% effective due to escalation factors that can cause a control to degrade, fail, or not work consistently or as expected. An escalation factor does not directly cause the top event or consequence rather it increases the likelihood that the scenario will progress because the associated control will be degraded or fail (ASSP TR-31010-2020).

Figure 10.3
Risk Transfer Options.

Transfer Risk

Unacceptable risks that cannot be avoided, eliminated, or reduced through risk control measures may be transferred to third parties through insurance, noninsurance contracts, or hedging as illustrated in Figure 10.3.

Insurance

A common means of meeting the financial consequences of hazard and operational risk is the purchase of insurance coverage. Insurance is a form of risk transfer that involves transferring the potential financial consequences of certain specified events from the covered insured to the insurer. This form of risk treatment provides the insurance buyer a "known" financial cost—the insurance premium—in place of an "unknown," possibility larger, financial loss from covered claims paid by the insurer. As part of the agreed contract, the insurance carrier agrees to pay for all of the organization's losses that are covered by the insurance contract as well as provide any specified services, such as risk control services, and claims handling.

Insurance is an important risk treatment component of a risk management program, and can include multiple layers of coverage (primary, secondary, excess, umbrella coverage) for liability, workers compensation, property, marine, inland marine, boiler and machinery, fleet, crime, cyber, directors and officers, business interruption, errors and omissions, and other coverages.

Contracts

Contractual risk transfer or noninsurance contracts are sometimes used as a risk treatment to transfer financial consequences of an event or activity to a third party. As with any contract, contractual risk transfer is an agreement between the risk owner and a third party to transfer financial or legal responsibility associated with specified activities, events, injuries, or damages. The contracted third party agrees to indemnify and hold the risk owner harmless in a contract, transferring the risk. Noninsurance contracts that assign responsibility for a particular event or activity that can produce risk to a third party are known as hold-harmless agreements or indemnity agreements.

Hedging

A form of risk treatment for financial risks where there are uncertainties associated with costs or returns is known as "hedging." In essences, it is a form of diversifying one's risks, so as to not have too much risk in one place. Hedging is often used to reduce risk of adverse price variability of an investment and requires making a second investment that offsets the potential consequences or losses of the original investment.

> **"Hedging" Example:** Hedging might involve spreading a company's exposure to global investments to balance out their US investments. Or the use of a "futures contract" with a supplier committed to purchase a quantity of a product or commodity at a pre-agreed price to avoid price fluctuation. For example, during the fuel crisis, Southwest Airlines purchased jet fuel for a set price to avoid price fluctuations and uncertainty.

Share Risk

Risk sharing is the practice of distributing or sharing risks among other industries, organizations, company divisions, investors, and other external or internal stakeholders. The theory is that the risk burden and its financial consequences are lessened to a level that is acceptable to each individual risk owner. It involves sharing or dividing risk among two or more entities for financial gain. Risk sharing is a measure used to diversify and reduce the concentration of risks retained by a single organization.

> **"Risk Sharing" Example:** Financial institutions use risk sharing practices in large loans to organizations where they share in the profits, as well as potential losses. Other examples of risk sharing include insurance products designed to "pool" risks among companies within a region or industry group, and the forming of partnerships.

Retain Risk

Risk retention is an organization's decision to intentionally retain a particular risk rather than transfer the risk with insurance or noninsurance contracts. Risk retention generally involves setting aside self-funding reserves by an organization to pay for losses as they occur, rather than shifting the risk to an insurer. An organization may choose to retain risks when they believe that the cost of doing so is less than the cost of fully or partially insuring against it.

Self-funding risk retention is generally used for pure risks (hazard or operational) when there is an internal fund within the organization to pay the cost of losses and when the cost for insurance is prohibitive or unavailable. For these reasons, it is sometimes the risk financing treatment of last resort.

Selecting Risk Treatments

Risk treatment strategies and options should be selected according to their perceived effectiveness, reliability, advantages, and benefits as well as their costs, potential disadvantages, and other possible negative factors. Selection of the most appropriate risk treatment options requires an optimum balance of expected benefits and gains over the potential costs and negative aspects. Methods such as cost-benefit analysis, financial and non-financial benefits analyses, pay-back period analysis, return on investment (ROI), and others can be useful in selecting and justifying appropriate risk treatments.

The combination of risk treatments is also often used as illustrated in Figure 10.4. For example, an organization may decide to accept and retain low severity/high frequency risks, while transferring high severity/low frequency risks through insurance. Such decisions are very often based on previous claims experience and statistical analysis.

In Figure 10.4, it is readily visible that the low severity events will have the highest frequency. However, the monetary losses will be represented in an inverted pyramid because the greater number of low severity risks will represent lower financial loss

Relative Severity	# of Loss Events	$ Amount
Low severity	70	<10,000
Medium severity	20	10,000 - <100,000
High severity	15	>100,000

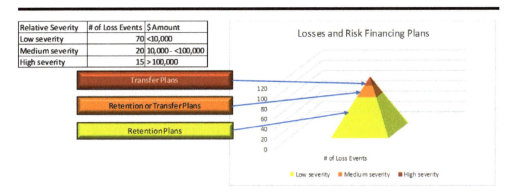

Figure 10.4
Risk Treatment Combinations.

than one high severity catastrophic event. The medium severity risks may or may not be that predictable. Some organizations may decide to retain or transfer the risk for medium severity risks. High severity risks in most cases are transferred. However, some organizations may decide to self-insure the whole operation including high severity low likelihood risks. Such high severity-low likelihood events are very often described as "black swan" events. On the other hand, high frequency-high likelihood events are sometimes described as "grey rhino" events. High likelihood events are not random surprises but occur after a series of warnings and visible evidence.

One way to make decisions regarding risk retention and risk transfer is to apply the approach developed by Richard Prouty. He proposed an analysis and evaluation of risk exposures based on loss frequency and severity. This proposed methodology has since become widely known as the "Prouty Approach." The Prouty Approach can be presented in a 3 x 4 risk matrix as represented in Figure 10.5.

Risk professionals should be aware of possible shortcomings of a qualitative risk matrix approach. For instance, slight and moderately severe outcomes are placed in the same category "Reduce or Prevent." The monetary difference between "Slight,"

Loss Severity	Loss Frequency: Almost Nil	Slight	Moderate	Definite
Severe	Transfer	Reduce or Prevent	Reduce or Prevent	Avoid
Significant	Retain	Transfer	Reduce or Prevent	Avoid
Slight	Retain	Transfer	Prevent	Prevent

Figure 10.5
The Prouty Approach Model.

"Moderate," and "Severe" outcomes could be millions of dollars. In addition, some modern methods would suggest a combination of prevention and mitigation layers. For instance, even for the "Slight Severity" events that are branded "Definite" on the Prouty matrix, both preventive and mitigation measures can be added. A good example is a slippery floor in a food processing facility where it is almost "Definite" that slips and falls will occur. In the event the organization cannot "Prevent" 100% of the slips, mitigation controls such as return to work management plan can be implemented to reduce the severity of impact or loss.

The Hierarchy of Risk Treatment Strategies

The selection of risk treatments and controls for risk sources resulting from hazards and operations (pure risk) should be made in accordance with the hierarchy of risk controls concept. The concept is based on the ranking of control strategies from most effective and reliable in risk reduction to the least effective and reliable. There are a number of existing hierarchy models, most of which include five strategies: elimination, substitution, engineering, administration, and personal protective equipment. Several include additional strategies including avoidance, minimization, simplification, passive engineering, active engineering, and warning devices. An example of a risk control hierarchy is provided in Figure 10.6.

The hierarchy of risk controls model includes three areas: design-level controls, engineering controls, and administrative controls (Lyon, Walline, Popov 2019). Design/redesign level risk control strategies are the only risk treatments that are long lasting and typically do not degrade over time. When hazards are avoided, eliminated, or replaced with less hazardous elements through design, the risk level will not change unless the design feature is changed. Engineering controls are less resilient and can be circumvented. Such controls can degrade, wear-out, or lose effectiveness or reliability over time due to lack of maintenance or damage. These types of controls also require ongoing inspection, testing, maintenance, and repair. Administrative controls are the least effective and least reliable since they degrade more quickly due to variations in the quality of training, application, and management, as well as organizational influences and human fallibility. Administrative controls including procedural, training, and personal protective equipment are considered the last resort in the hierarchy. The following are brief descriptions and examples of each risk control strategy:

Design-level Risk Control Strategies
Risk Avoidance

The most effective and reliable risk control strategy is the avoidance of a potential risk sources. This strategy is applied in the design phase by intentionally identifying and designing facilities, processes, products, or activities that avoid the introduction of specific hazards/risk sources. This strategy is also used in redesigns, modifications, and additions to existing systems and workplaces.

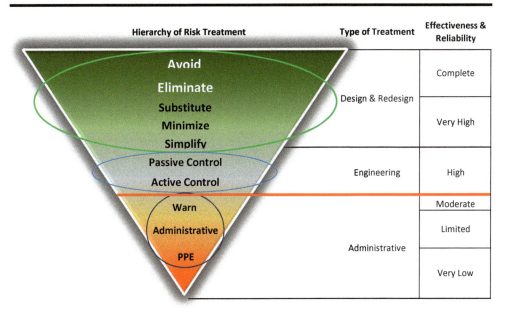

Figure 10.6
Hierarchy of Risk Treatment Model.

Risk Elimination

A second strategy is the elimination of existing risk sources from a system. Existing hazards/risks are eliminated or removed from systems/workplaces through redesign. Risk elimination is achieved by eliminating the need for a hazard or hazardous element in an existing process by redesigning the process. This may include removing and isolating a particular hazard away from people or assets.

Risk Substitution

A third strategy that should be considered when the first two options are not feasible is risk substitution. Risk substitution can be applied for new or existing hazards/risks. The strategy involves intentionally selecting less hazardous materials, equipment, methods, or activities that meet the needs of the system/workplace, while reducing the potential risk.

> **Examples of Risk Substitution**
> - To reduce the risk of exposure to pure sulfur dioxide liquid used to protect the quality of wine, a winery substitutes a less hazardous product, granulated potassium meta-bisulfite.
> - The risk of exposure to COVID-19 from in-person meetings is reduced by using virtual meetings instead.

Risk Minimization

Another strategy that can be used is minimizing the quantity or intensity of a particular risk. The amount or quantity of a particular hazard is minimized to a level that presents a lower severity risk.

> **Examples of Risk Minimization**
>
> - A food process operation reduces the size and weight of materials and ingredients handled by employees.
> - An existing chemical processing operation is redesigned to reduce the quantities of hazardous materials needed and reduced on-site storage.
> - A new manufacturing facility is designed to operate at lower voltages, lower temperatures, and lower pressures, and overall, less energy.

Risk Simplification

Complicated or confusing systems and methods are potential risk sources for errors and adverse effects. Risk simplification is the strategy of reducing complexity in the layout, controls, and methods to reduce the likelihood of error and improve the likelihood of expected performance.

> **Example of Risk Simplification**
>
> - An automobile manufacturer simplifies the design of controls and displays to improve ergonomics and human performance.
> - A complex chemical storage, piping, and connecting system is simplified, color coded, and streamlined to reduce the potential for mis-matching chemicals.
> - The number of steps to complete a critical task are reduced and simplified to reduce the potential for human error.

Engineering-level Risk Control Strategies

Passive Engineering Controls

For risk sources that cannot be avoided, eliminated, or reduced through design, engineering controls should be considered. Passive-type engineering controls are controls that function continually without activation. Passive engineering controls provide more reliable control that active-type controls.

> **Examples of Passive Engineering**
>
> - Containment dikes and secondary containment around hazardous material storage tanks
> - Fixed or permanent guarding on machines
> - Guard rails on highways and bridges

Active Engineering Controls

Active-type engineering controls are controls that only function upon activation. Active engineering controls are less reliable since they can fail to function or be bypassed. They should not be the sole control measure; however, they can be incorporated in addition to other risk controls in a "layer of controls" fashion.

> **Examples of Active Engineering**
>
> - Presence sensing devices on machines
> - Two-hand trips and interlocks
> - Process controls and safety instrumented systems (SIS)
> - Automatic fire suppression systems and sprinkler systems

Warnings and Awareness Controls

Warning and awareness controls are devices, sensors, alert systems, signage, labeling, or other methods that inform or warn of residual risks by sight, sound, or touch. They provide limited protection since they require the individual to detect and respond to the warning.

> **Examples of Warning and Awareness Controls**
>
> - Carbon monoxide detectors and fire alarms
> - Tornado warning sirens
> - Forklift backup alarm and flashing red light
> - Perimeter warning cones, rope, or tape
> - Warning or instructional signage
> - Highway "rumble strips" to indicate drifting off road

Administrative-level Risk Control Strategies

Administrative Controls

Administrative controls are measures developed by management to educate, guide, and monitor employee performance. They are widely practiced; however, administrative controls should be used in support of higher-level controls rather than as the sole measure due to their lack of effectiveness and reliability.

> **Examples of Administrative Controls**
> - Written operating procedures and safety programs
> - General lockout/tagout procedures; machine-specific lockout/tagout procedures
> - Work instructions
> - Orientation, training, education, and meetings
> - Supervision, equipment spotter, permit system, confined space entry attendant
> - Behavior-based safety efforts

Personal Protective Equipment

Personal protective equipment (PPE) is the least effective and least reliable control strategy, and the last line of defense. In this strategy, the exposure to hazards is hopefully reduced by proper donning and wearing of protective clothing and equipment. PPE is used to prevent or reduce contact, reduce exposure, and reduce impact or harm from physical, chemical, or biological hazards. Proper selection of appropriate equipment for the risk exposure is necessary for this control measure to be useful.

> **Examples of PPE**
> - Respiratory protection
> - Flame resistant clothing
> - Fall protection harness and lanyard
> - Hands, body, head, eye, face, and foot protection

Selecting Risk Treatments

Risk treatment strategies are selected according to their effectiveness and reliability using the hierarchy of risk controls concept. Beginning with the most effective strategy, risk avoidance or elimination, each risk treatment strategy should be considered for its feasibility in reducing risk to "as low as reasonably practicable" (ALARP). This approach to selecting risk control strategies in accordance with the hierarchy model is illustrated in the risk treatment decision tree in Figure 10.7. Decision makers should begin by asking is it possible to avoid or eliminate the risk? If not, then is it possible to substitute a less hazardous element to achieve ALARP? Decision makers continue down the decision tree until they are satisfied that the risk is as low as reasonably practicable. This often requires multiple layers of controls such as a combination of engineering-level devices, administrative procedures and training, supervision and inspection, and finally personal protective equipment.

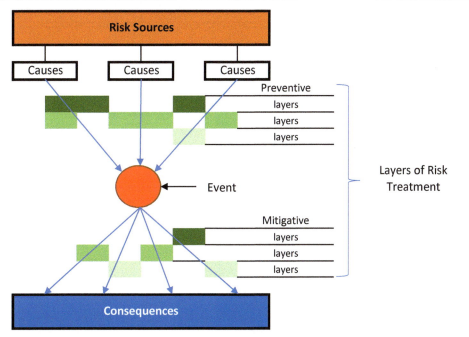

Figure 10.7
Risk Treatment Decision Tree.

Layering Risk Treatments

The concept of applying different risk treatments in layers to address more complex risks is an important aspect of reducing and managing risk. Rarely is a single control adequate in reducing and maintaining risk to a level that is considered acceptable. Layers of risk treatments and controls should be selected in accordance with their effectiveness and reliability using the hierarchy of risk treatments concept (Lyon, Popov 2020).

"Layers of Protection" is a concept whereby several independent devices, systems, or actions are provided to reduce the likelihood and severity of an undesirable event

(API RP 780- 2013). Such control layers should be constructed, implemented, verified, and monitored to achieve a level that is as low as reasonably practicable or ALARP. Figure 10.8 provides an illustration of using layers of risk treatments.

A comprehensive approach using layers of controls is often required to reduce more challenging risks to an acceptable level. By using stratified layers of controls that incorporate preventive measures such as (barriers between the hazards and the exposure to reduce the likelihood of the occurrence); mitigation measures (those measures that are reactive to an event and reduce the severity of the impact such as emergency action plans, fire suppression systems, and warning systems); and risk transfer (insurance coverage and noninsurance contractual risk transfer), a higher-level risk can be reduced and maintained at an acceptable level. Layering of risk controls provides not only more comprehensive coverage, but it also builds in redundancies in case of the failure of a single control.

Techniques such as barrier analysis, layers of protection analysis (LOPA), bow-tie analysis, and modified methods such as Layers of Control Assessment (LOCA) can be used to assess existing controls and determine whether risk is at an acceptable

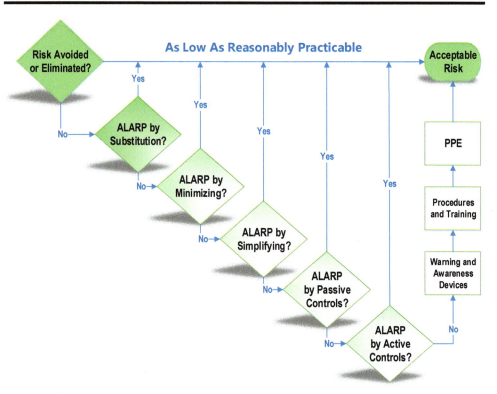

Figure 10.8
Layering of Risk Treatments Example.

level or if further risk reduction strategies are necessary to achieve and maintain ALARP.

Acceptable Risk and ALARP

Attaining a level of "zero risk" is not possible. After applying risk treatments, risks can be reduced; however, there will always be some level of residual risk. Therefore, an organization must strive for a level of risk that is relatively acceptable in terms of the potential severity and likelihood. Acceptable risk is defined as "that risk for which the probability of an incident or exposure occurring and the severity of harm or damage that may result are as low as reasonably practicable (ALARP) in the setting being considered" (ANSI/ASSP Z590.3-2011 R2016).

In ISO/IEC Guide 51: *Safety Aspects – Guidelines for its inclusion in standards*, Section 5 The Concept of Safety, states that "safety is achieved by reducing risk to a tolerable level, defined in this Guide as tolerable risk." The guide defines "tolerable risk" as the "level of risk that is accepted in a given context based on the current values of society." The guide further notes that the terms "acceptable risk" and "tolerable risk" are considered to be synonymous (ISO/IEC Guide 51-2014).

In his book, *Of Acceptable Risk: Science and the Determination of Safety*, William W. Lowrance wrote: "Nothing can be absolutely free of risk. One can't think of anything that isn't, under some circumstances, able to cause harm. Because nothing can be absolutely free of risk, nothing can be said to be absolutely safe. There are degrees of risk, and consequently there are degrees of safety" (Lowrance 1977).

> **Example:** A description of "acceptable risk level" is provided in NASA-STD-8719.7, Facility System Safety Guidebook. The National Aeronautics and Space Administration (NASA) technical standard describes their definition of acceptable risk as "Loss of life as a result of hazards in this facility is unlikely. Hazards may result in no lost workday injuries or no restricted duty cases, loss of facility operational capability of less than 1 day, or damage to equipment or property less than $25,000." (NASA, 1998)

Acceptable risk is a function of many factors and varies considerably across industries. For instance, industries that are typically higher risk such as mining, oil and gas, or farming might have higher acceptable risk levels than lower risk industries. Local or region cultures also play a role in risk acceptability as evidenced by those that have experience in global operations. Risk acceptability is also dynamic and time dependent. Risk levels that are currently acceptable may not be acceptable tomorrow, next year, or the next decade.

Each organization has its own "accepted risk" level. More sophisticated and risk-aware organizations will have a formalized written definition of their acceptable risk level. Depending upon the context, and the organization's culture, industry, environment, social-economic situation, or other factors, the level of risk that is considered acceptable may vary.

ALARP is defined as "that level of risk which can be further lowered only by an increase in resource expenditure that is disproportionate in relation to the resulting decrease in risk (ANSI/ASSP Z590.3-2011 R2016). Risk treatment involves the selection and application of one or more risk control options to reduce "pure" risk to a level that is as low as reasonably practicable (ALARP) and acceptable to the organization.

Risk Treatment Plans

As a result of the risk assessment, plans are made for treating the risk. Such plans can involve a single treatment or control; however, it is more likely that multiple risk treatment measures will be required to reduce and manage risk to an acceptable level. The plan should also specify the sequence and order in which various risk treatments are to be integrated and implemented. As outlined in ISO 31000, risk treatment plans should include information regarding: proposed actions and their timeline for implementation, rationale and justification for risk treatment selections, benefits to stakeholders, responsibilities and accountabilities for their implementation, performance metrics, and monitoring and communicating results.

Risk treatment plans may incorporate strategies such as "inherently safer designs," "layers of protection," "recognized and generally accepted good engineering practices," and "safer technology and alternatives" selected according to the hierarchy of controls.

- *Inherently safer design* is a concept that requires designers to attempt to eliminate or reduce hazards that are identified at each stage in the system's life cycle and design safety systems to control hazards rather than accept them. The concept focuses on eliminating or reducing the hazards associated with a set of conditions and is closely aligned with the prevention through design (PtD) concept (CCPS 2008).
- *Layers of protection* (discussed earlier) is a concept whereby several independent devices, systems, or actions are provided to reduce the likelihood and severity of an undesirable event (API RP 780-2013).
- *Recognized and Generally Accepted Good Engineering Practices* (RAGAGEP) was introduced in 1992 by OSHA in the process safety management (PSM) standard (29 CFR 1910.119). RAGAGEP involves the selection and application of appropriate engineering, operating, and maintenance knowledge when

designing, operating, and maintaining chemical facilities with the purpose of ensuring safety and preventing process safety incidents. (Lyon, Popov 2019).
- *Safer Technology and Alternatives* or STAA is the concept of integrating various risk reduction strategies that work toward making a facility and its chemical processes as safe as possible (EPA 2015; OSHA 2017).

It may be necessary to include a combination of options or strategies in a risk treatment plan that includes: (1) "avoiding a new risk," (2) "eliminating an existing risk," (3) "reducing the likelihood of occurrence," (4) "reducing the severity of impact," (5) "transferring risk," (6) "sharing risk" among other parties, and (7) "retaining a portion of the risk" (Lyon, Popov 2019).

It should be noted however, with the treatment of risk, there is the potential to cause additional risk or unintended consequences sometimes referred to as secondary risk. This potential concern must be considered carefully during the selection of risk treatments and monitored after implementation to verify that secondary risks have not occurred.

The Concept of Residual Risk

Residual risk is the risk remaining after risk treatment. It is also known as "retained risk" (ISO Guide 73-2009) and can contain unidentified, unknown risk as well. The concept of residual or "remaining" risk is important to understand when managing risks both internally and externally. Risk and its management are "dynamic" in nature and treatments continue beyond the initial risk treatment, similar to continual improvement. For this reason, risks that remain after an assessment and treatment should be continually monitored and assessed for secondary risk, hidden risk, or previously undiscovered risks. Following the implementation of risk treatments such as risk avoidance, elimination or risk control, the residual risk should be evaluated to verify that it is acceptable to the organization.

The "initial risk" levels from identified risks are estimated in the risk analysis. Then, a risk evaluation is performed comparing the initial risk level to the established risk criteria to determine whether it is acceptable or if it requires risk reduction treatment. Risk treatment options are considered, and the estimated risk reduction factors calculated to determine "future state risk level" or the projected "residual risk" level.

By comparing the estimated level of risk before and after treatment, a basis for determining which risk treatment option provides the lowest residual risk can be made. Prioritization of risk treatments should be based on the organization's risk tolerance and the estimated residual risk levels. Resources should be devoted to those residual risks that are of the greatest concern or greatest criticality.

Selected risk treatment efforts may not always produce the expected risk reductions. Therefore, it is important that implemented risk treatments be monitored, verified, and reviewed to determine their effectiveness, and action taken upon any treatments needing adjustment or replacement. As noted earlier, risk treatments can introduce new risks or increase existing risks that require managing and monitoring. Residual risk levels must be estimated and evaluated through follow-up risk assessments. The residual risk should be documented and subjected to monitoring, review and, where appropriate, further treatment (ANSI/ASSP/ISO 31000-2018).

Treating Risk throughout the Continuum

Risk will change with the variables, conditions, or risk drivers affecting it and will change over time. Risk can be viewed as being in a continuum depending upon its point in the risk management cycle. For this reason, risk must be continually managed and treated as it evolves or changes in the organization. Existing, new, or emerging risks as well as those risks that have been previously treated should be continually monitored and assessed. An illustration of the risk continuum, which includes inherent or untreated risk, initial risk, secondary and residual risk, and future state risk is shown in Figure 10.9.

Emerging Risks

New risks are created from new risk sources introduced into the system and can also develop and emerge from new technologies, activities, or expansions into different areas which requires scanning, detecting, and monitoring. Such emerging risks can come from known risks that previously were not considered a threat (pure risks) or an opportunity (speculative risks), which have increased in new or unfamiliar way that have a potential to affect the organization's objectives. Detection systems should be in place to identify and monitor their development.

Inherent Risk

Inherent risk is described "as the risk to an entity apart from any action to alter either the likelihood or impact of the risk" (Elliott 2017). It is the "untreated risk" that resides in an existing in the system before any risk management is applied. With new acquisitions, systems, or activities there are associated inherent risks, which require assessment and management. Inherent risks are derived from risk sources, risk drivers, and potential exposures associated with the endeavor or system.

Initial Risk

Initial risk is defined as "the first assessment of the potential risk of an identified hazard. Initial risk establishes a fixed baseline for the hazard" (MIL-STD-882E-2012). It is estimated and determined in the initial risk assessment and can be considered a "baseline" risk level. The initial risk level considers the effectiveness of existing controls and is used to determine whether further risk treatment is required.

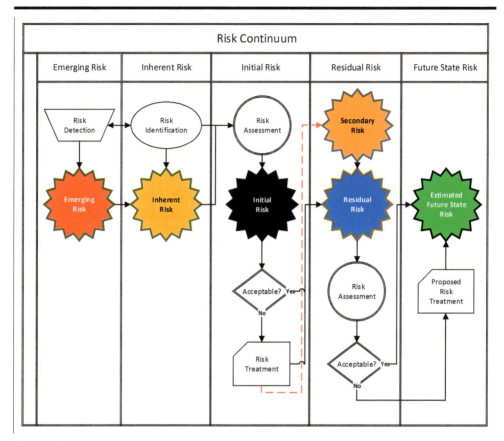

Figure 10.9
The Risk Continuum.

Residual Risk

Since risk cannot be completely eliminated, there will always be some "residual risk." Residual risk is the risk level that remains after applying the selected risk treatments from the initial risk assessment. Residual risk can also include previously unidentified or hidden risks, secondary risks, knowingly retained risks, shared risks, or transferred risked.

Secondary Risk

As previously mentioned, risk treatments can inadvertently cause new risks or increase existing ones. A secondary risk is a risk that arises as the result of implementing a risk treatment or control measure. If the risk treatment were not taken, the secondary risk would not exist.

The creation of secondary risks or "side-effects" must be carefully considered when selecting and developing risk treatments. The potential for secondary risks should be assessed when considering the various risk treatment options, anticipating and identifying possible unintended affects or interferences with other controls. Ongoing monitoring and reviewing of treatments should be performed to detect and correct any additional risks that might develop or be created. Proposed risk treatments that pose a potentially high secondary risk may be disqualified from consideration if the secondary risk falls outside of the project risk tolerance.

Future State Risk

Future state risk is the estimated risk level expected from the application of prescribed risk controls. Future state risk is used to show a measure of risk reduction or risk reduction percentage (RR%) for a proposed control compared to the current risk level or initial risk level. When proposing additional control measures for a current risk level, a "future state" risk level is estimated by considering the new control measures' anticipated effect on risk level.

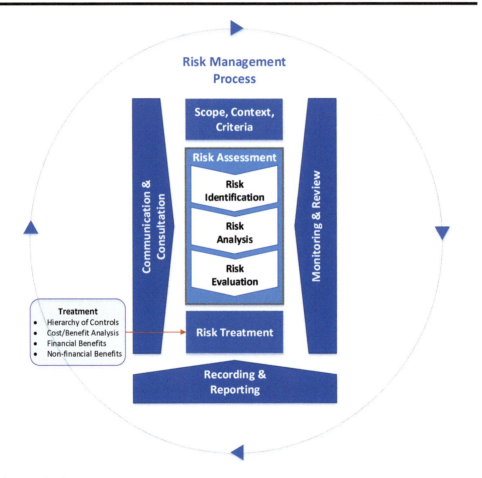

Figure 10.10
Risk Management Process and Risk Treatment Techniques.

Methods for Selecting Risk Treatment

There are multiple methods and tools available to can be used to select and justify risk treatment options as illustrated in Figure 10.10. ISO 31010 and other standards provide some guidance on such methods and their use. Table 10.1 provides a listing of several common methods with brief descriptions.

Table 10.1. Risk Treatment Selection Methods.

Risk Treatment Methods	Descriptions
Hierarchy of Controls	The concept of the hierarchy of controls is that control strategies are stratified according to their effectiveness and reliability in a top-down fashion. This is commonly represented in a table or pyramid graphic.
Cost-Benefit Analysis	Cost-benefit analysis weighs the total expected costs of options in monetary terms against their total expected benefits in order to choose the most effective or the most profitable option. It can be qualitative or quantitative or involve a combination of quantitative and qualitative elements and can be applied at any level of an organization.
Multi-Criteria Analysis	MCA uses a range of criteria to transparently evaluate and compare the overall performance of a set of options. In general, the goal is to produce an order of preference for a set of options. The analysis involves the development of a matrix of options and criteria which are ranked and aggregated to provide an overall score for each option.
Financial and Non-Financial Benefits	In financial analysis, a monetary value is assigned to all known direct and indirect costs. Non-financial benefits are positive business impacts that cannot be directly or easily quantified. They are also known as "soft" benefits.
Business Impact Analysis	Business impact analysis (BIA) is a systematic method used to determine and evaluate potential effects of an interruption to critical business operations as a result of a disaster, emergency, or serious incident.

Continued on next page

Risk Treatment Methods	Descriptions
Cost Savings	Cost savings is a simple calculation that provides a gross cost saving from an EHS proposal using number of incidents and their costs and a treatment that reduces frequency and costs.
Expanded ROHSEI	Expanded Return on Health, Safety, and Environmental Investment is a formula used to calculate and project costs before and after related to EHS program proposals.
Net Present Value	Net present value is a calculation used to compare the future cash amounts of a proposed investment after they are discounted by a specified rate of return.
Payback Period	Payback period is a simple formula used to calculate the time in which the initial cash outflow of an investment is expected to be recovered from the cash inflows generated by the investment.
Return on Investment	ROI is the difference between the gain from the SH&E investment and the cost of investment and the cost of investment.
Internal Rate of Return	Internal rate of return (IRR) is a formula used to express the interest rate at which the net present value of all the cash flows (both positive and negative) from a project or investment equal zero. IRR is used to evaluate the attractiveness of a proposed risk treatment.

Summary

Risk treatment, the process of modifying risk to an acceptable level is the primary reason to assess risk. It is considered the most important step in the risk management process. Without treating risks that have been assessed, a risk assessment is of little value to an organization. An iterative approach to selecting the most appropriate risk treatments should be part of the risk management process.

Review Questions

1. Define the terms *risk treatment* and *risk control*. List and describe the seven risk treatment options.
2. Identify and describe four different terms used in risk reduction.

3. Identify and describe the options used in risk transfer.
4. Explain how the hierarchy of risk treatment is used in selecting risk treatments. Identify and describe the three strategy groups in the hierarchy.
5. Describe what a risk treatment plan is and why is it important.
6. Describe the concept of residual risk. Identify and describe the various stages of risk in the risk continuum.
7. Identify and describe five methods used to select risk treatment.

References

ANSI/ASSP Z590.3-2011 (R2016). 2016. *Prevention through Design: Guidelines for Addressing Occupational Hazards and Risks in Design and Redesign Processes*. Park Ridge, IL: American Society of Safety Professionals.

ANSI/ASSP Z690.1-2011. 2011. *Vocabulary for Risk Management*. Des Plaines, IL: American Society of Safety Professionals.

ANSI/ASSP/ISO 31000-2018. 2018. *Risk Management - Guidelines*. Park Ridge, IL: American Society of Safety Professionals.

API RP 780. 2013. 2013. *Security Risk Assessment Methodology for the Petroleum and Petrochemical Industries*, First Edition, May 2013.

ASSP TR-31010-2020. 2020. *Technical Report: Risk Management – Techniques for Safety Practitioners*. Park Ridge, IL: American Society of Safety Professionals.

CCPS. 2008. *Inherently Safer Chemical Processes: A Life Cycle Approach,* 2nd ed. Hoboken, NJ: Wiley.

Elliott, Michael W. 2017. *Risk Management Principles and Practices*, 2d ed., Malvern, PA: The Institutes.

Environmental Protection Agency (EPA). 2015. "Chemical safety alert: Safer technology and alternatives" (EPA 550-F-15-003). www.epa.gov/sites/production/files/2015-06/documents/alert_safer_tech_alts.pdf.

ISO/IEC Guide 51:2014 *Safety Aspects – Guidelines for its inclusion in standards*. 2014. Geneva, Switzerland: International Organization for Standardization.

Lowrance, William F. 1976. *Of Acceptable Risk: Science and The Determination of Safety*. Los Altos, Calif.: William Kaufman Inc.

Lyon, Bruce K., and Georgi Popov. 2016. "The Art of Assessing Risk: Selecting, Modifying, and Combining Methods to Assess Operational Risks." *Professional Safety,* March 2016, 40–51.

Lyon, Bruce K., and Georgi Popov. 2019. "Risk Treatment Strategies: Harmonizing the Hierarchy of Controls & Inherently Safer Design Concepts." *Professional Safety,* May 2019, 34–43.

Lyon, Bruce K., and Georgi Popov. 2020. "Managing Risk Through Layers of Control." *Professional Safety,* April 2020, 25–35.

Lyon, Bruce K., David Walline, and Georgi Popov. 2019. "Moving Risk Assessments Upstream to the Design Phase." *Professional Safety*, November 2019, 24–35.

Manuele, Fred A. 2010. "Acceptable Risk: Time for SH&E professionals to adopt the concept." *Professional Safety,* May 2010, 30–38.

MIL-STD-882E. 2012. *Department of Defense Standard Practice: System Safety*. Washington, DC: Department of Defense.

NASA-STD-8719.7. 1998. *Facility System Safety Guidebook*. Washington, DC: National Aeronautics and Space Administration.

OSHA. 2017. "Process safety management for petroleum refineries: Lessons learned from the petroleum refinery process safety management national emphasis program" (OSHA 3918-08 2017). www.osha.gov/Publications/OSHA3918.pdf.

CHAPTER 11
Monitoring and Reporting Risk

Introduction

For risks to be managed throughout their life cycle, an organization must have systems in place to continually monitor, review, record, and report risk to decision makers. Such a continual feedback loop provides the organization the necessary information and assurance that risk treatments are effective, that new and emerging risks are detected, that secondary risks are detected and managed, and that the organization's objectives are being met. Without such ongoing review and communication of the development of risks to management, it is difficult for an organization to consistently make decisions or successfully achieve their objectives. These activities are closely linked with and tend to overlap risk communication and consultation efforts within an organization.

In the ISO 31000 risk management process shown in Figure 11.1, there are three components that surround the risk assessment and treatment process: (1) monitoring and review, (2) recording and reporting, and (3) communication and consultation. These components are the "check" points in the Plan-Do-Check-Act continual improvement model, and the key input to "communication and consultation" in the risk management process.

Interactive tools and supplemental materials are available at assp.org/ermtools.

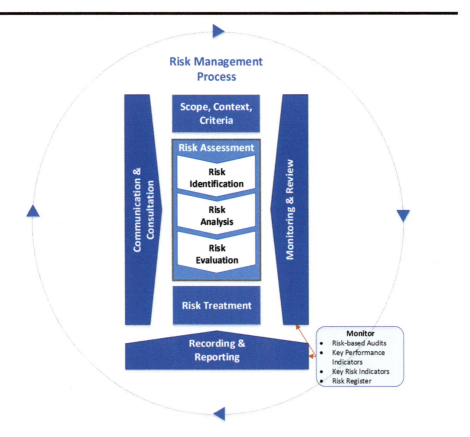

Figure 11.1
The Risk Management Process, Adapted from ANSI/ASSP/ISO 31000-2018, Highlighting Methods Used in Monitoring and Communicating Risk.

Continual Improvement

Managing risk requires a continual improvement cycle of planning, doing, checking, and acting. If plans and their execution are not "checked" and their progress communicated, there can be no action for improvement. Therefore, a system should be in place that monitors, validates, verifies, records, and communicates risk performance within an organization.

One of the guiding principles of risk management found in ISO 31000 is "continual improvement." Continual improvement is achieved through learning and experience using a Plan-Do-Check-Act (PDCA) cycle approach. "Management systems" such as ANSI/ASSP/ISO 45001 and ANSI/ASSP Z10.0 are also built upon a PDCA cycle as shown in Figure 11.2. In its Introduction, ANSI/ASSP Z10.0 explains that the PDCA model, although the elements appear linear, they are in fact interdependent and dynamic as illustrated in Figure 11.3.

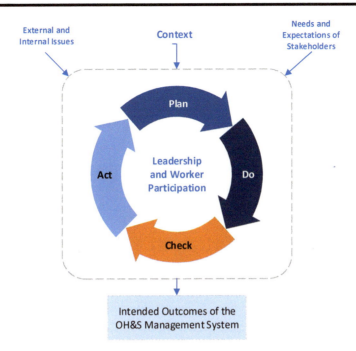

Figure 11.2
Plan-Do-Check-Act Model, Adapted from ANSI/ASSP/ISO 45001-2018.

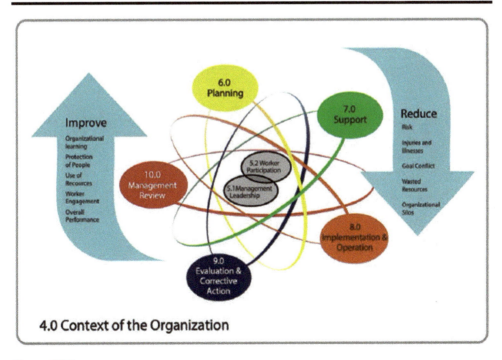

Figure 11.3
PDCA Model, Reprinted from ANSI/ASSP Z10.0-2019.

The PDCA model was originally developed by Walter Shewhart in the 1930s, and later made popular by W. Edwards Deming. The model is an iterative, systematic approach that enables an organization to manage and continually improve a system, process, or product. The PDCA model, which is a continuous cycle, provides a simple and effective process for managing change through planning, implementing, testing, and improving ideas before fully implementing them.

The checking and communicating function of PDCA should be applied throughout the risk management process and used to validate and verify outcomes; identify deviations, changes, or gaps; and track and measure performance. These "key performance indicators" should be incorporated into risk-based audits, gap analysis, compliance audits, and progress reviews.

The Continuing Evolution of Risk

Continual monitoring, review and communication of the risk management process and its outcomes are critical components and should occur in all stages of the process. Risk is dynamic in nature and continually changing with conditions, technologies, risk drivers, synergistic effects, exposures, escalating factors, and other elements. As illustrated in Figure 11.4, the dynamic nature of risk requires continual monitoring, review, recording, and reporting as it evolves within the organization.

Monitoring for new and emerging risks derived from new risk sources introduced into the system or its components must be incorporated into the risk

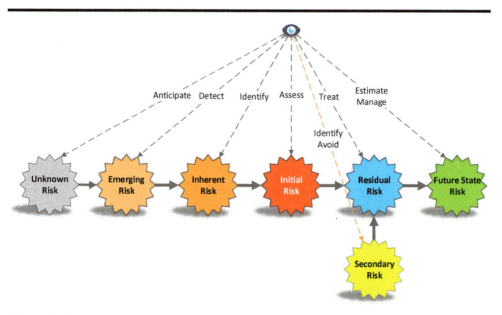

Figure 11.4
Monitoring throughout the Risk Continuum Model.

management and monitoring process. New risks can develop and emerge from new technologies, activities, or expansions into different areas which requires scanning, detecting, and monitoring. A systematic approach for scanning and early detection of emerging risks and their triggers should be in place.

Monitoring for secondary risks created by risk treatments is an important component of the monitoring process. Such risks can be inadvertently created increasing the overall risk. An example of a secondary risk might be an added risk control measure that reduces the effectiveness of another existing control; or that a new measure creates a false sense of security among users; or introduces a completely new risk. The potential for creating secondary risks should be included in the risk treatment selection, as well as follow-up detection and monitoring of implemented treatments.

Future state risks are the projected risk levels considering the application of proposed risk treatment(s). Current residual risks that require further reduction are assessed and additional risk treatments are proposed along with a projected "future state risk level" that is reduced based upon the proposed future treatments. Future state risk is estimated to communicate to decision makers the importance or justification of proposed controls. Monitoring and review of these risks and their continuum should be integrated into the risk management process.

Monitoring and Review

ISO 31000 states that the purpose of monitoring and review is to assure and improve the quality and effectiveness of process design, implementation, and outcomes. This involves planning for the monitoring process, gathering and analyzing the information, and documenting and communicating the results to stakeholders. Responsibilities and accountabilities must be clearly defined and communicated and the results integrated into the overall performance management system. As in other aspects of the business, risk management performance requires ongoing monitoring, measuring, and communication internally.

Monitoring and review can be broken down by definitions. *Monitoring* is defined by ANSI/ASIS/RIMS RA.1 as "ongoing scrutiny, oversight, evaluation of situational awareness, for determining the current status and to identify changes in the internal and external environment as well as performance." In ISO Guide 73, it is defined as "continual checking, supervising, critically observing or determining the status in order to identify change from the performance level required or expected." (ISO Guide 73/ANSI/ASSP Z690.1-2011). It is an active process used to understand the current performance or output of a system.

In addition to monitoring, risks must also be reviewed. Risk *review* is defined by ANSI RA.1 as an "activity undertaken to determine the suitability, adequacy and effectiveness of the management system and its component elements to achieve established objectives." It is also defined by ISO Guide 73 as an "activity undertaken to determine the suitability, adequacy and effectiveness of the subject matter to achieve established objectives" (ISO Guide 73/ANSI/ASSP Z690.1-2011). Like "risk evaluation," the process of risk review is used to determine if the current performance is acceptable in terms of the context and the objectives.

Monitoring and review are performed together and provide a means of comparing actual outcomes with the expected results which in turn allows for a determination of the adequacy of performance. Where risk performance is not meeting the expected levels, actions can be taken to adjust and improve performance. Monitoring and review help identify precursors and early indicators of potential consequences that were identified by the assessment. Monitoring and review are also used to collect data needed for understanding risk and determining when re-assessment is needed. Previous risk assessments should be periodically reviewed to determine if any changes have occurred in the context or if new information is available.

A method that is used to review and check risk performance is risk-based auditing. Risk-based auditing, to be effective, should be performed by a qualified and unbiased party(s) and conducted in a systematic method. Auditing should document the observed performance based on physical or material evidence including observations, interviews, and data and document reviews. In addition, audit findings should be evaluated objectively to determine the extent to which the risk management framework, or any selected part of it, is adequate and effective (ISO Guide 73/ANSI/ASSP Z690.1-2011). Monitoring and review ("checking") functions such as risk-based audits, gap analysis, and risk performance evaluations allow an organization to know the current status of their risk management efforts and residual risks.

Key Performance Indicators

For monitoring and review to be effective, key performance measures tied to the organization's objectives must be used. Key performance measures or key performance indicators (KPI) are a set of specific, quantifiable measures that an organization tracks to gauge performance over time. Such metrics are used to determine progress in achieving strategic and operational goals and to benchmark an organization's position or performance in comparison to baselines, internally or externally. Measurement of KPIs allows an organization to estimate its performance in comparison to its expected performance in support of the organization's strategic objectives.

Selecting the right KPIs requires an understanding of the organization's mission, goals, and objectives and what is currently measured related to achieving objectives. KPIs will vary from one organization to another, as well as between departments or business units, depending upon the stakeholders' needs and objectives. KPIs must be measurable and relevant to achieving the objective. For each KPI identified, the desired target and the baseline are established. Performance measures can be input-based or leading-type indicators and others may be outcome-based or lagging indicators. A combination of indicator types is often needed and may include:

- Qualitative or subjective measures, signal words, and descriptions.
- Quantitative or objective measures such as percentages, numbers, and ratios. Often times qualitative and quantitative indicators are used together to provide a more holistic picture of performance.
- Input-based or action measures that are designed to achieve a desired outcome sometimes called leading indicators. Input-based measures are activity-oriented measures that signal a change in performance. Input-based measures indicate changes in improvement in the process and detect changes that require adjustment. Examples of input- or action-based KPIs might include quarterly evaluation of the assessment process, number of process improvements completed per month, number of stakeholders trained in risk assessment (trained risk assessors) per quarter, or number of emerging risks identified prior to any incidents in a year.
- Output-based or result measures that produce numbers indicating the level of success are sometimes referred to as lagging indicators. Output-based measures are used to analyze events, successes or failures, and results or trends to determine if the process is effective and working. Examples of result type KPIs include the number of near miss incidents per quarter, number of corrective actions successfully completed, average number of days to complete corrective action, and incident rate numbers.
- Process measures used in measuring and evaluating a processes' efficiency or productivity.

For KPIs to provide value, they must be measurable, not too complex to understand or interpret, and tied to a specific business objective. They should be standardized measures, however, there is need for flexibility or ability to adjust with changes. Selected KPIs should be clearly defined and communicated to stakeholders to enhance their understanding and meaning as to the purpose of their measure and use. Selected key metrics and performance indicators must be included in the monitoring process with the findings recorded and reported to decision makers. Depending upon the specific KPI, they may be recorded each day and plotted over time to give senior management an overview of the risk management performance of the business at a glance.

Sparkline Charts

One method that can be used to capture and illustrate measurement data is a simple sparkline chart. A sparkline provides a linear graph typically drawn without axes or coordinates to communicate the movement up and down for a certain period of time. Examples of sparkline charts are the stock market price changes during a trading session or temperature ranges for a 24-hour period. Sparklines can be embedded in text or grouped together to show comparisons of several KPIs. The following example and Figure 11.5 illustrate how a sparkline chart using performance indicators can be used.

> **Example:** A global company with operations in four different countries keeps record of number of injuries in each location. The risk manager needed a quick overview and wanted to present that at the C-Suite annual meeting. The risk manager decided to use sparkline instead of complex graphs and charts. The value of a sparkline is that it has no axes, labels, or scales. The risk manager can get a quick visual understanding of the recordable injuries trends in four different locations in a global company. It saves time without reading in-depth annual performance numbers.

Performance Metrics and Indicators

Location	2014 # Recordable Injuries	2015 # Recordable Injuries	2016 # Recordable Injuries	2017 # Recordable Injuries	2018 # Recordable Injuries	Sparkline
US	7	4	3	2	1	
Canada	5	7	2	1	3	
Mexico	11	7	9	3	17	
Australia	3	5	2	1	3	

Figure 11.5
Example of Sparkline Chart.

Risk Performance Measurement

ISO 31000 states that risk management performance should be periodically reviewed and measured to determine if the risk management framework, policies, and plan are still appropriate for the external and internal context and the organization's objectives. This periodic review and measure of risk can be accomplished by implementing a "risk performance measurement" system.

An organization's overall risk performance is driven by the risk-based decisions and actions taken to achieve the desired results. Specific types of risk such as hazard-based risk can be managed by incorporating a risk performance measurement system that encompasses all levels of management and employees. This requires management leadership and commitment in the performance of risk-based actions and the involvement and participation of all levels of stakeholders. By structuring a process to establish and measure risk-related actions by stakeholders, risk performance can be successfully measured and tracked. A risk performance measurement (RPM) system is a system that establishes:

- specific actions for each level of management and employees,
- accountabilities for the completion of specific actions,
- periodic measurement of the percent completion of actions by group, and
- reporting of performance in a dashboard to senior management.

The periodic auditing of the RPM should be conducted by qualified objective reviewers to audit, measure key performance indicators, and evaluate and report performance to stakeholders. In addition, risk performance measures provide decision makers a "report on risk" indicating the effectiveness of the risk management plan. This requires a continual improvement process approach in risk management using performance goals, measurement, review, and modification of processes, systems, resources, capability, and skills.

Risk performance is driven by the daily performance of critical actions aligned with organizational objectives. To establish and sustain an effective risk process, it is well recognized that top management must be committed to leading the effort. Risk performance management (RPM) is a process of establishing and measuring risk and safety related actions or duties for each level of management and employees. The RPM process is outlined in Figure 11.6 and further described in the process steps.

Key Risk Indicators

While key performance indicators (KPIs) focus on performance measures important to the organization's objectives, another set of parameters are necessary to monitor and manage emerging or developing risk. These are known as key risk indicators (KRIs) and are risk measures that provide indications of the detection and identification of new, emerging, or developing risks. KRIs are used to determine when it has become necessary to address emerging or developing risks and are used in risk profiles and other risk tracking methods to understand severity and likelihood levels within the organization.

While performance indicators provide insights into known risks, key risk indicators (KRIs) provide an early warning of emerging risks that have reached a threshold level of concern. KRIs are used to develop strategies to identify and manage new risks and can be identified through analysis methods such as root cause analysis and causal factors analysis of previous incidents. In addition, outside sources such as industry trends or developments, technology and research, economic indicators, and competitor actions can be helpful in developing KRIs (Lyon, Popov 2018).

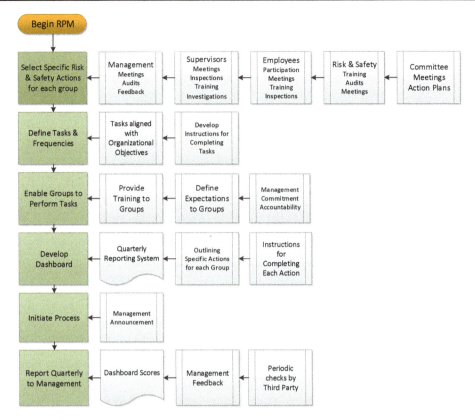

Figure 11.6
Risk Performance Measurement Process Example.

Verifying and Validating Results

ISO 31010 includes a section on verifying and validating results. It states that "where practicable, results of analysis should be verified and validated. Verification involves checking that the analysis was done correctly. Validation involves checking that the right analysis was done to achieve the required objectives. For some situations verification and validation can involve independent review processes" (ANSI/ASSP/ISO/IEC 31010-2019).

Verification is used to check and test the accuracy and consistency of the process and its results. According to Merriam-Webster online dictionary, the term *verify* is defined as the act "to establish the truth, accuracy, or reality of" something. (Merriam-Webster n.d.-a) It is an important element of monitoring and reviewing and can include checking or verifying the validity of calculations and the results produced. Verification can include comparing results or feedback with past experience, existing data, or previous input to determine accuracy.

Validation is used to determine appropriateness of the process and its results. It is defined as the act "to recognize, establish, or illustrate the worthiness or legitimacy of" something (Merriam-Webster n.d.-b). For the risk management process, validation is performed alongside verification, and should include reviewing and testing the assessment's scope, assumptions, methods, models, and data to validate conclusions.

Recording and Documenting Risk

There is an adage that says if something isn't documented, it didn't happen. This notion applies to risk management and the risk recording and documenting process. Risk management steps and their outcomes should be properly recorded in accordance with the organization's documentation policies and communicated to decision makers and appropriate stakeholders. ISO 31000 indicates that recording and reporting should communicate related actions and outcomes across the organization and provide decision makers the appropriate information.

One method of recording risk is through a risk register or risk log. A risk register is a spreadsheet type document used to record risk-related information about identified risks. Risk registers are used to communicate and track baselines and benchmarks for risks within an organization. Basic information on risks can include description, location, category, risk source, likelihood, severity, risk level, risk reduction percentage, etc. However, certain risks may be more complex and require a more description than can be accommodated in a register. For instance, risks with multiple risk sources, multiple potential outcomes, secondary or cascading effects, or multiple control failures will require more information. The risk register and residual risk levels should be updated when appropriate risk treatments are selected and implemented. Updates to the risk register may also include agreed-upon risk treatment strategies; specific actions to implement; trigger conditions, symptoms, and warning signs of a risk occurrence; budgets and schedule activities needed; contingency plans and their risk triggers; residual risks that are expected to remain after planned treatments; accepted risk levels; and secondary risks that arise as a direct outcome of implementing a risk treatment. An example of a risk register is presented in Figure 11.7.

Once risks are documented and entered into a spreadsheet or a database, they can be integrated into the organization comprehensive risk portfolio or profile. Comprehensive risk portfolios usually include a risk hierarchy organized by the organization's unit or division, and by risk type. According to COSO ERM-Risk Assessment in practice guidance, the term *risk profile* represents the entire portfolio of risks facing the enterprise. Some organizations represent this portfolio as a hierarchy, some as a collection of risks plotted on a heat map (COSO 2012). An example of a risk hierarchy is presented in Figure 11.8.

Risk Register

Case #	Location	Task	Hazard #	Hazard	Current State Risk Level	Additional Controls	Completion Date	Future State Risk Level
1	QC Lab - Weld	Plasma cutter	1.1	Electrical Shock	14	Yes	2/20/15	12
1	QC Lab - Weld	Plasma cutter	1.2	burns	15.2	Yes	3/15/15	12
1	QC Lab - Weld	Plasma cutter	1.3	arc flash	11.2	Yes	2/20/15	9.8
1	QC Lab - Weld	Plasma cutter	1.4	noise	19	Yes	3/15/15	8.4
1	QC Lab - Weld	Plasma cutter	1.5	fire	14	Yes	3/15/15	12
1	QC Lab - Weld	Plasma cutter	1.6	dust	11.2	Yes	3/15/15	9.6
2	QC Lab - Weld	Weld Destruct	2.1	ergo-strains	14	Yes	4/15/15	14
2	QC Lab - Weld	Weld Destruct	2.2	vibration	19	Yes	4/15/15	4.8
2	QC Lab - Weld	Weld Destruct	2.3	noise	11.2	Yes	4/15/15	10.8
2	QC Lab - Weld	Weld Destruct	2.4	struck by	15.2	Yes	2/20/15	14.4
2	QC Lab - Weld	Weld Destruct	2.5	dust	16	Yes	4/15/15	8.4
2	QC Lab - Weld	Weld Destruct	2.6	struck against	11.4	Yes	3/15/15	6.3
2	QC Lab - Weld	Weld Destruct	2.7	falls same level	16	Yes	3/15/15	11.2
3	Finishing	Wash Station	3.1	hot liquid	9	Yes	4/15/15	6.3
3	Finishing	Wash Station	3.2	struck against	14.25	Yes	4/15/15	0.2
3	Finishing	Wash Station	3.3	chem-corrosive	11.2	Yes	4/15/15	4.2
3	Finishing	Wash Station	3.4	hot surfaces	14.25	Yes	4/15/15	2.1
3	Finishing	Wash Station	3.5	mechanical	9.6	Yes	3/15/15	4.8
3	Finishing	Wash Station	3.6	ergo-strains	11.2	Yes	4/15/15	0.2

Figure 11.7
Risk Register Example.

ISO Guide 73 defines *risk profile* as a "description of any set of risks. The set of risks can contain those that relate to the whole organization, part of the organization, or as otherwise defined" (ISO Guide 73/ANSI/ASSP Z690.1-2011).

Reporting Risk

Reporting risk-related information is critical to an organization's governance and should be designed to improve overall risk communications and understanding of risks. ISO Guide 73 defines risk reporting as a "form of communication intended to inform particular internal or external stakeholders by providing information regarding the current state of risk and its management" (ISO Guide 73/ANSI/ASSP Z690.1-2011).

When designing risk reporting systems, there are several key factors to consider. First, defining the audience and their needs is critical. Internal decision makers and stakeholders will require specific risk-based information presented in a way that is useful to them. Dashboards, risk matrices, heat maps, and key performance metrics are helpful in communicating risk performance at a glance and may be most useful to the organization's senior management and decision makers. Striped bow tie diagrams can be useful in presenting more complex risk scenarios.

Of course, more detailed, supporting data should be available to decision makers and stakeholders as needed. For external stakeholders, risk reporting should be limited to specific information that is required (regulatory agencies for instance) or risk information that affects their objectives (suppliers, customers, partners, etc.) and that is appropriate to share. Other considerations include the reporting methods used, the expected (budgeted) costs of reporting, and frequency and timing of reports.

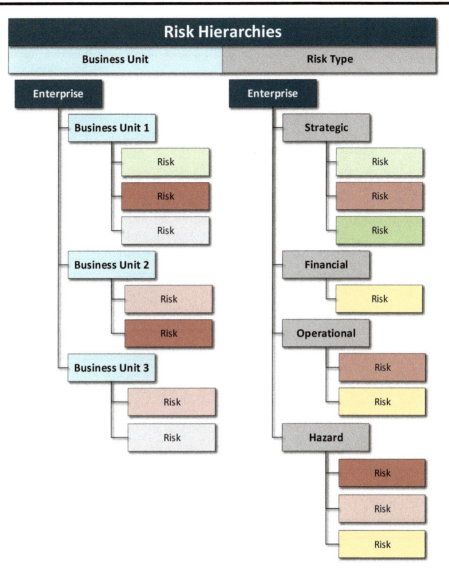

Figure 11.8
Example of a Risk Hierarchy.

Risk Assessment Information

A key component in risk communication is the documenting and communicating of risk assessments and their results to decision makers and stakeholders. This should include the names, titles, and qualifications of the risk assessment team; the methods employed; the risk sources identified and risks assessed; the risk treatments implemented; and follow-up actions taken. One method that could be used to communicate risk assessment information and assign responsibilities is the RACI chart.

RACI is an acronym derived from the four key responsibilities most typically used: Responsible, Accountable, Consulted, and Informed. RACI charts help describe the participation by various roles in completing tasks, projects, or business process.

> **RACI Example:** The following example is taken from the OSHA publication OSHA3902, Small Entity Compliance Guide for the Respirable Crystalline Silica Standard for Construction. Using this example of two projects/activities, a Responsibility Assignment Matrix – RACI chart is presented in Figure 11.9. The chart can be used for clarifying and defining roles and responsibilities in cross-functional projects and processes. Figures 11.10 and 11.11 show the projects/activities listed in the RACI chart (Figure 11.9). The EHS manager will be responsible for developing plans and control measures to protect the operators from silica dust, the risk manager will be accountable, and the CEO will be informed. Figure 11.12 provides a second matrix with general task assignments for responsible parties.

Number	Project Name	CEO	Risk Manager	Project Champion	EHS manager	Business analyst	Production manager	Engineer	Employees Representative
1	Stationary masonry saw - Dust Suppression	I	A	R	R	C	C	C	I
2	Handheld power saw for cutting fber-cement board (with BD of 8 inches or less) - Dust Collection	I	A	R	R	C	A	C	I

Responsible (R), Accountable (A), Consulted (C), and Informed (I). - Use the drop down menu to select responsibility.

Figure 11.9
RACI Chart example.

Figure 11.10
RACI # 1- Stationary Masonry Saw—Dust Suppression from www.osha.gov/Publications/OSHA3902.pdf.

Figure 11.11
RACI #2—Handheld Power Saw.

Tasks	Roles		
	Operations Engineer	OSH Manager	Project Manager
Prepare design	R	C	I
Prepare Operating Procedures	R	C	C
Prepare H&S plan	C	R	I
Manage Project	I	C	A

Responsible (R), Accountable (A), Consulted (C), and Informed (I)

Figure 11.12
Roles/Tasks Responsibility Assignment Matrix example.

Ongoing monitoring and reporting of risk-related actions should be traceable and track progress. Table 11.1 provides a brief summary of risk reporting and communicating methods that are available.

Table 11.1. Methods used to Monitor and Report Risk.

Method	Description
Risk Matrix	Compares individual risks by selecting a consequence likelihood pair and displaying them on a matrix with consequence on one axis and likelihood on the other. Matrices can be used to report information about the magnitude of risks from different sources to monitor risk performance.
Risk Register	A means of recording information about risks and tracking actions.
S Curves	A means of displaying the relationship between consequences and their likelihood plotted as a cumulative distribution function (S curve).
Bow Tie Diagram	A diagrammatic way of describing the multiple pathways from risk sources to outcomes and reviewing controls. It can be used where risks require a more complex description than can be accommodated in a traditional risk register. For example, a description might need to include multiple sources of risk leading to a single event, multiple possible outcomes from a single event or source, knock on effects, and potential control failures.
Key Performance Indicators	Key performance indicators (KPIs) are considered business metrics used to assess critical performance aspects that help an organization assess progress towards declared goals.
Key Risk Indicators	Key risk indicators (KRIs) are measures that tend to predict changes in risk or development of new emerging risks.
Risk Performance Measurement	A measurement system used to monitor and measure risk performance within an organization. Assigned duties or actions for stakeholders are measured on a periodic basis and reported to management.

Summary

The ultimate purpose of monitoring, reviewing, recording, and reporting risk information is to provide the necessary risk-based information to decision-makers and stakeholders to properly manage risk. Risk-related documents and information provide a record and justification for decisions made and preserve the results of risk management efforts for future use and reference. They also allow for the verification of results and provide an audit trail (Lyon, Popov 2018).

The risk management process is a continual improvement cycle that is designed to help an organization create and protect value. It requires the integration of the risk management framework and process into the organization's management system, and it must have top management leadership and stakeholder involvement. As organizations mature and improve their ability to identify, analyze, evaluate, and treat risks, they will become more competitive and successful in the achievement of their business objectives.

Review Questions

1. Identify the three process steps that follow risk treatment in the ISO 31000 risk management process. Briefly describe each of these three steps.
2. Compare the similarities of the risk management process with the Plan-Do-Check-Act continual improvement process cycle.
3. Explain the differences between monitoring and reviewing.
4. Describe what is meant by a key performance indicator (KPI). Provide five examples of KPIs.
5. Describe what is meant by a key risk indicator (KRI). Provide examples of KRIs.
6. Explain the differences between verifying and validating.
7. Identify several key factors to consider when designing risk reporting systems.
8. List and briefly describe five methods used to monitor and report risk.

References

ANSI/ASIS/RIMS RA.1-2015. 2015. *Risk Assessment*. Alexandria, VA: ASIS International and The Risk and Insurance Management Society, Inc.

ANSI/ASSP Z10.0-2019. 2019. *Occupational Health and Safety Management Systems*. Park Ridge, IL: American Society of Safety Professionals, 2019.

ANSI/ASSP Z690.1-2011. 2011. *Vocabulary for Risk Management*. Park Ridge, IL: American Society of Safety Professionals.

ANSI/ASSP/ISO 31000-2018. 2018. *Risk Management – Guidelines*. Park Ridge, IL: American Society of Safety Professionals.

ANSI/ASSP/ISO 45001-2018. 2018. *Occupational Health and Safety Management Systems – Requirements with Guidance for Use*. Park Ridge, IL: American Society of Safety Professionals.

ANSI/ASSP/ISO/IEC 31010-2019. 2019. *Risk Management – Risk Assessment Techniques*. Park Ridge, IL: American Society of Safety Professionals.

COSO. *ERM-Risk Assessment in Practice Guidance*. 2012. www.coso.org/Documents/COSO-ERM-Risk-Assessment-in-Practice-Thought-Paper-October-2012.pdf.

Lyon, Bruce K., and Georgi Popov. 2018. *Risk Management Tools for Safety Professionals.* Park Ridge, IL: American Society of Safety Professionals.

Merriam-Webster.com. n.d.-a. "Verify." Accessed October 13, 2020. www.merriam-webster.com/dictionary/verify.

Merriam-Webster.com. n.d.-b. "Validate." Accessed October 13, 2020. www.merriam-webster.com/dictionary/validate.

OSHA. 2017. *Small Entity Compliance Guide for the Respirable Crystalline Silica Standard for Construction.* Publication OSHA 3902-07R 2017. Washington, DC: OSHA.

CHAPTER 12
Communicating Risk

Introduction
The process of communication is a two-way exchange of sending and receiving information to reach a mutual understanding among the affected parties. This requires active listening by each party to not only hear or read the information, but to comprehend its intended meaning. The verification that the message has been properly understood requires a further exchange among the sender and receiver(s) to clarify and verify the meaning of information sent, and to acknowledge it has been received and understood. This is of the upmost importance when it involves risk and its uncertainty of effects on objectives.

Risk Communication
Risk assessment, without effective communication does not enable an organization to successfully achieve its objectives. Risk communication and consultation are required to understand and reduce uncertainty and ultimately manage risks. Through consistent and effective risk communications, decision makers are kept better informed and will be more confident in decisions they make (Lyon, Popov 2017). Successful risk assessment depends on effective communication with stakeholders before, during, and after the process, otherwise the result will be a less-effective assessment. A quality risk assessment involves stakeholders as well as

---

Interactive tools and supplemental materials are available at assp.org/ermtools.

customers, investors, partners, suppliers, and vendors throughout the process and seeks their input (Lyon, Hollcroft 2012).

"Communication and Consultation" is a major provision in the ISO 31000 standard. It states that "communication seeks to promote awareness and understanding of risk, whereas consultation involves obtaining feedback and information to support decision-making" (ISO 31000-2018). These terms are defined in ISO Guide 73, *Risk Management – Vocabulary,* as follows:

> Communication and Consultation. Continual and iterative processes that an organization conducts to provide, share, or obtain information, and to engage in dialogue with stakeholders (3.2.1.1) regarding the management of risk. NOTE 1: The information can relate to the existence, nature, form, likelihood (3.6.1.1), significance, evaluation, acceptability and treatment of the management of risk. NOTE 2: Consultation is a two-way process of informed communication between an organization and its stakeholders on an issue prior to making a decision or determining a direction on that issue. Consultation is a process which impacts on a decision through influence rather than power; and an input to decision making, not joint decision making (ISO Guide 73/ANSI/ASSP Z690.1-2011).

Risk communication can be described as the exchange of timely information and opinions relevant to risk and related factors with internal stakeholders (decision makers, risk assessors, risk managers, management, affected parties, etc.) and external stakeholders (suppliers, contractors, investors, local community, regulatory agencies, etc.). The fundamental purpose of risk communication and consultation is to facilitate a higher degree of understanding of the nature of the risk among affected stakeholders so that risk can be effectively managed to an acceptable level. Figure 12.1 illustrates the risk management process and communication techniques.

Where communications are ineffective or inconsistent, problems are likely (Lyon, Popov 2017). Incidents where communications have failed have often led to unwanted and sometimes severe consequences. Investigators determined that NASA's space shuttle Columbia explosion on February 1, 2003, which claimed seven lives, was partially due to a lack of effective communication of critical safety information. They concluded that organizational causes, including lack of communication, contributed to the incident.

> Cultural traits and organizational practices detrimental to safety were allowed to develop, including: reliance on past success as a substitute for sound engineering practices . . . organizational barriers that prevented effective communication of critical safety information and stifled

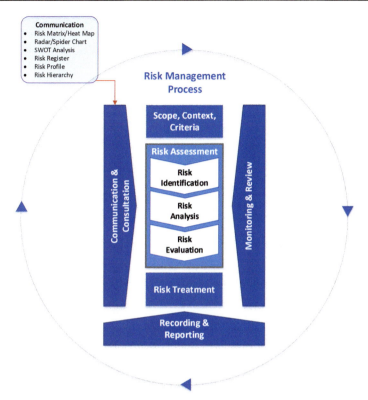

Figure 12.1
Risk Management Process and Communication Techniques.

professional differences of opinion; lack of integrated management across program elements; and the evolution of an informal chain of command and decision-making processes that operated outside the organization's rules (CAIB 2003, p. 9).

> **Examples of Communication Breakdown**
> Many catastrophic events can be linked to breakdowns in communication as a contributing factor to its cause, or as an escalating factor. Some of these include:
>
> - Texas City Refinery explosion;
> - Toyota Worldwide vehicle recall;
> - Hurricane Katrina;
> - Three Mile Island incident;
> - multiple medical malpractice deaths;

- Deepwater Horizon oil spill;
- aircraft disasters;
- Bhopal pesticide plant explosion;
- space shuttle Challenger and Columbia explosions. (Abkowitz 2008)

The breakdown or failure of communication is a common cause or contributing factor associated with disasters, severe incidents, and emergencies. In addition, the impact of disasters can be intensified if there is not adequate communication in mitigating and managing risk.

Communication Process

In addition to ISO 31000, other national and international standards on risk and safety management systems include provisions for establishing effective communication processes including ANSI/ASIS/RIMS RA.1, ISO 22301, ISO 45001, ANSI/ASSP Z10.0, and the OSHA Voluntary Protection Program.

The ISO 45001 OH&S management systems standard requires an organization to "establish, implement, and maintain the process(es) needed for the internal and external communications relevant to the OH&S management system." Communication processes should include determining what information is to be communicated, when it should be communicated, those with whom to communicate and methods of communication. In addition, communication processes should consider legal and regulatory requirements, and be consistent with the organization's other communication practices and policies. As part of the communication process, document retention policies should be followed (ANSI/ASSP/ISO 45001-2018).

Similar to 45001, ANSI Z10.0 Section 7.3, Awareness and Communication, requires an organization to "establish a process to determine what, when, to whom and how OHS information will be communicated both internally and externally" (ANSI/ASSP Z10.0-2019). Z10.0 also outlines considerations for legal requirements; diversity, cultural and language aspects; response to communications; consistency with other information systems; and specific information needs. Document control processes (Section 7.4) are required to create and maintain records related to the OHS management system. These same communication and document control processes should be integrated with the risk management process.

Communicating Risk-related Information

Throughout the risk management process, effective communication and consultation is required with internal and external stakeholders. An understanding of the nature of the risk and the reasons behind risk management decisions are necessary for stakeholders. To improve communication, the stakeholders and their background must be considered. Globally, stakeholders will have various cultural backgrounds, values, assumptions, and perspectives that affect their perceptions of a risk. Stakeholder perceptions will likely influence their judgments and decision-making regarding the risk. Some cultures are more reserved and less likely to share information about risks than others. The culture, interests, and perceptions of internal and external stakeholders must be considered when constructing the risk communication and management process.

Specifically, risk communications should seek to provide timely, relevant, and effective information to the appropriate stakeholder(s) and decision makers. Communication delivery and methods should be consistent, and when appropriate it should involve stakeholders to improve ownership, trust, and confidence in the process. Figure 12.2 outlines some key design criteria for effective communication systems.

Figure 12.2
Risk Communication Systems Design Criteria.

Risk communication systems that document and communicate the steps of the risk management process should be put in place. These systems should ensure documents align with the organization's documentation control procedures and are used in on-going communications with management. The extent of documentation will depend upon the purpose and use of the document. Considerations for risk related records include its purpose, objectives, and scope; description; summary of the external and internal context; how it relates to the situation, system, or circumstances being assessed; risk criteria; limitations and assumptions; assessment method; risk analysis results and their evaluation; discussion of results; conclusions and recommendations (Lyon, Popov 2018).

Risk-related information that is necessary in communicating risk can be grouped into four categories. These categories are (1) the nature of the risk, (2) the potential benefits and costs, (3) information on uncertainty, and (4) the risk management options are shared and exchanged with various stakeholders during the process. These four categories of risk-related information are illustrated in Figure 12.3.

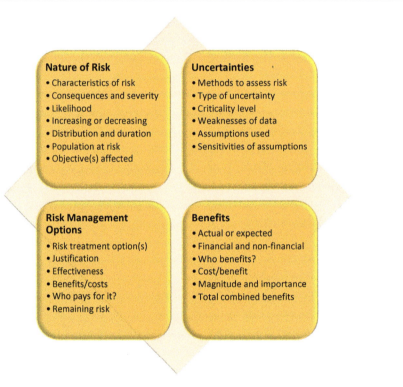

Figure 12.3
Risk-related Information.

Nature of Risk

Characteristics of the risk source
Information regarding the risk source type, its description, triggers, or causes for exposure.

Type of consequence(s)
Descriptions of the types of potential consequences that would result from the risk and their effect on the organization.

Severity of Risk
Estimated worst credible case and the degree or magnitude of harm that could credibly occur from exposure to the risk source.

Urgency or Criticality
Degree of concern in relationship with other risks and the level of action required. May require accelerating process or escalating decision to top management.

Trending of the Risk
Information on the trajectory of the risk over a period of time and whether the risk is increasing or decreasing.

Likelihood of Occurrence
Information on how often the exposure or event may occur within the organization, including a determination or estimation of its probability or likelihood.

Exposure Distribution and Duration
Information on the extent of the exposure when it occurs and how many parties or assets it may affect. This may include the time period the exposure is expected to last when exposure occurs, and the number exposed.

Significant Risk
The determined level where the risk is considered unacceptable by the organization based on their risk criteria and acceptable risk level or as low as reasonably practicable (ALARP).

Nature and Size of the Population at Risk
Information on the internal and external stakeholders that are potentially exposed to the risk and a determination of the risk levels to each.

Greatest Risk
Information on those parties at greatest risk to the potential exposure, including a quantitative, semi-quantitative, or qualitative estimation of the risk level.

Uncertainties

Risk Assessment Methods
Information on the risk assessment process used, including establishment of context, development of risk assessor(s) or team, and techniques used for risk assessment (*i.e.,* risk identification, analysis, and evaluation methods).

Types of Uncertainties
The type of uncertainties such as lack of knowledge or lack of predictability, and the degree of importance to the organization should be determined and communicated to stakeholders in order to prioritize resources and manage uncertainties.

Weaknesses of Data

Any weaknesses in the data used to assess risk should be acknowledged by decision makers and shared as appropriate with affected stakeholders. Informing those responsible for managing risks that there are potential uncertainties in the data allows for a more cautious approach.

Assumptions

Assumptions made and the reasons for those assumptions should be communicated, as appropriate, to affected stakeholders. As the risk management process unfolds, these assumptions may change. New or better data should be communicated to stakeholders as it becomes available.

Sensitivity

Information on assumptions with a sensitivity to change should be communicated.

Effect of Changes

When changes in the estimates are planned to occur, communication of the anticipated effects of those changes should be provided to affected stakeholders.

Risk Management Options

Risk management and treatment options—A review of available options for treatment and management of risks should be provided to decision makers and affected stakeholders.

Selected Treatments

Prior to implementation, the selected risk reduction controls or actions and their reasons for selection should be properly communicated to affected stakeholders.

Justification

In addition to the reason for selection, some degree of justification for the reasoning—including financial and non-financial benefits, costs, or other supporting data—should be made available.

Effectiveness

As part of the justification, an estimate of the selected treatment's effectiveness based on experience, industry practices, historical data, or other supporting data should be made and communicated.

Benefits

For each selected risk management option, a description of the specific anticipated benefits—including those that are financial and those that are non-financial (*i.e.,* reputational, ethical, humanitarian, legal, cultural, etc.)—and an estimate of the amount or degree of each benefit to be expected should be communicated to stakeholders and decision makers.

Costs
Information regarding the party or department that will be funding the measure as well as the initial and any ongoing costs of implementing and maintaining the selected control option should be determined and communicated to stakeholders and decision makers.

Residual Risk
As part of the risk assessment process, an estimation of the residual risk after the selected option is put into place should be determined and communicated.

Benefits of Treating the Risk
Actual or Expected Benefits
Following implementation of the selected option, the recognized and anticipated benefits from the implementation should be communicated with affected stakeholders.

Beneficiaries
Any benefits derived by those who are directly or indirectly affected, such as the organization or community, should be determined and communicated to further justify such implementations.

Cost-Benefit
Tools, such as cost-benefit analysis and return on investment, can be used to quantify the benefits and overall costs so that decision makers can evaluate justification and further actions.

Magnitude and importance
Information on the various benefits derived from the selected option and the level of impact each benefit creates should be provided to stakeholders and decision makers.

Total benefits
The combined sum of benefits from the selected option should be determined or estimated and communicated to stakeholders and decision makers. Financial benefits can more easily be totaled, while non-financial benefits require some qualification and explanation.

Summary
Risk assessment, by itself, does not achieve its objectives. Risk communication is required to reduce uncertainty and manage operational risks. Assessing risks within an organization enables decision-makers to properly manage risks and make plausible decisions. (Lyon, Popov 2017).

"Communication and Consultation" is a major provision in the ISO 31000 standard. Risk communication can be described as the exchange of timely information and opinions relevant to risk and related factors with internal stakeholders (decision makers, risk assessors, risk managers, management, affected parties, etc.) and external stakeholders (suppliers, contractors, investors, local community, regulatory agencies, etc.). The fundamental purpose of risk communication and consultation is to facilitate a higher degree of understanding of the nature of the risk among affected stakeholders so that risk can be effectively managed to an acceptable level.

Review Questions

1. Describe why communication and consultation are important in the management of risk.
2. Identify key design criteria for effective communication systems.
3. Identify and describe the four risk information categories.
4. For each risk information category, list and describe five examples of each.

References

Abkowitz, M.D. 2008. *Operational Risk Management: A Case Study Approach to Effective Planning and Response.* Hoboken, NJ: John Wiley & Sons.

ANSI/ASIS/RIMS RA.1-2015. 2015. *Risk Assessment.* Alexandria, VA: ASIS International and The Risk and Insurance Management Society, Inc.

ANSI/ASSP Z10.0-2019. 2019. *Occupational Health and Safety Management Systems.* Park Ridge, IL: American Society of Safety Professionals.

ANSI/ASSP Z690.1-2011. 2011. *Vocabulary for Risk Management.* Des Plaines, IL: American Society of Safety Professionals.

ANSI/ASSP/ISO 31000-2018. 2018. *Risk Management – Guidelines.* Park Ridge, IL: American Society of Safety Professionals.

ANSI/ASSP/ISO 45001-2018. 2018. *Occupational Health and Safety Management Systems – Requirements with Guidance for Use.* Park Ridge, IL: American Society of Safety Professionals, 2018.

ANSI/ASSP/ISO/IEC 31010-2019. 2019. *Risk Management – Risk Assessment Techniques.* Park Ridge, IL: American Society of Safety Professionals.

Columbia Accident Investigation Board (CAIB). 2003. Columbia accident investigation board report (Vol.1). Washington, DC: NASA. www.nasa.gov/columbia/home/CAIB_Vol 1.

Lyon, Bruce K., and Bruce Hollcroft. 2012. "Risk Assessments: Top 10 Pitfalls & Tips for Improvement." *Professional Safety,* December 2012, 28–34.

Lyon, Bruce K., and Georgi Popov. 2017. "Communicating & Managing Risk: The Key Result of Risk Assessment." *Professional Safety,* November 2017, 35–44.

Lyon, Bruce K., and Georgi Popov. 2018. *Risk Management Tools for Safety Professionals.* Park Ridge, IL: American Society of Safety Professionals.

CHAPTER 13
Practical Applications of Risk Management Methods

Introduction

The purpose of this chapter is to demonstrate how risk management principles and methods can be put into practice. The chapter contains a number of case studies with examples of practical applications of various risk management methods that help demonstrate their use. The reader is encouraged to modify and combine these and other methods to properly address risks in their work environments.

The chapter is broken up into sections according to the risk management process steps including: Section 1—Establishing Context; Section 2—Identifying Risk; Section 3—Analyzing Risk; Section 4—Evaluating Risk; Section 5—Treating Risk; Section 6—Monitoring and Reporting Risk; and Section 7—Communicating and Consulting.

While the methods shown in Figure 13.1 are linked to specific steps in the risk management process, most if not all are used in various stages of the risk management process with a great deal of overlap as demonstrated in the following sections and case studies.

Interactive tools and supplemental materials are available at assp.org/ermtools.

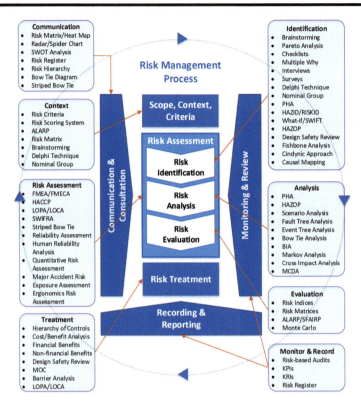

Figure 13.1
Risk Management Process and Associated Methods, Expanded from ANSI/ASSP/ISO 31000.

Risk is fluid and therefore, its management must be fluid and ongoing. These examples are designed to provide readers with ideas on how some methods can be applied throughout the risk management process, while acknowledging that there are many different ways of identifying, analyzing, assessing, and treating risk.

Section 1—Establishing Context

In the planning process before the risk assessment can be conducted, the context must be established. There are many considerations necessary when setting the parameters of a risk assessment including its scope, purpose, variables, limitations, risk criteria, resources, and stakeholders, among other elements. As discussed in Chapter 4, Planning the Assessment, various methods can be used to establish the context and plan the assessment. Some of these methods such as selecting risk criteria, risk assessment matrices, and defining acceptable risk and risk action levels are covered in Chapter 4. Here, several additional examples of methods including SWOT Analysis, Radar/Spider charts, and Pareto Analysis are presented.

Pareto Analysis

Pareto analysis or Pareto charting is a method used to identify and evaluate factors that contribute to the greatest frequency of unwanted outcomes displayed in a diagram or chart. It is a data analysis tool which is based on Italian economist Vilfredo Pareto's 1906 observation that 80% of the land in Italy was owned by 20% of the population (Lavinsky 2014).

The Pareto principle states that 80% of the impact of the problem will show up in 20% of the causes and is referred to as the "vital few" concept. It is most useful as a method to analyze and select among multiple competing outcomes or options at an operational level. Specifically, it is used to prioritize elements or areas of focus when establishing the context and planning the risk assessment. For example, risk professionals may use Pareto Analysis to screen, analyze, and select which hazards cause the costliest losses or which operational issues are most significant and in need of assessment and treatment.

Pareto analysis is typically presented as a bar chart (as shown in Figure 13.2) in which the horizontal axis represents categories of interest and the vertical axis represents a numerical factor such as frequency, monetary value, or another performance indicator (*e.g.,* injuries, illnesses, types of accidents, operations, parts, time, etc.) A cumulative percentage line is sometimes added to aid visualization. The basic steps in a Pareto analysis are presented in the following steps:

1. Define Scope—First, the scope of the concern must be clearly defined and understood. Typically, this is an operational type issue that has multiple causes, options, or categories.
2. Identify Categories—Based on the scope, the data is reviewed to identify the causes, categories, or problems that are believed to create the concern. This may require some research and data review to identify potential categories of interest. Such categories may be types of hazards that lead to large losses identified in workers' compensation loss runs or defect types in a product that lead to product recalls or product liability claims.
3. Identify Numerical Values—For each category or cause of interest, a numerical value is identified from the available data. Numerical values can be frequencies of occurrence, dollar amounts of losses, or percentages of an occurrence or amounts. For example, numerical values may represent the frequency that a problem or category occurs; the direct dollar costs paid by the workers' compensation insurance carrier for claims tied to specific hazard causes; or the percentage of product failures related to specific product defects.
4. Create Chart—Once the categories and their numerical values are determined, they are entered into a spreadsheet and sorted in descending order to create a column chart or histogram, as shown in Table 13.2. The cumulative sum of the

categories can be added to a third column in descending order, and percentages in a fourth column.

5. Create Line Graph—Using the sorted data from the column chart, a line graph is generated from the cumulative percentage, which provides a visual comparison of the categories and their significance and allows for prioritization of treatment.
6. Take Action—Using the findings of the Pareto analysis, prioritized treatment or corrective action can be taken to address the greatest problems first, making better use of available resources.

Top 10 Causes and Direct Costs of the Workplace Injuries		
Causes	Direct Costs $	Cumulative %
Back injuries due to overexertion	200000	52.15123859
Strain from pushing and pulling	107000	80.05215124
Slips, trips and falls	25000	86.57105606
Struck by object or equipment	20000	91.78617992
Other exertions	10000	94.39374185
Minor cuts	8000	96.4797914
Slip or trip without fall	5000	97.78357236
Struck against object or equipment	4000	98.82659713
Repetitive motions—micro-tasks	3500	99.73924381
Paper cuts	1000	100

Figure 13.2
Pareto Chart Example.

In the example presented in Figure 13.2, an auto supply company analyzed the types of injuries and the associated average cost per injury type. The first two causes (back injuries from overexertion, and strains from pushing and pulling) contribute to 80% of the direct costs of the workplace injuries. In Section 6 of this chapter, the readers will notice how this company was able pinpoint where they have concentrated their efforts to reduce their hazard, operational, financial, and strategic risks.

Radar/Spider Charts

A radar chart or spider chart is a graphical method of displaying multiple variates of data in a two-dimensional chart with three or more quantitative variables represented on axes (or spokes) starting from the center point and radiating outward much like a spider web. Each spoke has a graduated data length proportional to the variable for each data point and consistently proportioned across all data points. A line is drawn connecting the data values for each spoke which gives the plot a star-like appearance. Radar charts are suited for showing outliers and commonality and imbalances among chart variables.

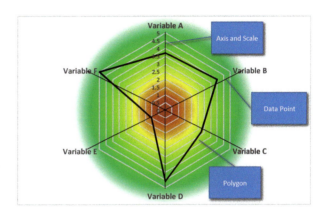

Figure 13.3
Anatomy of a Radar Chart.

As shown in Figure 13.3, each variable is provided an axis or spoke that starts from the center point and radiates outward with equal distances between each other, while maintaining the same scale between all axes. Each variable's data point value is plotted along its individual axis or spoke. Then, all the variables in a dataset are connected to form a polygon or star-shaped graph. While radar charts can be helpful, too many variables and spokes make the chart hard to read, confusing, and cluttered. Typical Radar Charts use four to ten variables for this reason.

For example, Figure 13.4 provides a Radar Chart with risk management related variables including (1) OSH Management System, (2) Quality Management, (3) Hazard Risks, (4) Operational Risks, (5) Financial Stability, and (6) Strategic Risks. Each category has data points plotted on its own axis/spoke and the data points are connected to create the star-shaped polygon graph. The OSH Management System is visually displayed as deficient in comparison with the other variables providing an indication that efforts in this area will be most appropriate.

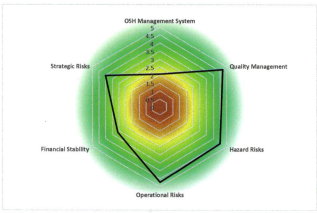

Figure 13.4
Risk Management Radar Chart Example.

SWOT Analysis

There are many methods that can be used to establish the context. One in particular is a Strengths, Weaknesses, Opportunities, and Threats analysis or SWOT analysis. SWOT analysis, sometimes referred to as a SWOT matrix, is a strategic planning method used to help an organization identify its strengths, weaknesses, opportunities, and threats related to achieving business objectives or project planning. Strengths and weakness are generally internal, while opportunities and threats typically come from the external environment.

Strengths

Strengths are considered abilities that empower the organization to accomplish its objectives. They are the beneficial characteristics of the organization and may include variables such as:

- Human capital
- Innovation
- HSE (Health, Safety, and Environmental) excellence compared to competition
- Products
- Services
- Quality
- Financial capital
- Profitability

Weaknesses

Weaknesses are qualities that may prevent the achievement of objectives. They are often associated with negative effects on the organizational performance and may include such variables as:

- Waste of materials and time
- Poor design
- Inefficient operations
- High turnover rate
- Negative debt to income ratio
- High incidence rate
- High Experience Modification Rate (EMR greater than 1.00)

Opportunities

Opportunities represent the chances to benefit from an external environmental condition. Organizations can benefit from opportunities identified early in the process to help them make more carefully calculated risks to achieve the objectives. Opportunities variables may include:

- Increased demand for product or services
- New innovative products
- Favorable currency exchange rate (for global organizations)
- New regulations
- Improved reputation
- Market conditions

Threats

Threats represent elements associated with external environmental conditions that may endanger the organization. In some cases, certain threats can't be controlled, only recognized. Threats variables may include:

- New competitors
- Financial instability
- Regulations
- Liabilities
- Tariffs imposed on major suppliers
- Inability to hire talented employees
- Unstable environment or political climate

Applications

SWOT analysis is used to specify the business objectives and to identify the internal and external factors that are favorable and unfavorable to achieving those objectives. SWOT analysis is useful in decision-making situations where the objective is clear and well-defined. It may also be used in creating a recommendation during a viability study/survey.

Users of a SWOT analysis often ask and answer questions to generate meaningful information for each category to make the tool useful and identify their competitive advantage.

SWOT analysis is usually presented as a 2 × 2 matrix with strengths and weakness related to internal factors, and opportunities and threats to external factors as shown in Figure 13.5. Brainstorming sessions can be used to generate ideas, and the nominal group technique used to identify consensus on the most significant elements to populate the quadrants.

Furthermore, the categories can be subdivided into risk categories with risk ratings from 1 to 5 as shown in Figure 13.6. Note that for Strengths and Opportunities a rating of 5 is the most beneficial outcome, while for Weaknesses and Threats, the highest value is the most negative outcome. These categories/rankings are somewhat subjective; however, they provide a way to visualize the results. An example is provided in Figure 13.7.

In this example, the organization has a patent that expires in two years and ships most of the product to another country. The organization has difficulties hiring and retaining talented employees due to significant number of shoulders, neck,

	SWOT Analysis				
	Beneficial	Rate	Negative		Rate
Internal	Strengths 1 2 3		Weaknesses 1 2 3		
External	Opportunities 1 2 3		Threats 1 2 3		5.00

Figure 13.5
SWOT.

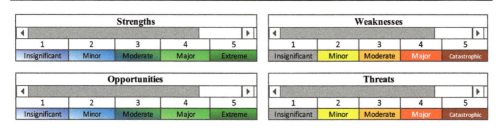

Figure 13.6
SWOT Category Ratings.

Figure 13.7
Cardboard Boxes Operation.

and back injuries/disorders. By the time the packaging employees are trained and productive, they complain about shoulder and back pain. Due to low unemployment rate in the area, HR informed upper level management that they have to increase the hourly rate by $3 per hour. However, due to recently imposed tariffs by the receiving country, ABC Supply cannot afford to increase the hourly rate. In addition, the US dollar declined in value relative to the other currency. That creates additional financial pressure.

Fortunately, ABCs Research and Development department created a new formulation that will reduce the size of the individual packages and increase productivity. The new product will increase crops yield by 15%. No such product exists on the market. In addition, our engineering department in collaboration with the risk manager had developed a plan to completely redesign the current operation. It is estimated that the new operation will reduce the MSDs by 75%.

A SWOT analysis can be completed for this situation. First the top two or three benefits or negative effects for each category are selected and entered into the spreadsheet. Each SWOT element identified is rated on the 1–5 scales presented in Figure 13.8. The ratings are automatically averaged for each category.

Furthermore, the authors developed a simple four-variable radar chart based on the SWOT analysis. The average rate for each category is transferred to the radar chart. The radar chart in Figure 13.9 is a good visual representation of the SWOT analysis results.

230 | Assessing and Managing Risk: An ERM Perspective

	SWOT Analysis			
	Beneficial	Rate	**Negative**	Rate
Internal	Strengths 1 R&D department 2 New product	4 5 4.50	Weaknesses 1 Number of MSDs 2 Financial instability 3 Expiring patent	4 4 2 3.33
External	Opportunities 1 Automate operation 2 Improve productivity 3 Reduce MSD risk by 75%	4 3 3 3.33	Threats 1 Currency rate 2 Tariffs 3 Turnover rate	4 4 3 3.67

Figure 13.8
SWOT with Ratings.

SWOT Analysis Radar Chart		AVG Rate
Strengths: characteristics of the organization that give it an advantage over others.	S	4.50
Weaknesses: characteristics of the organization that place it at a disadvantage relative to others.	W	3.33
Opportunities: elements in the environment that the organization could exploit to its advantage.	O	3.33
Threats: elements in the environment that could endanger the organization.	T	3.67

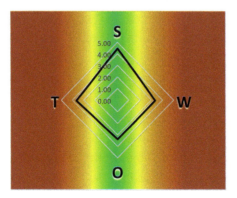

Figure 13.9
SWOT Analysis Radar Chart Example.

Section 2—Identifying Risk

The first step of risk assessment is identifying risks, their risk sources, existing controls, exposures, risk drivers, and causes or failure modes, as well as the potential consequences they could impose. There are a number of methods available including those covered in Chapter 5. In this section, several additional methods are reviewed using a case study that includes incident mapping, barrier analysis (for existing controls), change analysis, 5 Why analysis and multiple 5 Why, and a causal factor tree diagram. Also, a Trending Analysis tool used by the US Bureau of Labor Statistics (BLS) is briefly discussed.

Trending Analysis Tool

As risk management efforts continue to make progress in reducing injuries and illnesses, their remains a serious concern—the number of fatalities and serious incidents (FSI) events that occur each year. In fact, the numbers for fatalities are trending upward. Recent numbers cited by BLS indicate a total of 5,147 workers died from an occupational injury in 2017. BLS published a new interactive tool that visualizes the number of fatal work injuries by employee status (BLS n.d.). The latest available data is presented in Figure 13.10, and it shows alarming increase of fatal work injuries from 2013 to 2017.

Not surprisingly, a significant number of the fatalities are related to transportation incidents (BLS: www.bls.gov/iif/oshwc/cfoi/cfch0016.pdf). This alarming trend seems to suggest that many organizations have flaws within their management systems—in the way they plan, organize, implement, execute,

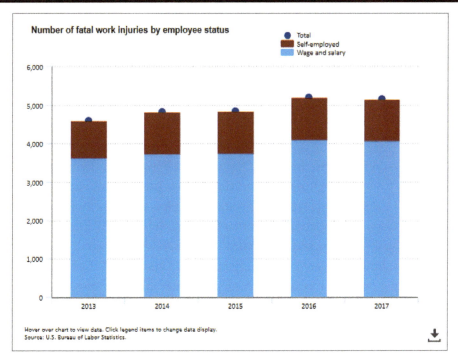

Figure 13.10
Number of Fatal Work Injuries by Employee Status (BLS n.d.)

monitor, communicate, and improve. One particular way risk professionals can help organizations improve their management systems is through more effective analyses of incidents (Lyon, Popov, and Roberts 2018). To demonstrate effective analysis of an incident, the authors would like to present the following case study.

Case Study

Drilling Rig Site Forklift Incident

At the ABC Drilling Rig Site, around 4:05 P.M. on 8/7/19 the work crew were about to "nipple up" (assemble the blowout preventer stack on the wellhead at the surface). There were three employees using an all-terrain forklift in muddy conditions to hang pipe near the catwalk. Another employee (injured party—IP) was working on a choke manifold adjacent to the forklift work approximately 15 feet away.

Figure 13.11
Forklift Operating between Pipe Rack and Manifold.

    The operation required the forklift to maneuver between the manifold unit and the pipe rack to supply employees connecting pipe on the opposite end as pictured in Figure 13.11. As the employees were connecting pipe, the (IP) employee working on the manifold was completing his work. Once completed, the IP knelt and leaned over one of the diverter lines to reach inside the manifold unit to grab a wrench he left behind as shown in the reenactment pictured in Figure 13.12. As he reached from a kneeling position, he extended his leg into the path of the moving forklift as it was backing. With the employee's leg in the direct line of the forklift tire, the forklift operator began backing up to re-position without seeing the IP. As the operator backed up, he did not know the employee was there in the path of the forklift and backed over his ankle in the soft mud (reenactment picture in Figure 13.13). The IP screamed, notifying the operator of his presence and the forklift pulled forward.

Figure 13.12
Reenactment of Injured Party Position before Incident.

Figure 13.13
Reenactment of Injured Party's Leg in Path of Forklift and the Soft Mud.

Incident Map

With the information and facts collected during the investigation, the team lays out the sequence of events and related conditions of the incident. Only events and conditions that lead to the incident are used. Four events were identified in this incident which included (1) forklift operating in congested area between pipe rack and manifold unit; (2) the injured employee was working on a manifold unit adjacent to the forklift activity; (3) the injured employee was unaware of the forklift and extended his led in the path of the forklift; (4) the forklift operator could not see

234 | Assessing and Managing Risk: An ERM Perspective

the other employee when backing up. Two conditions were identified which were (1) reduced visibility on the site, and (2) muddy conditions, which reduced the severity of the injury.

Barrier Analysis

After completing the incident map, a barrier analysis of available controls is performed. Using the color-coded legend, controls are labeled, placed in the map, and connected to the affected events and/or conditions as shown in Figure 13.14. In the case study, the barrier analysis determined:

- One new control needed (pre-job planning)
- Seven existing controls were ignored or not used including:
    - Pre-shift briefing
    - Review of the JSA
    - Pre-job walk-around inspection
    - Stop Work Authority
    - Use of a spotter
    - Use of tool belt
    - Use of high-visibility vests.
- One control failed (forklift backup alarm)

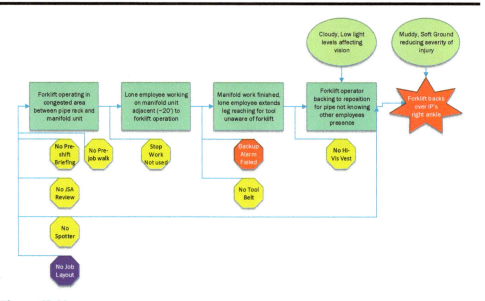

Figure 13.14
Barrier Analysis of Forklift Incident.

Change Analysis

The significant events are described and compared to what should have occurred to determine discrepancies. Using the form in Table 13.3, the most significant event from the case is described, along with existing controls, deviations that occurred causing the control to be ineffective, the underlying causal factors tied to the deviation, and actions necessary to address the underlying causes.

Table 13.3. Change Analysis of Forklift Incident.

1. Event Describe the Event	2. Controls Describe existing controls that should prevent the event	3. Deviation What happened and why were controls ineffective	4. Causal Factors Underlying Elements	5. Actions Describe needed actions to prevent future events
Forklift operator was backing near another worker	Pre-shift briefing	Site management did not hold a pre-shift briefing leading to unsafe work near forklift.	Planning. Accountability.	Implement safety performance measurement system to track safety tasks performed at sites. Measure and reward site management based on performance of duties. No tolerance for non-performance.
	Review of JSA	Site management did not require employees to review JSA.	Accountability. Employee involvement.	Safety tracking system same as above. Review JSAs for clarity, and accuracy.

Continued on next page

1. Event	2. Controls	3. Deviation	4. Causal Factors	5. Actions
Describe the Event	Describe existing controls that should prevent the event	What happened and why were controls ineffective	Underlying Elements	Describe needed actions to prevent future events
	Pre-job inspection	Site management did not require a pre-job inspection.	Planning. Accountability.	Safety tracking system same as above.
	Spotter	Site management and forklift operator did not require a spotter.	Enforcement. Accountability. Employee involvement.	Safety tracking system same as above.
	Stop Work Authority	Site management and employees did not use Stop Work Authority.	Enforcement. Accountability. Employee involvement.	Safety tracking system same as above.
	Hi-vis vest	Site management did not provide hi-vis vests.	Budgeting & resources. Accountability.	Review management's allocations for safety equipment.
	Forklift backup alarm	No PM schedule: Site management did not correct.	Maintenance. Accountability.	Include safety features for all equipment in the PM schedule. Create a priority work order for safety related repairs.

5 Why Analysis

To dig down to the underlying management system causal factors, a 5 Why Analysis can be used. In this case, a Multiple Path 5 Why Analysis was used to analyze the

Practical Applications of Risk Management Methods | 237

multiple contributing causal factors that were discovered for the event as shown in Figure 13.15.

Causal Factors Tree Diagram

The incident's causal factors are broken down and traced back to the management level elements using a causal factor "fault-tree" diagram shown in Figure 13.16. Along with the diagram, a report narrative is provided to management. The report describes the facts of the incident, the events and conditions, the performance of

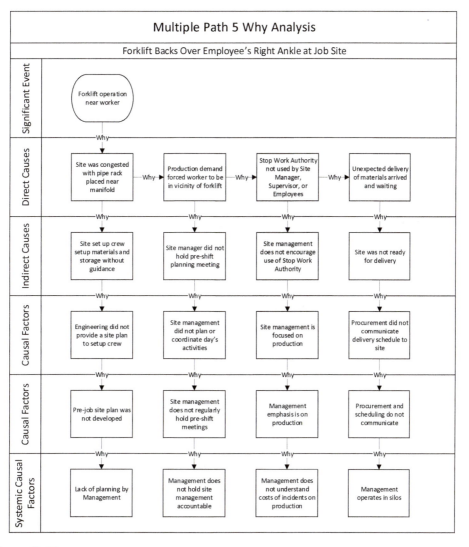

Figure 13.15
Multiple Path 5 Why Analysis of Forklift Incident.

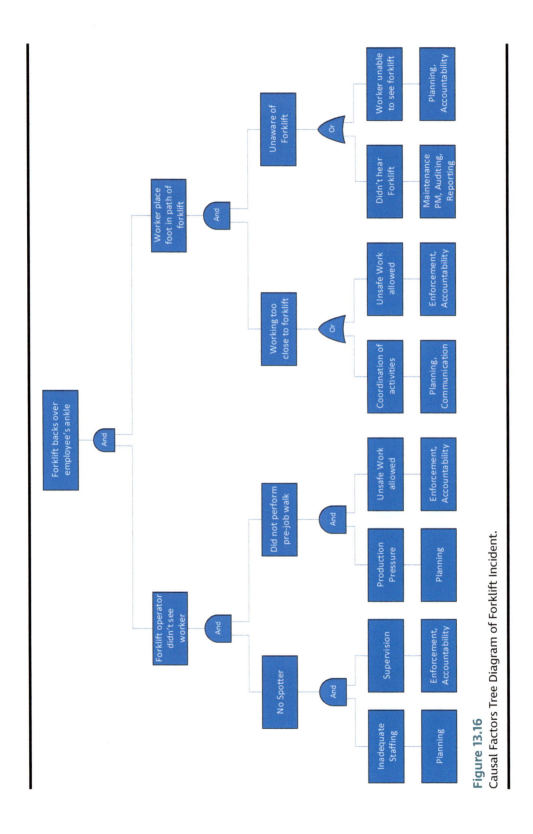

Figure 13.16
Causal Factors Tree Diagram of Forklift Incident.

control measures, and the recommended actions that will address direct causes, intermediate causes, and most importantly, the management-level causal factors.

As a result of the analysis, several key management system level causal factors were uncovered. Those included a "lack of planning," "lack of consistent enforcement of rules and lack of accountability," "lack of effective communication," and "inconsistent or ineffective preventive maintenance, auditing, and reporting."

Section 3—Analyzing Risk

The second step in risk assessment is risk analysis. As discussed in Chapter 8, risk analysis is used to estimate the risk level and is the input for the risk evaluation step. Several methods are used in risk analysis. Some methods however only analyze the hazard without estimating the risk. A brief review of the terms hazard analysis, risk analysis, and risk assessment follows.

Hazard analysis is the process to determine if a hazard-based risk source can lead to an undesired event. Hazard analysis involves analyzing identified hazards, existing controls, and potential exposures and produces a range of possible consequences and severity estimates.

Risk analysis is the "process to comprehend the nature of risk and to determine the level of risk." It includes the steps of a hazard analysis (analysis of identified hazards, existing controls, and potential exposures), and selects a consequence to determine how the event could occur, and estimates its severity (S), likelihood (L), and risk level (R). A risk analysis estimates the risk level; however, it does not determine whether the risk is acceptable.

Risk assessment is the process of identifying, analyzing, and evaluating risk. It goes beyond a risk analysis by including an "evaluation" or judgement of risk acceptability. A comparison of the "estimated risk level" with the established risk criteria is performed to determine whether the risk level is acceptable or if actions are needed to reduce the risk to an acceptable level. Figure 13.17 shows a comparison of the steps of a hazard analysis, risk analysis, and risk assessment.

Hazard Analysis Case Study

To demonstrate practical applications of hazard analysis, the following case study is presented which is based on the U.S. Chemical Safety and Hazard Investigation Board (CSB) investigation from a chemical release in October 2016.

CSB Investigation Summary

On October 21, 2016, a chemical release was caused by inadvertent mixing of incompatible chemicals at a chemical processing facility in Atchison, Kansas. The mixture of the two chemicals, sulfuric acid and sodium hypochlorite (bleach), produced a cloud containing chlorine and other compounds. The cloud impacted

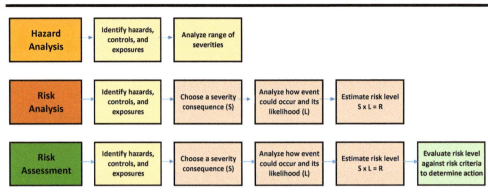

Figure 13.17
Comparison of Hazard Analysis, Risk Analysis and Risk Assessment Steps.

workers onsite and members of the public in the surrounding community. The incident occurred during a routine chemical delivery of sulfuric acid from a chemical supplier cargo tank motor vehicle (CTMV) at the chemical facility tank farm. The Atchison County Department of Emergency Management (ACDEM) ordered thousands of community members to shelter-in-place and other community members to evacuate in some areas. Over 140 individuals, including members of the public, employees of the chemical processor, and a chemical supplier employee, sought medical attention; one employee and five members of the public required hospitalization as a result of exposure to the cloud produced by the reaction.

While two specific substances were involved in this incident, the accidental mixing of many acids and bases or other incompatible chemicals during unloading operations and other activities can lead to potentially dangerous reactions. Chemical unloading operations from CTMVs may be perceived as simple compared to other processes in fixed facilities, but because these operations can involve extremely large quantities of chemicals, the consequences of an incident may be severe (CSB 2018).

As described in the CSB report, CTMV drivers rely on operators to unlock and identify the fill line designated for the chemical being transferred. Operators then show drivers the appropriate fill line. Once the equipment is unlocked, operators return to the control room. Drivers then remove the dust cap and connect their chemical discharge hose from the cargo tank to the fill line. The readers should be aware that both connections, sulfuric acid and sodium hypochlorite, looked the same and they were very close to each other. Figure 13.18 presents the connectors as-found post-incident. Sulfuric acid fill line padlock (circled) placed on angle iron. Sodium hypochlorite dust cap on ground beneath fill lines (CSB 2018).

The CSB found that the proximity of the sulfuric acid fill line to the sodium hypochlorite fill line increased the *likelihood* for an incorrect connection during

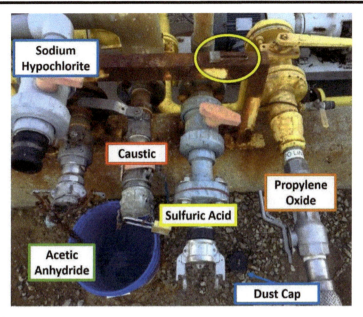

Figure 13.18
State of Connection Area.

chemical unloading. The five chemical fill lines in the Mod B chemical transfer area were all located near each other; significantly, the sodium hypochlorite fill line was about 18 inches from the sulfuric acid fill line presented in Figure 13.28 (in the next section). In addition to the incompatibility of sodium hypochlorite and sulfuric acid, the other chemicals delivered to Mod B presented reactivity hazards if mixed.

The CSB recommended physically isolating or using distance to separate fill lines, which can lower the risk of incorrect connections. Physical separation is considered a passive control and can be especially important when receiving various classes and types of chemicals (CSB 2018). CSB also recommended a combination of fill line shapes and sizes to avoid incorrect connections during deliveries presented in Figure 13.33 (next section).

What-if Analysis

"What-if" is a powerful question when used in a risk assessment approach. The concept of using the what-if question to determine potential effects is important and fundamental to assessing and controlling risk. It is essentially reasoned curiosity for the purpose of discovery to reduce uncertainty (Lyon, Popov 2020b).

The what-if analysis technique is well described in Chapters 7 and 8. Some of the benefits of using what-if analysis technique are—easy to use, employees with little risk assessment expertise can participate meaningfully, and it leads to deeper insight, especially for persons/people conducting the analysis. Some of the limitations are:

- it is only useful if you ask the right questions,
- it relies on the intuition of team members,
- it could be subjective and create greater potential for bias.

However, the what-if technique could be more difficult to translate results into convincing arguments for change. The success of the what-if risk reduction technique depends on the experience of the facilitator. The facilitator will have to consider the big picture and avoid the silo approach. It is important to expand the what-if questions beyond unsafe acts and explore the causal factors underneath. It is sometimes common for management to focus the blame on the operator or rely upon training as the primary control. What-if the inexperienced team had decided that training alone would be sufficient to avoid future mix-ups. Imagine if the company had conducted a traditional what-if analysis and asked:

- What-if it were possible to mis-match connections?
- What if an operator inadvertently connects the wrong chemical while filling tanks?
- What if the operator had noticed that lines were mixed and was able to shut down the supply line on time?
- What if only minor quantities of chlorine gas were released?

The traditional what-if analysis may look like the one presented in Figure. 13.19.

#	What if?	Consequences	Causes	Controls	Recommendations - Additional Controls
1	the operator mixes connections?	Chlorine gas generation	Lack of communication; lack of experience	Verbal communication	Better training
2	the operator is exposed to Chlorine gas?	Possible fatality	Experience and improper controls	Training	Install additional emergency supplied air packs along the egress path and provide respirators
3	local population is exposed to Chlorine gas?	Possible multiple fatalities	Task complexity or design; communication; experience	Alarm, Social Media	Add new emergency shutdown devices to complement the existing devices; upgrade monitoring and detection equipment to decrease the risk of chemical releases

Figure 13.19
Traditional What-if Analysis—Mixed Connections.

A what-if analysis of the system could prove beneficial in preventing such incidents; however, a traditional what-if analysis has certain limitations and possible deficiencies. For example, an inexperienced facilitator may lead the team to brand it as a "near miss" and recommend better procedures and additional training. A more experienced facilitator would use what-if with a risk reduction model and continue to ask what-if questions. The facilitator may consider what-if questions where the consequences from the previous what-if question would become the next what-if question exploring the potential cascading effects, much like a "5 Why Method." A question might be: What if chlorine gas was released? The consequences might be a Clean Air Act violation and EPA fine of up to $1.7 million. Such consequences of a $1.7 million fine and severely damaged reputation of the organization might be considered catastrophic. In the CSB case, both companies were indicted by the US Attorney's office for violations of the federal Clean Air Act (CAA) and, if convicted, are looking at fines of up to $1.7 million.

Transitioning to What-If Risk Analysis

A traditional What-If Hazard Analysis usually does not include a risk level estimation. However, the Structured What-if technique (SWIFT) described in the ISO 31010-2019 Risk Assessment standard suggests that the risks should be summarized as the team considers current controls in place. It also suggests that the description of the risk, its causes, consequences, and expected controls are confirmed with the team and recorded.

If the control measures are less than satisfactory, the team further considers risk treatment tasks and potential controls are defined. It is normal to use a qualitative or semi-quantitative risk assessment method to rank the actions created in terms of priority (ISO 31010). To estimate risk levels based on the possible consequences, risk professionals can add severity of consequences, likelihood, and risk level columns to the traditional what-if analysis. To demonstrate the additional risk assessment steps, a simple 5 × 4 risk assessment matrix can be used. Risk matrices can be qualitative, semi-quantitative, or both as in the example provided in Figure 13.20.

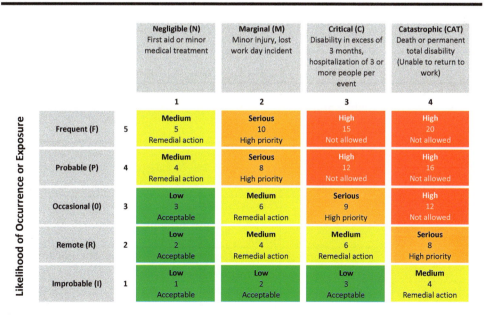

Figure 13.20
Qualitative/Semi-quantitative Risk Assessment (5 x 4) Matrix Example.

The likelihood and severity ratings are presented in Table 13.4 along with the descriptions for severity of consequences in Table 13.5. Table 13.6 provides the risk level scores and required actions for each level.

A traditional what-if analysis can be transitioned into a what-if risk assessment technique by adding risk estimation and evaluation steps. For example, beginning with what-if questions such as, "what if the operator mixes sulfuric acid and sodium hypochlorite connections?" the answer might be "chlorine gas generation." The causes may be found in the design of the filling ports and filling nozzles. If it is possible to inadvertently insert and fill the wrong chemical into a tank, an unwanted event is possible. The designers could have considered incompatible connections for these two chemicals. Imagine if the only control of preventing this event is to

Table 13.4. Qualitative and Semi-Quantitative Descriptions for Likelihood of Occurrence.

Numerical Rating	Likelihood of Occurrence (L)	%	Description
5	Frequent (Almost Certain)	90–100	Almost certain to occur. Has occurred more than once within the last 12 months. Conditions exist for it to occur.
4	Probable	70–90	Very likely to occur. Has occurred once within the last 12 months. Conditions often exist for it to occur.
3	Occasional	50–70	Likely to occur if conditions exist. Has occurred within the last 24 months. Conditions can exist for it to occur.
2	Moderate	10–50	May occur if conditions exist. Has occurred within the last 36 months. Conditions sometimes exist for it to occur.
1	Unlikely	1–10	Unlikely to occur. Has not occurred within last 5 years. Conditions rarely exist for it to occur.

Table 13.5. Qualitative and Semi-Quantitative Descriptions for Severity of Consequence.

Numerical Rating	Severity of Consequences (S)	Description
4	Catastrophic	One or more fatalities, multiple serious hospitalizations; incident resulting in more than $250K
3	Critical	Disabling injury or illness; permanent impairment; incident resulting in more than $50K
2	Marginal	Medical treatment or restricted work; recordable incidents; incident resulting in more than $1K
1	Low	First aid or non-treatment incidents; incident resulting in less than $1K

Table 13.6. Risk Scoring Levels and Action Example.

Risk Level	Risk Score	Action
Very High	12 or greater	Operation not permissible, stop work; immediate action required
High	8 to 10	Remedial action required; high priority
Moderate	4 to 6	Remedial action suggested
Low	1 to 3	Remedial action discretionary

rely on human verbal communication for two fill lines. Would this be considered an effective control measure? The likelihood of mixing the lines with only human verbal communication could be estimated as "Probable," with the consequence severity at "Critical" or higher. With the likelihood and severity estimates, a "High" risk level is determined on the Qualitative 5 × 4 risk matrix, which is considered an unacceptable risk level.

To simplify the process and avoid numerical calculations mistakes, a what-if risk analysis such as the one developed by the authors shown in Figure 13.21 can be used. An interactive version of this tool is available at www.assp.org/ermtools. A semi-quantitative model of the what-if risk analysis is presented in Figure 13.22 for those that prefer to use numbers. Not surprisingly, the risk levels for all three scenarios are in the high-risk category.

At this point, the risk has been estimated; however, the risk has not been evaluated. This is performed in the next section, Evaluating Risk.

Section 4—Evaluating Risk

Following the risk analysis, a judgement is made whether the risk is acceptable or if it requires some form of risk treatment known as risk evaluation. Continuing with the CSB investigation from a chemical release in October 2016, a Structured What-if Risk Assessment is used to illustrate risk evaluation as part of a full risk assessment.

SWIFRA Model

As briefly mentioned in Chapter 8, the Structured What-if Risk Assessment model incorporates structured what-if questions, followed by ask "how is it possible" and then "why is it possible." In this modified model, a risk estimation is added for current state and future state risk levels along with a risk reduction percentage to help communicate risk reduction to decision makers (Lyon, Popov 2020b). The steps for applying a SWIFRA are:

What If?	Consequences	Causes	Controls	L	S	Risk Level
...the operator mixes connections? 	Chlorine gas generation	Task complexity or design; communication; experience	Verbal communication	Probable (P)	Critical (C)	High
...the operator is exposed to chlorine gas?	Possible fatality	Experience and improper controls	Training	Probable (P)	Catastrophic (CAT)	High
...local population is exposed to chlorine gas?	Possible multiple fatalities	Task complexity or design; communication; experience	Alarm, social media	Occasional (O)	Catastrophic (CAT)	High

Figure 13.21
Qualitative What-if Risk Analysis.

What If?	Consequences	Causes	Controls	L	S	Risk Level
...the operator mixes connections? 	Chlorine gas generation	Task complexity or design; communication; experience	Verbal communication	4	3	12
...the operator is exposed to chlorine gas?	Possible fatality	Experience and improper controls	Training	3	4	12
...local population is exposed to chlorine gas?	Possible multiple fatalities	Task complexity or design; communication; experience	Alarm; social media	3	4	12

Figure 13.22
Semi-Quantitative What-if Risk Analysis.

- *Develop Questions*: The team conducts research reviewing relevant documents, past incidents, historical data analysis, and interviewing personnel (and making observations) to develop a list of valid and relevant what-if questions to uncover possible problems the system.

- *Create Spreadsheet*: The facilitator loads the list of what-if questions into the SWIFRA spreadsheet.
- *Team Answers Questions*: The team then goes through each what-if question with a multiple what-if or why question process to determine potential failure modes and their systemic causal factors, as well as controls. For instance, in the chemical release case study, the team would ask "what if the operator mixes sulfuric acid and sodium hypochlorite connections" during the filling of tanks process. Then, the next question might be "how would this possibly happen?" followed by "why is this possible?" This would likely lead to conclusions that the current design of the filling ports can be easily mis-matched with the only existing control measures being procedural and dependent upon the individual filling the tanks. The answers generated from the team are entered into the appropriate columns in the worksheet.
- *Identify Existing Controls*: The related controls for the possible what-if are identified and listed in the worksheet.
- *Analyze Risk*: Based on the answers developed and existing controls, the team estimates likelihood, severity, and risk level. Figure 13.28 provides an example using the case study. Considering the low-level controls, the team estimates likelihood of mixing the lines as "Probable" (4) and severity as "Critical" (3), producing a risk level of 12.

At this point, a risk analysis has been completed with the risk levels estimated for the chemical release case study. To complete the risk evaluation, Tables 13.4, 13.5, and 13.6 are used to compare and judge the estimated risk levels for acceptability and required action. Like Table 13.6, an ALARP model such as Figure 13.23 can be used to visually rank the risk levels according to their action levels.

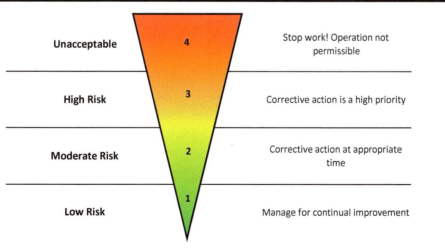

Figure 13.23
ALARP Model for Risk Evaluation.

Evaluating Risk Levels

Following the risk analysis performed in the SWIFA model shown in Figure 13.24, three what-if risk events are estimated.

1. "What-if the operator connects to the wrong chemical during filling?" The answer is chlorine gas would be generated and possibly released causing potential fatalities and injuries in the nearby community. It was determined that this could occur due to the fact that all connections are universal, allowing the possibility of mis-matching chemicals during filling. The original design of the port filling connections did not take this into account. The only controls currently used are signage, labeling, procedures, and training. This led to the risk level estimate of 12. Evaluating the risk level of 12 compared to the established risk criteria, it is determined that the risk is unacceptable, requiring immediate risk treatment.

2. "What if the operator is exposed to chlorine gas?" The answer would be possible death or severe injury. Inadvertently connecting and filling the wrong chemical could cause chlorine gas generation and a release. Universal port design allows for inadvertent filling, and the procedure requires the operator to be at the point of operation and exposure. Only signage, labeling, procedures, and training are used to control the risk. The risk level is estimated at 12 which is unacceptable and requires immediate attention.

3. "What if local population is exposed to chlorine gas release?" The answer would be potential catastrophic results with multiple fatalities, injuries, and disruptions. The current universal port design allows inadvertent mixing, and the local community is approximately 1 mile away from the tank filling

Structured What-if Risk Assessment (SWIFRA)								
#	What If?	How?	Why?	Current Controls	L	S	Risk Level	Risk Level Acceptable (Y/N)
1	...the operator connects to the wrong chemical during filling? **Answer: Chlorine gas generation and possible release, possible fatalities and injuries.**	The filling ports are all the same allowing mismatching of chemicals.	Original design not previously considered. Management not aware.	Signage/labeling; procedural training	4	3	12	No
2	...the operator is exposed to chlorine gas? **Answer: Probable death or severe injury**	Inadvertently connecting and filling wrong chemical causing Chlorine gas release. Operator at point of connection in proximity of release.	Universal ports allow mismatching. Connecting procedure requires operator to be a point of release.	Signage/labeling; procedural training	4	3	12	No
3	...local population is exposed to chlorine gas release? **Answer: Possible multiple fatalities and injuries to public and workers, business interruption**	Inadvertently connecting and filling wrong chemical generating and releasing Chlorine gas that drifts over community	Univeral ports allow mismatching. Community within 1 mile of tank farm. Task complexity or design; communication; experience	Signage/labeling; procedural training	4	4	16	No

Figure 13.24
SWIFA, Risk Evaluation Stage.

operation. The prevailing winds are typically out of the southwest which would cause the cloud plume to travel toward/over the community. The risk level is estimated at 16, which is unacceptable requiring immediate attention.

Section 5—Treating Risk

Following the risk evaluation, risks that are judged to be unacceptable require risk treatment. In Chapter 10, Treating Risk, the importance of achieving risk levels that are "as low as reasonably practicable" or ALARP is discussed. To achieve and maintain ALARP, a combination of prevention and mitigation measures are typically needed (Lyon, Popov 2020a).

In the CSB chemical tank filling case study, the SWIFRA model was used and determined that three risk events were considered unacceptable and require immediate attention. The following actions were taken to treat risks in this case:

> The facility managers examined their processes and equipment to identify ways that the risks could be reduced, both from a likelihood of occurrence and severity of impact. Using the hierarchy of controls model (shown in Figure 13.25) to select risk control measures, the company implemented several layers of controls specific to the facility's ventilation system and chemical transfer equipment. Special focus was placed on the fill lines, transfer valves, transfer piping, tanks, and associated equipment including:

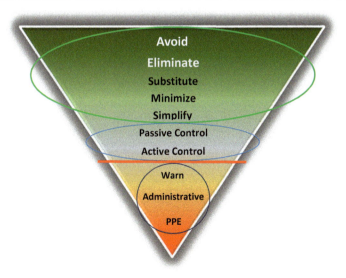

Figure 13.25
Hierarchy of Risk Treatment Model (Lyon, Popov 2019).

- Upgrading chemical unloading and transfer equipment with chemical portal separation, signage, and unique locks and fittings. (Preventive— combination of redesign, engineering, warnings, and administrative controls)
- Implementing an innovative key control and chemical unloading sequences. (SOPs —Preventive—Administrative)
- Improving movement within the control room by moving the center control console from the middle of the control room to the walls. (Preventive redesign—Administrative)
- Conducting several Process Hazard Analyses (PHAs) covering propylene oxide, phosphorus oxychloride, and acetic anhydride. (Preventive— Risk Assessment—Administrative)
- Removing the acetic anhydride process entirely, leaving only four liquid bulk chemicals at the facility as opposed to five, thus reducing the number of bulk flammable chemicals from two to only one. (Preventive— eliminate and minimization)
- Upgrading monitoring and detection equipment to decrease the risk of chemical releases. (Mitigation—Warning equipment)
- Adding new emergency shutdown devices to complement the devices that were already in place. (Mitigation—engineering)
- Installing more emergency supplied air packs along the egress path. (Mitigation—PPE) (CSB 2018).

The risk treatments added to the chemical tank filling operation are presented in their hierarchal layers for preventive controls and mitigative measures in Figure 13.26.

After the implementation of the layers of controls, the updated SWIFRA may look like the one presented in Figure 13.27. The chemical filling portals arrangement is presented in Figure 13.28. The new unique fill line shapes and sizes incorporated into the filling process to avoid mis-matching chemicals during deliveries is pictured in Figure 13.29.

As mentioned in Chapter 1, operational risks are derived from people or a failure in processes; and hazard risks are derived from property, liability, or personnel loss exposures, and are generally insurable. This real-world practical example demonstrates how the operational risks can become hazard risks. Unfortunately, both lead to negative consequences.

With a proactive risk assessment and management process, organizations can reduce uncertainty and the potential for serious incidents. Methods such as What-if analysis and SWIFRA can be powerful tools in identifying, assessing, and communicating risk within an organization. Risk professionals should equip themselves with such tools. The time to ask "what if" is now.

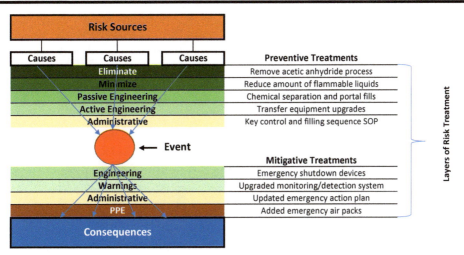

Figure 13.26
Additional Layers of Control for the Chemical Filling Operation.

#	What if?	How?	Why?	Current Controls	L	S	Risk Level	Risk Level Acceptable (Y/N)	Additional Controls	L2	S2	Risk Level 2	% RR
1	...the operator connects to the wrong chemical during filling? **Answer: Chlorine gas generation and possible release, possible fatalities and injuries.**	The filling ports are all the same allowing mismatching of chemicals.	Original design not previously considered. Management not aware.	Signage/labeling; procedural training	4	3	12	No	Design unique connections for each chemical. Upgrade chemical unloading and transfer equipment with chemical portal separation, signage, locks, and fittings; update procedures and training.	2	3	6	50%
2	...the operator is exposed to chlorine gas? **Answer: Probable death or severe injury**	Inadvertently connecting and filling wrong chemical, causing chlorine gas release. Operator at point of connection in proximity of release.	Universal ports allow mismatching. Connecting procedure requires operator to be a point of release.	Signage/labeling; procedural training	4	3	12	No	Design unique connections for each chemical. Upgrade chemical unloading and transfer equipment with chemical portal separation, signage, locks, and fittings; update procedures and training. Provide emergency escape respiratory protection.	2	3	6	50%
3	...local population is exposed to chlorine gas release? **Answer: Possible multiple fatalities and injuries to public and workers, business interruption**	Inadvertently connecting and filling wrong chemical, generating and releasing chlorine gas that drifts over community.	Univeral ports allow mismatching. Community within 1 mile of tank farm. Task complexity or design; communication; experience	Signage/labeling; procedural training	4	4	16	No	In addition to above controls, add new emergency shutdown devices to complement the devices that were already in place. Upgrade monitoring, detection, and warning equipment to decrease the risk of chemical releases.	2	3	6	63%

Figure 13.27
SWIFRA with Proposed Controls.

The Concept of Layers of Control

As indicated in the previous chapters and examples, no single risk treatment is sufficient to adequately manage risk. Similarly, no single risk assessment tool is adequate to address all possible needs or scenarios. In this next section, scenario and sensitivity analyses are reviewed as well as the concept of using layers of defenses and a Layers of Control Analysis (LOCA) methodology.

Layers of protection, lines of defense, and *depth in defenses* are terms adopted from the military strategy of using multiple layers of defense to withstand an attack and maintain adequate defenses to resist rapid penetration (Lyon, Popov 2020a).

252 | Assessing and Managing Risk: An ERM Perspective

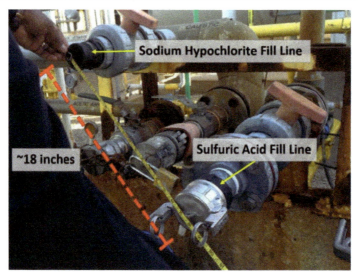

Figure 13.28
Distance between Fill Lines (CSB 2018a).

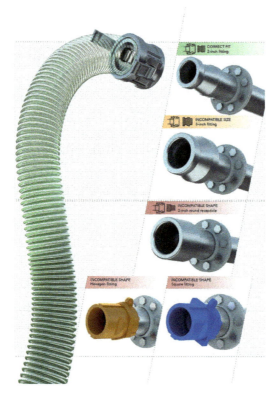

Figure 13.29
Unique Fill Line Shapes and Sizes to Avoid Mis-matching Chemicals during Deliveries (CSB 2018).

This strategy is designed to slow the attack, fortify around critical elements, and yield rather than exhaust themselves. The American Petroleum Institute (API) standards provide the following definitions of the layers of protection concept:

> A concept of providing multiple independent and overlapping layers of protection in depth. For security purposes, this may include various layers of protection such as counter surveillance, counterintelligence, physical security, and cyber security. A second consideration is the balance of the security measures such that equivalent risk exists regardless of the threat's pathway or method (API RP 781 Security Plan Methodology for the Oil and Natural Gas Industries. First Edition, September 2016.)
>
> A concept whereby several independent devices, systems, or actions are provided to reduce the likelihood and severity of an undesirable event (API RP 780, Security Risk Assessment Methodology for the Petroleum and Petrochemical Industries, First Edition, May 2013.)

In the chemical processing industry, layers of protection are constructed with "independent protection layers" or IPLs. An IPL is defined as a device, system, or action capable of preventing an event or exposure from occurring that is independent from other controls and is verifiable or auditable for effectiveness. IPLs are considered physical barriers or devices (typically engineering controls) that prevent the "initiating cause" of an event from proceeding to an unwanted consequence. Control types used in a layered fashion include design-level controls (prevention through design or PtD), prevention controls, and protection controls and mitigation controls as illustrated in Figure 13.30.

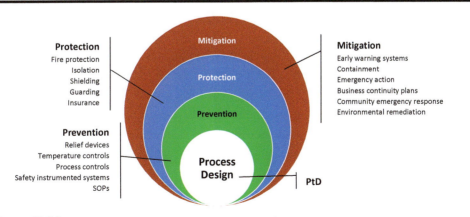

Figure 13.30
Layers of Controls Model.

James Reason's Swiss cheese model illustrates the concept of using layers of protection (Figure 13.31). Reason postulates that all workplace accidents have at least three common features: (1) hazards, (2) failed defenses, and (3) losses. Of these three features, the "failed defenses" offer the greatest potential for risk reduction improvement. Controls can exist at many levels and take a variety of forms, however each control serves one or more of the following functions: to create understanding and awareness of the hazards; to give guidance on how to operate safely; to provide alarms and warnings when danger is imminent; to place barriers between the hazards and the potential losses; to restore the system to a safe state after an event; to contain and eliminate the hazards should they escape the barriers and controls; and to provide the means of escape and rescue should the defenses fail catastrophically (Reason 2016).

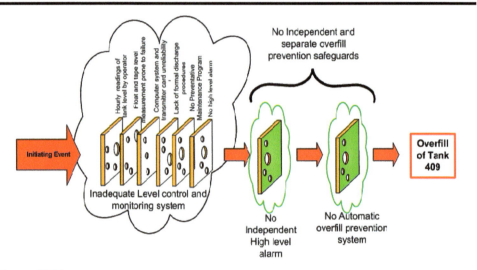

Figure 13.31
The Swiss Cheese Model taken from the CSB Investigation (CSB 2015).

The "depth in defenses" concept can be effective in making complex technological systems, such as nuclear power plants, largely protected from single point failures. But, as Reason points out, no defense is perfect. Controls can contain weaknesses, flaws, and gaps such as "holes in Swiss cheese slices." Under certain conditions, these holes or weaknesses can "line up" allowing an accident to occur as illustrated by the Swiss cheese model (Reason 2016).

Case Study

Petroleum Tank Terminal Explosion and Fires

In the US Chemical Safety and Hazard Investigation Board (CSB) Final Investigation Report Caribbean Petroleum Corporation (CAPECO) Tank Terminal Explosion and

Multiple Tank Fires (2015), an example of the Swiss cheese model demonstrating layers of protection can be found. The following statement and Swiss cheese diagram in Figure 13.31 are from the report:

> The CSB determined that numerous technical and systemic failures contributed to the explosion and multiple tank fires at the CAPECO tank terminal. The CSB found that multiple layers of protection failed within the level control and monitoring system at the same time. In addition, a lack of independent safeguards contributed to the overfill. James Reason's Swiss Cheese Model best demonstrates these systemic failures that led to the accident. Reason postulates that an accident results from the breakdown of the "interaction between latent failures and a variety of local triggering events (active failures)" and although rare, the "adverse conjunction of several causal factors" from various layers. The deficiencies or holes at each layer of protection are constantly increasing or decreasing based on management decisions and operational deviations.

Case Study

Metal Dust Explosion and Fire

This case study is taken from the metal dust explosion and fire at the AL Solutions facility in New Cumberland, West Virginia, as reported by the CSB. The incident resulted in three employee fatalities and one contractor injury. The explosion and ensuing fire damaged the production building and ultimately caused the shutdown of the plant (CSB 2014). The final report is available at: www.csb.gov/al-solutions-fatal-dust-explosion/. To visualize the risk pathway of the event, Figure 13.32 is presented.

The CSB report states:

> Like all fires, a dust fire occurs when fuel (the combustible dust) is exposed to energy (an ignition source) in the presence of oxygen (typically from air). Removing any one of these elements of the classic fire triangle (depicted in Figure 13.33) eliminates the possibility of a fire. A dust explosion requires the simultaneous presence of two additional elements: dust dispersion and confinement (as shown in the dust explosion pentagon in Figure 13.34). Suspended dust burns rapidly, and confinement enables pressure buildup. Removal of either the suspension or the confinement element can prevent an explosion, although a dust fire can still occur (CSB).

256 | Assessing and Managing Risk: An ERM Perspective

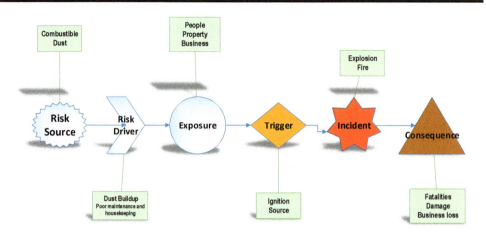

Figure 13.32
Risk Pathway for Combustible Dust Explosion.

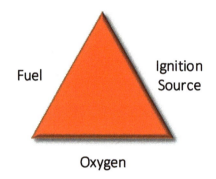

Figure 13.33
Fire Triangle.

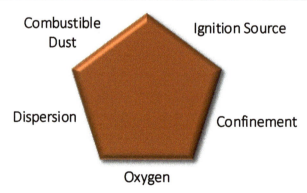

Figure 13.34
Dust Explosion Pentagon.

Using this case study, a modified what-if risk assessment shown in Figure 13.35 indicates that there were no sufficient risk *prevention* measures available at the time of the accident. As a result, additional preventive measures were added including the re-designed blender and an inert gas blanket creating "layers of prevention."

What If?	Consequence	Human Error & Systems Issues	L	S	Risk Level	Risk Level Acceptable (Y/N)	Additional Controls	L2	S2	Risk Level 2	% RR
Metal blender is not functioning properly?	Ignition source	Task complexity or design	4	4	16	No	Re-design the blender. Inert gas (no Oxygen). New procedures.	2	3	6	63%
Sufficient concentration of combustible dust is present?	Explosion possible	Task complexity or design	4	4	16	No	Re-design the blender. Inert gas (no Oxygen). Improve ventilation to reduce combustible dust concentration. New housekeeping procedures.	1	4	4	75%
Explosion generates toxic gases?	Operators and EM personnel exposure	Task complexity or design. Experience	4	3	12	No	Re-design the whole operation to eliminate operator exposure.	1	3	3	75%

Figure 13.35
Modified What-if Risk Assessment.

In this example, likelihood and severity could be reduced for all three hazards by 63% and 75%. The remaining 37% and 25% respectively may be retained if the organization assumes that the risk is within acceptable limits.

Section 6—Monitoring, Reviewing, Recording, and Reporting Risk

As discussed in Chapter 11, a crucial part of risk management is verifying that risks are properly controlled, monitoring and reviewing their status, and recording and reporting results to stakeholders. These steps obviously tie into the communication and consultation aspects of risk management.

Monitoring, Reviewing, Testing, and Validating

Part of monitoring and review is the testing and validating of outputs from the selected risk management model, which is critical in reducing uncertainty and improving a model's value. Such testing is needed to evaluate the model's representation of the actual situation to be assessed and decided upon. In this example, an auto supply company is examined.

Auto Supply Company Case Study

An auto supply company operates an auto parts fulfilment center in the Midwest. The company rents a warehouse facility for $50,000 annually. The fulfillment center sells 25000 auto parts per year and the average price per auto part is $50. The company's average cost to buy the auto parts is $25 per part. The fulfillment associates are among those on the front-line fulfilling customers' orders within the fulfillment center. The fulfillment associates perform production duties like pick/pack orders, receive/stow product at elevated levels, ensure inventory accuracy, and unload/load trucks.

Unfortunately, during the past year, four associates suffered back injuries and average cost per injury was $50,000 for a total of $200,000. This increase in injury costs was unexpected and affected the bottom line of the company. The company lost $125,000 that year. As a result, the risk manager constructed a Pareto Analysis (see Figure 13.2) and discovered that "back injuries from overexertion" was the highest loss category. The obvious solution was to reduce the exposure to back injuries from overexertion; however, that would require a complete redesign of the warehouse and the addition of process automation. As a result, management decided to perform a sensitivity analysis and evaluate all the options.

Management estimated that if they increase the average auto part price, they will sell fewer auto parts. On the other hand, if they lower the price, they will sell more auto parts, but the profit margin will be significantly reduced. The risk manager was experienced in performing sensitivity analysis and developed an Excel file. A sensitivity analysis example is presented in Figure 13.36.

Current Operation	
# of Auto Parts Sold	25000
Average price per auto part	$50
Our average cost per auto part	$25
Warehouse rent	$50,000
Injuries/Illnesses Cost	$200,000 4 back injuries
Payroll	$500,000

Annual Profit/Loss	
Revenue	$1,250,000
Cost of sales	$625,000
Gross Profit	$625,000
Expenses (Rent, I&I, Pay)	$750,000
Operating Profit/Loss (P or L)	-$125,000

Price	# of Auto Parts Sold				
-$125,000	15000	17000	25000	27000	29000
$75	$0	$100,000	$500,000	$600,000	$700,000
$70	-$75,000	$15,000	$375,000	$465,000	$555,000
$50	-$375,000	-$325,000	-$125,000	-$75,000	-$25,000
$45	-$450,000	-$410,000	-$250,000	-$210,000	-$170,000
$35	-$600,000	-$580,000	-$500,000	-$480,000	-$460,000

Figure 13.36
Sensitivity Analysis.

It is easy to see that the supply company lost money last year. The risk manager can demonstrate how the values are interdependent. For instance, if the management decides to increase the auto parts price to $75 and assume that they will sell 15,000 parts instead of 25,000, the company will break even next year. The obvious preference would be to keep the price constant and reduce the cost of injuries. The sensitivity analysis shows that at the current price per auto part, $50, even if the parts sales increase to 29,000 the operation is still not profitable—in fact, they will lose $25,000. Therefore, a decision was made to evaluate several different branching scenarios. The risk management team decided that they can improve the operation using robots. It is estimated that four warehouse robots would cost $500,000 and the annual payment would be $113, 896 at 4.5% interest rate as shown in Table 13.7.

Table 13.7. Cost of Robots Projection.

Cost of Robots	$500,000.00
Interest Rate	0.045 annual
Loan term	5 years
Annual Payment	($113,895.82)
Loan term	60 months
Monthly Payment	($9,321.51)

However, the proposed solution will eliminate the back injuries (no manual tasks). It is difficult to convince the management of a mid-size company to invest $500,000 without proper analysis. Based on the author's experience, it is better to present three or four different scenarios to the upper level management. Therefore, the risk manager prepared a branching scenario with four different options. Scenario analysis, as described in Chapter 6, is a process of analyzing possible future outcomes by considering alternative scenarios used to identify risk and explore consequences or potential financial outcomes in our case study. Scenario analysis consists of developing a plausible scenario and analyzing what might happen given various possible future developments. The branching scenario is very similar to an event tree analysis or decision-making tree. An example is presented in Figure 13.37.

Considering the current cost of back injuries at $200,000, it is estimated that fully automated operation would reduce the cost of back injuries by 80–100%. At a conservative estimate of 80% back injuries cost reduction, the expected annual cost avoidance would be $160,000. Partially automated operation may reduce the back injuries costs by an estimated 20–50%. However, that will reduce the back injuries

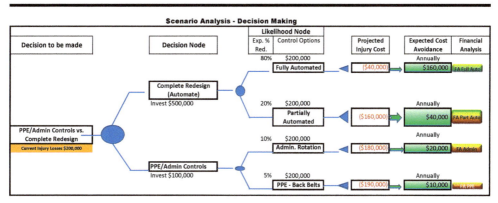

Figure 13.37
Branching Scenario.

cost by only $40,000. On the "lower end" of the branching scenario, we could see that administrative and PPE (back belts) type of controls would be a lot cheaper option—only $100,000. However, the annual cost reduction would be between $10,000 and $20,000. Therefore, a longer-term financial analysis would be a good supplement to the branching scenario analysis. All four different financial analyses are available in the supplemental interactive tools and presented in Figures 13.38, 13.39, 13.40, and 13.41.

The analyses indicate that the initial investment for PPE is a lot less ($100,000 vs. $500,000), however, the Net Present Value, return on investment (ROI), and internal rate of return (IRR) for PPE are all negative. It follows the old British maxim, "I'm not that rich to buy cheap things." While a payback period of 3.1 years for the fully automated operation is not ideal, it represents *opportunity cost*.

If the risks and opportunities are further analyzed using another sensitivity analysis, it would indicate that the best option is the fully automated/robotized operation. This would also reduce the payroll by $100,000 making the operation profitable—generating $61,104 in profit. Future state sensitivity analysis is presented in Figure 13.42.

The warehouse operation is a good example of how hazard and operational risks can become financial risks due to back injuries affecting the profitability of the

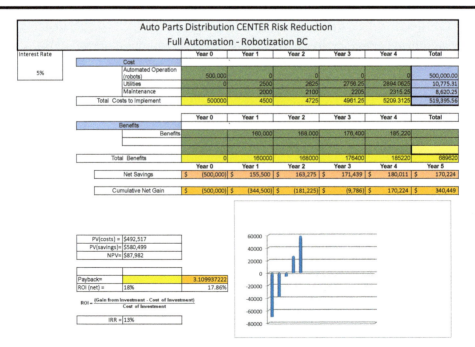

Figure 13.38
Full Automation.

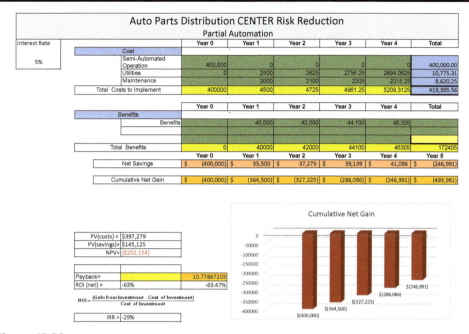

Figure 13.39
Partial Automation.

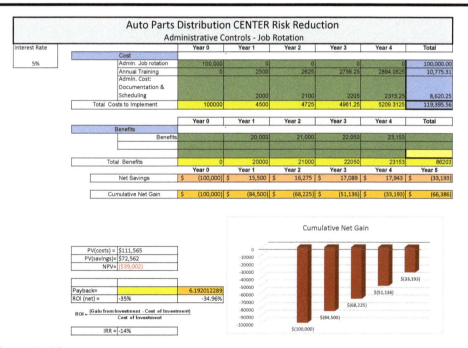

Figure 13.40
Administrative Controls—Job Rotation.

Auto Parts Distribution CENTER Risk Reduction
PPE - Back Belts

Interest Rate		Year 0	Year 1	Year 2	Year 3	Year 4	Total
5%	**Cost**						
	PPE Back belt + Initial training	100,000	0	0	0	0	100,000.00
	Annual Training	0	2500	2625	2756.25	2894.0625	10,775.31
	Replacement cost		2000	2100	2205	2315.25	8,620.25
	Total Costs to Implement	100000	4500	4725	4961.25	5209.3125	119,395.56

	Year 0	Year 1	Year 2	Year 3	Year 4	Total
Benefits						
Benefits		10,000	10,500	11,025	11,576	
Total Benefits	0	10000	10500	11025	11576	43101

	Year 0	Year 1	Year 2	Year 3	Year 4	Year 5
Net Savings	$ (100,000)	$ 5,500	$ 5,775	$ 6,064	$ 6,367	$ (76,294)
Cumulative Net Gain	$ (100,000)	$ (94,500)	$ (88,725)	$ (82,661)	$ (76,294)	$ (152,589)

PV(costs) =	$111,565
PV(savings)=	$36,281
NPV=	($75,283)

Payback=		17.36363636
ROI (net) =	-67%	-67.48%

$$ROI = \frac{(\text{Gain from Investment} - \text{Cost of Investment})}{\text{Cost of Investment}}$$

IRR =	-40%

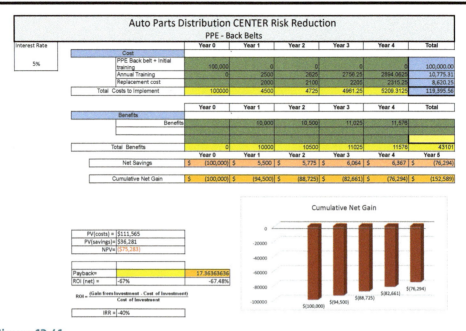

Figure 13.41
PPE—Back Belts.

Current Operation		
# of Auto Parts Sold	25000	
Average price per auto part	$50	
Our average cost per auto part	$25	
Warehouse rent	$50,000	
Injuries/Illnesses Cost	$0	No back injuries
Payroll	$400,000	

Annual Profit/Loss	
Revenue	$1,250,000
Cost of sales	$625,000
Gross Profit	$625,000
Expenses (Rent, I&I, Pay)	$450,000
Operating Profit/Loss (P or L)	$175,000
	($113,896)
	$61,104

Price	# of Auto Parts Sold				
$175,000	15000	17000	25000	27000	29000
$75	$300,000	$400,000	$800,000	$900,000	$1,000,000
$70	$225,000	$315,000	$675,000	$765,000	$855,000
$50	-$75,000	-$25,000	$175,000	$225,000	$275,000
$45	-$150,000	-$110,000	$50,000	$90,000	$130,000
$35	-$300,000	-$280,000	-$200,000	-$180,000	-$160,000

Figure 13.42
Sensitivity Analysis.

organization. In addition, the company was facing cancelation of contracts due to their experience modifier rate (EMR) approaching 1.00, since many organizations require their contractors and suppliers to verify that their EMRs are below 1.00. (EMR is a multiplier used by insurance carriers to calculate worker's compensation premiums based on an organization's past three years of claims experience.) The organization EMR affects much more than the annual insurance cost. Understanding and lowering EMR is essential for organizations looking to reduce insurance costs and even gain more new contracts. The number of injuries, delayed orders completions, financial losses, and EMR affecting the reputation of the company

Practical Applications of Risk Management Methods | 263

reflect on all four quadrants of the ERM model. All of them negative are outcomes in this example. However, with the elimination of manual material handling and the costs of back injuries, the company would have the opportunity to improve the profitability and the reputation of the company.

Risk Recording and Reporting

As indicated in ISO 31000, the steps taken to manage risk and the resulting outcomes should be recorded in accordance with the organization's documentation policies and reported to decision makers and appropriate stakeholders. Recording and reporting measures should be used to communicate related actions and outcomes across the organization and provide decision makers the appropriate information.

Some of methods used to record risk covered in Chapter 11 include risk profiles, risk registers and risk logs, risk hierarchies, and risk performance measurement. In addition, many organizations use software applications and spreadsheets to track risk performance, risk reduction, and the status of risk treatments.

Risk reporting is a form risk communication and it is critical for management and decision makers. Methods of risk reporting include dashboards, risk matrices, heat maps, and key performance metrics that provide a quick view of the current status. For more complex risk scenarios, a striped bow tie risk assessment diagram such as one provided in Figure 13.43 can be useful in presenting more complex risk scenarios.

Also, risk matrices can be designed to not only provide "pure risk" or negative risk ranges, but also "opportunity or strategic" risks such as the example provided in

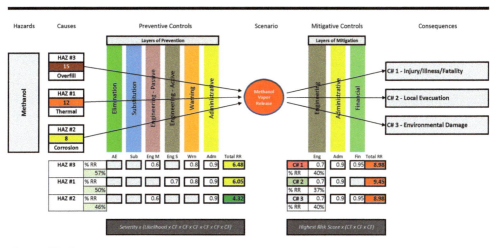

Figure 13.43
Striped Bow Tie Diagram Example Used to Visualize and Communicate Risk.

Figure 13.44. Visual tools such as these should be used along with more detailed and in-depth data. For external stakeholders, risk reporting should be limited to specific information that is required (regulatory agencies for instance) or risk information that affects their objectives (suppliers, customers, partners, etc.) and that is appropriate to share. Other considerations include the reporting methods used, the expected (budgeted) costs of reporting, and the frequency and timing of reports.

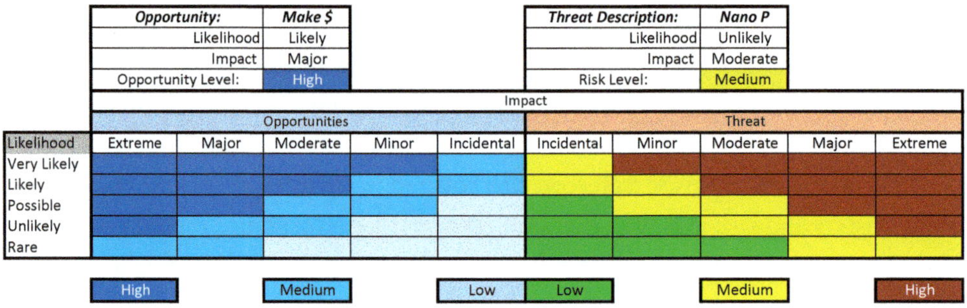

Figure 13.44
Combined Opportunity and Threat Matrix Example.

Risk Communication and Consultation

In Chapter 12, it was emphasized that an essential element to a successful risk management process is effective communication. Communication and consultation are major components of the risk management process as indicated in ISO 31000 and must be integrated throughout the process. ISO 31000 defines communication and consultation as "continual and iterative processes that an organization conducts to provide, share or obtain information, and to engage in dialogue with stakeholders regarding the management of risk. Consultation is a two-way process of informed communication between an organization and its stakeholders on an issue prior to making a decision or determining a direction on that issue" (ISO 31000-2018).

Communication and consultation are integrated into the entire process to enable effective risk dialogue with stakeholders, from establishing the scope, to assessing and treating risk, to monitoring, recording, and reporting risk. Where communication is ineffective or inconsistent, problems are likely. Most risk professionals can recount events and experiences where inadequate communication led to unwanted and sometimes severe consequences.

Risk Communication and Disasters

Communication breakdowns are cited as contributing factors in many catastrophic events such as the Texas City Refinery explosion, Three Mile Island, the Deepwater

Horizon oil spill, the Bhopal explosion, and NASA's space shuttle explosions (Lyon, Popov 2017).

Disasters, whether accidental, intentional, or natural, seem to share common risk factors. The question is "with all our knowledge, skill and technology, why can't we do something to prevent them or at least keep them from causing such devastation?" (Abkowitz 2008).

Research indicates that disasters, although different, when closely analyzed have remarkable similarities in how they were caused or allowed to develop (Abkowitz 2008). These common risk factors are listed in Table 13.8.

As indicated in Table 13.8, humans cause or contribute to the impact of disasters through their actions or inactions and, therefore, can/should control and influence these risk factors. To address these commonalities, a list of key practices for improving the management and communication of risk is provided in Table 13.9.

Those involved should understand how risk-based information is communicated to decision makers and emphasize that risk assessments are conducted with the organization's objectives in mind. Risk communication is essential for routine situations and also in times of crisis. Risk professionals must be well-versed in the use of effective risk communication principles, so they can determine how best to apply them to their own situations and needs among all of the challenges that exist.

While every situation is different and may require a different type of response, five common elements can help in developing a risk communication plan. First, prepare for plausible scenarios and crises; second, communicate the essential information effectively to the right audience; third, be timely and measured in the message; and finally, learn and improve (Ellis 2018).

Table 13.8. Commonalities in Disasters.

Commonalities in Disasters
1. Flaws in design and construction
2. Failure in communication
3. Lack of planning and preparedness
4. Deviation from set procedures
5. Economic pressure and lack of resources
6. Convergence of multiple risk factors overwhelming control measures
7. Political agendas
8. Individual and organizational arrogance
9. Lack of uniform safety standards
10. Not taken seriously by decision makers until a disaster occurs
11. Risk level is unknown and, thus, unmanaged

Table 13.9. Key Practices for Risk Communication and Management.

Key Practices for Risk Communication and Management
1. Prepare for plausible scenarios and crises;
2. perform formal assessments;
3. define the context and objective of each assessment;
4. understand the organization's acceptable risk level;
5. assemble the best team to perform the assessment;
6. use the most appropriate assessment techniques;
7. be objective and unemotional in the assessment process;
8. identify risk sources that create risks and consider the whole-system risk;
9. consider the hierarchy of controls and failure to prioritize based on risk;
10. perform assessment during the design/redesign phases;
11. communicate before, during, and after the assessment with affected stakeholders;
12. be timely and measured in the message; and
13. learn and improve.

Methods of Risk Communication

Examples of public or external risk communication may include the list in Table 13.10 taken from the US Federal Emergency Management Agency (FEMA 2014).

Organizations can provide general risk communication to stakeholders (external and internal) through Annual and Quarterly Reports and other formal

Table 13.10. FEMA List of Risk Communication Methods.

FEMA List of Risk Communication Methods
• Public addresses or alerts
• Warning systems
• Brochures or flyers (*e.g.*, At health care facilities, the DMV, etc.)
• Television ads
• Public awareness campaigns (*e.g.*, If You See Something, Say Something)
• Signs, videos, and announcements at the airport (particularly in the screening area)
• Briefs to leadership
• Emails/memos
• Reports
• Meetings at work
• Town hall meetings with the public

means. There are many digital and alternative methods for communicating in this complex information environment as well. However, with the steady stream of information immediately available around key issues such as public health risks, environmental concerns, and natural disasters, and the broadening array of traditional, alternative, and digital outlets, there is the potential for important information to be overshadowed, filtered out, or not provided in the proper context for the recipient. As a result, there's the danger that stakeholders may miss critical facts to guide their decision making, or may take specific actions based on misinformation, which can ultimately lead to unwanted outcomes (Ellis 2018). Organizations must be proactive in designing effective risk communication strategies, and these strategies must be implemented in a timely manner at the first sign of any risk to inform affected stakeholders.

Closing

The assessing and managing of risk, both pure risk and strategic risk (as shown in Figure 13.45), is critically important to an organization's ability to achieve their goals and objectives. Managing uncertainty and ultimately risk enables decision makers to have a level of confidence in their ability to make better decisions resulting in better outcomes. Organizations and risk professionals that recognize and implement the risk management principles, framework, and process presented in this manual will have greater opportunities for success.

Figure 13.45
The Quadrants of Risk.

References

Abkowitz, M.D. 2008. *Operational Risk Management: A Case Study Approach to Effective Planning and Response.* Hoboken, NJ: John Wiley & Sons.

ANSI/ASSP/ISO 31000-2018. 2018. *Risk Management – Guidelines.* Park Ridge, IL: ASSP.

ANSI/ASSP/ISO/IEC 31010-2019. 2019. *Risk Management – Risk Assessment Techniques.* Park Ridge, IL: ASSP.

API RP 781. 2016. Security Plan Methodology for the Oil and Natural Gas Industries. September 2016.

API RP 780. 2013. Security Risk Assessment Methodology for the Petroleum and Petrochemical Industries. May 2013.

Bureau of Labor Statistics (BOL). n.d. "Number of fatal work injuries by employee status." Accessed October 19, 2020. www.bls.gov/charts/census-of-fatal-occupational-injuries/number-of-fatal-work-injuries-by-employee-status-self-employed-wage-salary.htm#.

CSB. 2014. "AL Solutions: Fatal Dust Explosion." www.csb.gov/al-solutions-fatal-dust-explosion/.

CSB. 2015. "Final Investigation Report Caribbean Petroleum Corporation (CAPECO) Tank Terminal Explosion and Multiple Tank Fires." www.csb.gov/assets/1/17/06.09.2015_final_capeco_draft_report__for_board_vote.pdf?15462.

CSB. 2018. "MGPI Processing, Inc. Toxic Chemical Release," www.csb.gov/mgpi-processing-inc-toxic-chemical-release-/.

Ellis, Lisa. 2018. Harvard School of Public Health. "The Need for Effective Risk Communication Strategies in Today's Complex Information Environment." https://www.hsph.harvard.edu/ecpe/effective-risk-communication-strategies/.

EPA 2013. "AL Solutions, Inc. Settlement." www.epa.gov/enforcement/al-solutions-inc-settlement.

Lavinsky, D. 2014. *Pareto Principle: How to Use It to Dramatically Grow Your Business. Forbes.* January 20, 2014. www.forbes.com/sites/davelavinsky/2014/01/20/pareto-principle-how-to-use-it-to-dramatically-grow-your-business/#3792a35a3901.

Lyon, Bruce K., and Georgi Popov. 2017. "Communicating and managing risk: The key result of risk assessment." *Professional Safety,* November 2017, 62(11), 35–44.

Lyon, Bruce K., and Georgi Popov. 2019. "Risk Treatment Strategies: Harmonizing the Hierarchy of Controls & Inherently Safer Design Concepts." *Professional Safety*, May 2019, 64 (5), 34–43.

Lyon, Bruce K., and Georgi Popov. 2020. "Managing Risk through Layers of Control." *Professional Safety,* April 2020a, 65 (4), 25–35.

Lyon, Bruce K., and Georgi Popov. 2020. "The Power of What-if: Assessing and Understanding Risk." *Professional Safety,* June 2020b, 65 (6), 36–43.

Lyon, Bruce K., Georgi Popov, and A. Roberts. 2018. "Causal Factors Analysis: Uncovering Deficiencies within Management System Elements." *Professional Safety,* October 2018, 63 (10), 49–59.

Reason, J. 2016. *Organizational Accidents Revisited*. Boca Raton, FL: CRC Press.

The Review. "AL Solutions settlement ends civil claims." www.reviewonline.com/news/local-news/2016/10/al-solutions-settlement-ends-civil-claims/ (accessed June 23, 2019).

US Federal Emergency Management Agency (FEMA). 2014. "Lesson 3. Communicating in an Emergency." https://training.fema.gov/emiweb/is/is242b/student%20manual/sm_03.pdf.

Answers to Chapter Questions

Chapter 1

1. Explain what motivates an organization to manage its risks. List several reasons why risk should be managed.

    A. An organization manages risk to achieve its objectives. If it does not meet its objectives, the organization risks losing market share and value, failing to compete, having to downsize, or even going out of business. Uncertainty can be a significant obstacle to achieving objectives. To succeed and grow, organizations must be able to reduce uncertainty that impedes decision making so they can be in a position to successfully achieve their business objectives.

2. Determine whether risk is static or dynamic and explain why.

    A. Risk is dynamic, continuously changing with changes in conditions, risk drivers, risk treatments and other variables. Risk should be considered a continuum that requires continuous monitoring and management. Its dynamic nature begins with new conditions and developments that cause a new risk to emerge. As an organization detects and recognizes emerging risks, it should monitor them for their potential to become a concern. As conditions, risk drivers, and other variables occur, emerging risks become inherent risks, leading to risk assessment, treatment, and management. This continuous, dynamic process of risk is depicted in Figure 1.5 as the Risk Continuum.

3. Explain how emerging risks are different from inherent risks and how initial risks are different from residual risks.

   A. Emerging risks can be characterized as new, developing risks that have been anticipated and detected when they become apparent, or existing risks that are changing and increasing in new or unfamiliar conditions. These emerging risks create uncertainty about objectives due to new threats and hazards, changes in their frequency of occurrence, or changes in their consequences or the severity of their effects; in the case of speculative risks, there can also be new opportunities and potential gains. Inherent risk is the risk that exists in the system before any risk management is applied. Initial risk is the risk level determined by the initial risk assessment. It is in fact a baseline risk level first measured by a risk assessment. Initial risk also refers to the present risk level estimated from a risk assessment that takes into consideration any existing controls and their effects. Residual risk' (remaining risk) is the degree of risk that remains after applying the recommended risk treatment from the risk assessment. Residual risk can also include risks that are unidentified, knowingly retained, shared, or transferred.

4. Identify and describe the four risk quadrants.

   A. Hazard risks are derived from property, liability, or personnel loss exposures and are generally insurable. Operational risks are derived from people or failures in processes, systems, or controls, including exposures related to information technology (IT). Both hazard and operational risks are closely aligned and interrelated, so they are often managed as such. Financial risks are derived from the effects of market forces or financial assets or liabilities and include market risk, credit risk, liquidity risk, and price risk, Strategic risks are derived from trends in the economy and society, including changes in economic, political, and competitive environments, as well as demographic shifts

5. Describe the risk-based decision-making process.

   A. Risk-based decision making (RBDM) is a process that organizes information about possible unwanted outcomes into an orderly structure that facilitates decision making and produces more informed management choices. RBDM is, in essence, the practice of risk management in the decision-making process. It provides a consistent, systematic, structured means of making informed decisions that use risk-related information in a timely fashion. Its purpose is to reduce uncertainty of the effects and outcomes of the selected decision.

6. Identify and describe the four different types of uncertainty.

   A. (1) Epistemic uncertainty is a condition in which there is a lack of relevant knowledge of the system. (2) Aleatoric uncertainty is a condition in which a random, unpredictable nature exists surrounding the system. (3) Linguistic uncertainty is a vagueness or ambiguity inherent in spoken languages. (4) Decision uncertainty is uncertainty associated with value systems, professional judgement, company. values and societal norms

7. Explain what is meant by "black swan events."

   A. A "black swan event" can be characterized as unpredictable, meaning that there is no precedent or similar event history available, and that it is random in its nature. The frequency (or lack of frequency) of such events makes black swan events almost impossible to predict. Examples of black swan events include earthquakes and tsunamis, volcanic eruptions, the terrorist attacks against the United States on September 11, 2001, the global financial crisis of 2008, the September 2019 drone attacks on the world's largest oil processing facility and a major oil field in Saudi Arabia, sparking huge fires and halting about half of the supplies from the world's largest exporter of oil.

8. Provide four ways uncertainty might be reduced.

   A. Ways to reduce uncertainty include the following: reduce the size of the decision; understand the options; defer the decision until it is better understood; focus on one decision at a time; understand the credible worst-case scenario; clarify the potential outcomes; understand the context; be flexible and adaptative; remain objective and unemotional.

Chapter 2

1. Describe the origin of the word *hazard* and the word *risk*.

   A. The English word "hazard" is thought to come from the medieval French game *hazard,* a dicing game of chance; the word for the game was borrowed from the Arabic *az-zahr* (or *al-zahr*). The English word "risk" is believed to come from the French word *risque,* which came from the Italian *risco,* meaning "danger."

2. Explain when and why insurance began being used.

   A. In the era known as the Age of Exploration, which began in the early fifteenth century and lasted through the seventeenth century, the Dutch and English were sending ships around the world. This business was a highly profitable, but risky. The ships and the cargo required some form of insurance. To be able to ensure the ships and cargo, a group of underwriters started gathering at the Lloyd's coffee shop in London.

3. What is probability theory?

   A. Understanding risk requires some way to estimate the chance of an event and predict its consequences. For most of history, the concept of chance (now considered probability) was shrouded in mythology. Then, in the seventeenth century, probability theory was first introduced in "games of chance." It was used to calculate the odds of winning, and the mathematicians of the time were able to make predictions using numbers. The development of probability theory allowed the transition from risk being considered "an act of God" to the belief that risks could be understood, assessed, and controlled.

4. What is the law of large numbers?

   A. One of the significant developments in the field of risk management was the development of the law of large numbers. It was first stated by Gerolamo Cardano (1501–76), an Italian mathematician, who noted that the accuracy of empirical statistics tends to improve with the number of trials (Mlodinow). However, he could not prove the law mathematically. It was not referred to as a law of large numbers until Jacob Bernoulli was able to provide an adequately rigorous mathematical proof, which was published in his *Ars Conjectandi* (*The Art of Conjecturing*) in 1713.

5. What is the central limit theorem?

   A. The central limit theorem simply states that the distribution of sample means approximates a normal distribution as the sample size gets larger (assuming that all samples are identical in size), regardless of population distribution shape (Investopedia). This theorem is still used in risk management and insurance to explain pooling of losses as an insurance mechanism. The central limit theorem is related to the law of large numbers, which was first proven mathematically by Jacob Bernoulli in 1713.

6. Describe how modern risk management practices lead to enterprise risk management.

    A. In his book *Against the Gods: The Remarkable Story of Risk,* Peter Bernstein suggests that the actual dividing line between what we call ancient times and modern times is the concept of managing risk. Modern risk management practices consider prevention as an important part of managing risk. In fact, modern risk management practices include the concept of enterprise risk management (ERM). ERM is the process of integrated risk management that places a greater importance on cooperation among departments or functions to manage the organization's full range of risks. It is a relatively new concept that can be traced back to the early 1970s, when Gustav Hamilton of Sweden's Statsforetag proposed the "risk management circle" to describe the interaction of all elements in the risk management process: assessment, control, financing, and communication (Hamilton).

Chapter 3

1. Identify the primary objectives for managing risk and explain why each objective is important to an organization.

    A. The objectives for managing risk are to reduce uncertainty, improve decision making, enable the organization to achieve its business objectives, and protect people and assets. Uncertainty affects an organization's ability to achieve its objectives. Decision making is a critical element in achieving objectives and managing risk. A business or an organization establishes objectives that are important for its success. People (the most important asset), reputation, property, financial stability, and other similar areas are vital to an organization's sustainability and success.

2. List and describe the eight principles for risk management found in ISO 31000. Identify the core purpose of risk management.

    A. The eight principles are (1) integrating risk management into an organization's activities and decision making, (2) taking a structured and comprehensive approach, (3) customizing for an organization's needs and objectives, (4) including stakeholder perspectives, (5) being dynamic and responsive to organizational changes, (6) using the best available information, (7) taking human and cultural factors into account, and (8) learning and adapting for continual improvement. The core purpose is to "create and protect value."

3. Describe the framework for risk management found in ISO 31000.

   A. As outlined in ISO 31000, a risk management framework provides an organizational structure for the integration of risk management into important activities and functions. This framework, supported by management and stakeholders, should be designed to enable organizational leadership, process design, implementation and monitoring, and evaluation and continual improvement of the risk management process, as illustrated in Figure 3.4.

4. Describe in order the elements within the risk management process.

   A. The risk management process involves the systematic application of policies, protocols, and practices of activities in an organization and involves (1) communication and consultation; (2) scope, context, and criteria; (3) identifying risk; (4) analyzing risk; (5) evaluating risk; (6) treating risk; (7) monitoring and reviewing; and (8) reporting and recording, as shown in Figure 3.5.

5. Besides ISO 31000, list other standards for risk management and risk assessment.

   A. ANSI/ASSP/ISO 31010-2019, *Risk Management—Risk Assessment Techniques;* ANSI/ASIS/RIMS RA.1-2016, *Risk Assessment;* ANSI/ASSP Z590.3-2011(R2016), *Prevention through Design;* ASSP TR-31010-2020, *Technical Report: Risk Management—Techniques for Safety Practitioners*

6. In a paragraph, describe the prevention through design concept. Identify three unique requirements found in the standard ANSI/ASSP Z590.3 *Prevention through Design*.

   A. Prevention through design (PtD), also known as safety in design or safety through design, is defined by ANSI/ASSP Z590.3 (Z590.3) as "addressing occupational safety and health needs in the design and redesign process to prevent or minimize the work-related hazards and risks associated with the construction, manufacture, use, maintenance, retrofitting, and disposal of facilities, processes, materials, and equipment" (ANSI/ASSP Z590.3-2011, R2016). PtD is a concept that assesses and manages risk throughout the life cycle of a system. The prevention through design concept is considered the most effective and long-lasting way to avoid or reduce risk in an operation. By avoiding and reducing sources of hazard and risk through design, the resulting inherent risks are reduced. For this reason, prevention through design should be integrated into risk management process concepts and techniques. It is important to consider managing risk from the beginning stages of design throughout the system's life span to decommissioning and disposal, rather than just in the operational phase.

Chapter 4

1. List the seven elements that should be included in the context of a risk assessment.

    A. (1) Purpose, (2) scope and limitations, (3) external and internal environment, (4) stakeholders and decision makers, (5) risk criteria to be used, (6) decision or action to be determined, and (7) resources and timeframe

2. Identify the information needed in the planning process to establish the context.

    A. Type of decision(s) required; business objectives affected; outcomes; timeframe, location, boundaries and limits, inclusions, and exclusions; methods and techniques to be used; resources (internal and external), materials, equipment, training, experts, etc.; specific responsibilities and accountabilities; and documentation and recordkeeping.

3. List five internal factors and five external factors.

    A. The external factors include social and cultural environments; the perceptions, needs, objectives, and relationships of external stakeholders (customers, suppliers, public, etc.); the legal and political climate; regulatory aspects; competitive factors; key business drivers; financial influences; the economic climate and outlook; and potential changes and developments. Internal factors include culture, perceptions, and values; mission, goals, and objectives; strategy, structure, and management style; capabilities, resources, and knowledge; stakeholders and decision makers; and policies, practices, and protocols.

4. List the four general risk criteria needed in the context.

    A. Risk scoring; risk acceptability; the evaluation of the significance of risk; the selection of risk treatment options.

5. Besides likelihood and severity, what are the other six factors listed in ANSI/ASSP Z590.3 that may be needed in defining the context.

    A. Exposure, frequency, duration, failure detectability, control reliability, and prevention effectiveness.

278 | Assessing and Managing Risk: An ERM Perspective

6. List and describe the five elements in a risk scoring system.

   A. Elements within a scoring system include (1) risk characterization—whether it will be qualitative, semiquantitative, or quantitative; (2) risk factors—variables used to measure risk; (3) risk levels—a scale of graduated risk level categories; (4) risk actions—actions defined for each risk level category indicating how risk will be managed; and (5) risk screening and communication—a means of comparing risks to the established risk criteria that is used to evaluate and communicate risk.

7. List and describe four methods used to help establish the context.

   A. The methods include (1) risk criteria—established risk criteria for performing risk assessments, including risk factors, risk characterization, risk levels, risk actions, acceptable risk level, and a risk matrix, among other related criteria; (2) risk scoring system—a formula using risk factor variables to estimate a risk score that is used to measure, prioritize and manage risk; (3) ALARP—as low as reasonably practicable; and (4) risk matrix and heat map—a visual method for ranking risks according to their likelihood level and severity level.

Chapter 5

1. Five key elements should be factored into the selection of methods. List and describe each.

   A. (1) The point at which the effort is to be taken should be applied within the risk management process must be identified to select the proper method(s). (2) The specific target or application of the effort must be considered when selecting the method(s). (3) The level of complexity of the targeted application will influence the selection of the method(s). (4) The criticality level of the targeted effort or problem is an important factor to consider in selection as it determines the level of complexity and accuracy of the method needed. (5) The decision and the type of information or output necessary to help make the decision must be understood in the selection process. (6) Resource limitations such as budgets, time frames, internal and external resources, information and data, personnel, and skill levels, use of outside experts, and software and hardware all affect the selection of the method(s) to be used.

2. List four standards available to the risk professional that contain risk assessment and management methods.

A. ANSI/ASSP/ISO/IEC 31010, *Risk Management—Risk Assessment Techniques;* ANSI/ASIS/RIMS RA.1-2015, *Risk Assessment;* ANSI/ASSP Z590.3-2011 (R2016), *Prevention through Design;* ANSI/ASSP Z10.0-2019, *Occupational Health and Safety Management Systems;* and ASSP TR-31010-2020, *Technical Report: Risk Management—Techniques for Safety Practitioners.*

3. List the six factors that should be considered when selecting methods and provide two examples of each.

A. (1) Process Step—communication, context, risk identification, risk analysis, risk evaluation, risk treatment, monitoring, reporting. (2) Application Level—organizational, regional, location, department, system, job, task. (3) Hazard/Exposure—general hazards, energy sources, chemical, machinery, robotics, industrial hygiene, environmental, musculoskeletal, error-induced. (4) Criticality—degree of uncertainty, degree of FSI risk, criticality of sensitivity. (5) Output—degree of detail needed, availability of data, decision-making needs, regulatory or legal requirements, risk levels or scoring needs. (6) Resources—budget, timeframe, personnel and skill levels, external consultants, software.

4. Explain why a single risk management method may not be adequate for some situations.

A. Many risk management applications require multiple methods to accomplish the objective. Some situations are more complex or need multiple sources of information.

5. Explain why a risk management method may require modification or customization for some situations.

A. Even though numerous methods are available, most methods will require at least some minor customization to fit the needs of a specific application. Each risk assessment technique or risk management method has its own applications, along with strengths and weaknesses. It is up to the user to optimize methods by making modifications that serve the purpose of the risk management application. Some methods may require additional features to enhance the information produced, such as including a risk scoring mechanism. Other methods may be too complex for the application and require removing certain features.

Chapter 6

1. Explain the factors or elements that must be considered in determining the types of information needed.

    A. The types of information required by an organization are determined from the established context, purpose, and scope of the risk management initiative, as well as the type of decision being made. It is also necessary to determine the specific means of identifying the sources of information, how it will be collected, its storage and use, and its overall management

2. Describe some of the sources of data that may be gathered.

    A. Some sources for information include internal documents and knowledgeable stakeholders; external sources such as third parties, contractors, and suppliers; public agencies and governmental sources; industry groups and professional associations; and consultants and expert opinions related to the subject matter.

3. List some of the critical elements that the risk assessment team must understand from previous experiences.

    A. Types of consequences. Severity levels and impacts. Likelihood of past occurrences. Trends, cycles, patterns, and frequencies of occurrences. Circumstances and causal factors surrounding events. Risk controls or treatments that were in place at the time of previous occurrences and the state of their effectiveness. Escalating factors. Limitations and uncertainties in the existing information.

4. Identify the steps provided in ISO 31010 for constructing a decision-making model.

    A. Define the problem. Describe the purpose of the model and desired outcomes. Develop a model for solving the problem. Build the physical, mathematical, or software version of the conceptual model. Develop tools to analyze how the model behaves. Process the data. Review and validate outputs from the model. Draw conclusions from the model and the problem.

5. Identify and describe three methods used to validate decision models.

    A. (1) Sensitivity analysis is a systematic method used to understand how risk estimates and risk-based decisions are dependent on variability and uncertainty in contributing risk factors. (2) Scenario analysis is a process of analyzing possible future outcomes by considering alternative scenarios used to identify risk and explore consequences. (3) The Pareto principle (known as the 80–20 rule) states that, for many events, roughly 80% of the effects come from 20% of the causes.

Chapter 7

1. Explain how risk identification is more than simply identifying hazards.

    A. Risk identification is used to find, describe, and document risks that are important to the organization and warrant further assessment. Risk identification is more than simply identifying hazards or risk sources. It involves identifying and describing the uncertainties and their effects, the related circumstances or concerns, any existing controls and their effectiveness, how the risk may occur, related events in the past, and the potential human and organizational factors that might apply.

2. Identify the factors to be considered in the identification process as listed by ISO 31000.

    A. Tangible and intangible sources of risk; causes, triggers, conditions, and events; threats and opportunities; vulnerabilities and capabilities; changes in the external and internal context; indicators of emerging risks; the nature and value of assets and resources; consequences and their impact on objectives; limitations of knowledge and reliability of information; timeframes and time influences; and biases, assumptions, and beliefs of those involved.

3. Described how emerging risks can be characterized and why they are important.

    A. Emerging risks can be characterized by tangible and intangible sources of risk; causes, triggers, conditions, and events, threats, and opportunities; vulnerabilities and capabilities; changes in the external and internal context; indicators of emerging risks; the nature and value of assets and resources; consequences and their impact on objectives; limitations of knowledge and reliability of information; timeframes and time influences; biases, assumptions, and beliefs of those involved. It is important to have an understanding of the significance of emerging risks since they can develop into threats or concerns to the organization. All risks are dynamic and continually changing. Emerging risks may first appear as insignificant but can develop into more significant risks with changing conditions.

4. Explain what risk sources are and provide several examples.

   A. A risk source is generally defined as an element that, either by itself or in combination with other elements, has the potential to create risk and uncertainty. In other words, risk and uncertainty are derived from risk sources. For pure risk (risk that can only result in negative outcomes), the most effective means of managing the risk is at its source. If the risk source can be avoided, eliminated, or reduced to an acceptable level of risk (ALOR), it will require little if any management going forward. Sources of risk can include events, decisions, actions, or conditions that alone or combined create risk.

5. Describe the difference between pure risk and speculative risk.

   A. Pure risks, which are typically insurable, are derived from hazards and operations and present negative effects. Speculative risks, which are typically not insurable, are derived from financial and strategic aspects and can present effects that are positive, negative, or both.

6. Give four examples of fundamental causes.

   A. Among the examples are causes related to: machinery, processes, or facilities; human-related interactions; management; methods; materials; and the environment.

7. Define what a failure mode is and provide five examples.

   A. A failure mode is described as a condition in which a system fails to perform as expected or deviates from its design tolerances, resulting in a potential for harm or a hazardous event. Examples include premature operations, failure to start or stop, failure during operation, degraded operation, exceeded capacity, and misuse of operation.

8. As stated in ISO 31010, consideration should be given to what elements?

   A. Sources of risk, effectiveness of existing controls, ways certain events might occur, past experiences and incidents, and human aspects and organizational factors.

9. Identify and describe five methods used to identify risk.

   A. Brainstorming: This team-based method is used in workshops to stimulate imaginative thinking and generate ideas. Checklists: This simple form of identification uses a listing of typical hazards or exposures, often taken from industry experience, codes, or standards. Cause and effect analysis: This team-based method is used to identify and categorize possible causes and contributory factors so that all possible hypotheses can be considered. Cindynic approach: Semi-structured interviews are performed in a structured meeting or workshop to identify intangible hazards and sources of risk that can lead to different consequences. Delphi technique: This method is used to collect informed opinions on a topic through a set of sequential questionnaires. Participants provide their opinions anonymously while receiving others' responses after each set of questions. Design safety review: This method conducts a structured review of design plans, specifications, and safety-related factors using safety specifications and performance standards to identify hazards and failure modes. Failure mode and effects analysis: This qualitative or semiquantitative method systematically lists the failure modes, their effects, existing safeguards, and any additional controls that are needed to reduce risk to an acceptable level. Hazard identification study: This structured, qualitative method uses guidewords or checklists to identify potential hazards, causes, and potential consequences. See Table 7.2.

Chapter 8

1. Explain the purpose of risk analysis and the elements that are involved.

    A. Risk analysis is a process to comprehend the nature of risk and to determine the level of risk. Risk analysis provides the basis for risk evaluation and decisions about risk treatment. It assesses the likelihood and consequences of a risk to provide the basis for risk evaluation and risk treatment decision-making.

2. Describe the differences between the terms *hazard, risk, hazard analysis, risk analysis,* and *risk assessment*. List the steps in a hazard analysis, steps in a risk analysis, and steps in a risk assessment.

    A. A hazard is considered a source of risk. Risks are derived from risk sources such as hazards and operational aspects, which are considered pure risks that can only produce negative consequences. Hazard analysis is considered the fundamental process of determining if a hazard or failure can lead to an incident or undesired event. Hazard analysis involves analyzing the identified hazards, their existing controls, and potential exposures. As a result, the analysis produces a range of possible consequences and severity estimates. Risk analysis is the process to comprehend the nature of risk and to determine the level of risk. In a risk analysis, a consequence is selected to determine how the event could occur and estimate its severity (S), likelihood (L), and risk level (R). A risk analysis allows for the ranking and prioritizing of risks, using risk level estimations. Risk assessment is the sequential process of identifying, analyzing, and evaluating risk. It goes beyond a risk analysis by including an evaluation or judgement of risk acceptability. A comparison of the estimated risk level with the established risk criteria is performed to determine whether the risk level is acceptable or if actions are needed to reduce the risk to an acceptable level.

3. Identify and describe five methods used in hazard analysis.

   A. Bow tie analysis: This barrier-type analysis uses a visual diagram to describe and analyze risk pathways of hazards, their causes, preventive controls, the hazardous event, mitigating controls, and consequences. Causal mapping: A network diagram represents the events, causes, effects and their relationships. What-if analysis, What-if checklist, Structured What-if technique: These team-based processes use a structured, predetermined list of "what if" questions to identify deviations and analyze hazards of a system or process. See Table 8.1.

4. Identify and describe five methods used in risk analysis.

   A. Business impact analysis: - This is an analysis of the critical functions of an organization and the resources needed to maintain them in the event of a disruption or change. Event tree analysis: - This analysis models the possible outcomes from a given initiating event and the status of controls, thus analyzing the frequency or probability of the various possible outcomes. Failure mode and effect analysis (FMEA): This is a qualitative or semiquantitative method that systematically lists the failure modes, their effects, existing safeguards, and any additional controls that are needed to reduce risk to an acceptable level. Fault tree analysis: This deductive technique starts with an undesired event (top event), determines the ways in which it could occur, and uses a logical tree diagram. Hazard analysis and critical control points (HACCP): This is a systematic and preventive system for hazard identification and placement of controls at critical points in a process to effectively prevent hazards from occurring. It is used in processes related to in food safety. Hazard and operability study (HAZOP): - This qualitative method is used to identify hazards and operability problems by using "guide words" to prompt team members in identifying deviations that can lead to the failures. See Table 8.2.

5. List and describe the three elements that must be analyzed in risk analysis.

   A. (1) Severity of consequences: The potential impact and magnitude of the impact on the organization's objectives and assets must be identified and analyzed. (2) Likelihood of occurrence: Likelihood (sometimes referred to as probability) can refer to a specific event or consequence and must be clearly defined as part of the context of the assessment. (3) Risk level: The third element is the resulting estimated risk level.

6. Describe the difference between a traditional what-if analysis and a structured what-if risk assessment.

   A. A traditional What-if analysis does not include risk estimations and only analyzes the hazards, while a structured What-if risk assessment (SWIFRA) includes risk estimation and evaluation which is considered a risk assessment.

7. Explain the concept of risk summation.

   A. The potential effect of combined or whole-system risks is often greater than any single risk in a system. An important concept in risk assessment is understanding whole-system risk, the combined or synergistic effects of multiple risk sources. An example of such an effect might be found in the meat processing industry, where cold temperatures combined with vibration of workers' hands and arms from pneumatic hand tools increase the risk of soft-tissue damage.

Chapter 9

1. What are the primary reasons for evaluating risk? Why is the risk evaluation step important?

   A. The purpose of risk evaluation is to support decisions by comparing the results of the risk analysis with the established risk criteria to determine where additional action is required. As a result, the organization may decide to take no action, consider treatment options, conduct further analysis, maintain existing treatments, or reconsider the objectives. Risk evaluation is used to determine a risk's acceptability to the organization. Without judging the acceptability or tolerance of a particular risk, the organization could make no decision to prioritize or act upon risks.

2. Identify and explain several key elements that must be developed by the organization up front when establishing the context used in risk evaluation.

   A. The risk criteria and decision-making factors that are used in evaluating risk should be developed up front as part of the context of the risk assessment. The established risk criteria are used to make two fundamental decisions in risk evaluation: the significance of risk and the prioritization of risks.

3. What role does risk evaluation play in terms of decision making and risk treatment?

   A. The decision made in the risk-based decision making (RBDM) process is conducted in risk evaluation and risk treatment phases of the risk assessment. Risk evaluation uses the established risk criteria to determine whether the risk is acceptable or if risk reduction is required, and the priority level for action.

4. Describe what is meant by "risk significance," and list five elements that it is based on.

   A. Risk significance is based on the severity and likelihood of occurrence and is generally expressed in a risk matrix. Other factors in determining risk significance include potential worst credible consequences, effectiveness of existing controls, stakeholders' views and perceptions, the cost and practicability of treatments, and interactions between risks.

5. Risk-based decision making (RBDM) takes into consideration five key questions that must be answered in the process. What are these five questions?

   A. RBDM takes into consideration the following key questions about risk concerning the decision to be made: (1) what can go wrong, (2) the severity of the potential outcome, (3) the likelihood that the risk will occur, (4) the acceptability of the risk, and (5) the need for risk reduction.

6. List and describe five methods used in evaluating risk.

   A. Consequence likelihood matrix: This method compares individual risks by selecting a consequence-likelihood pair and displaying them on a matrix with the consequence on one axis and the likelihood on the other. F/N diagrams: This is a special case of a quantitative consequence likelihood graph applied to the consideration of the tolerability of risk to human life. Cause and consequence analysis: This is a combination of fault and event tree analysis that allows inclusion of time delays. Both the causes and consequences of an initiating event are considered. Risk indices: Risk indices are used in rating the significance of risks based on numerical ratings applied to factors that are believed to influence the magnitude of the risk. Risk heat maps: A risk heat map is a two-dimensional map used to plot and present the results of risk assessments to visually communicate risk to decision makers. See Table 9.1.

7. Describe the concept of ALARP.

   A. ALARP, as low as reasonably practicable, is the concept of achieving a risk level that can be lowered further only by increasing resource expenditure disproportionately in relation to the resulting decrease in risk. The concept of ALARP establishes risk level boundaries between unacceptable, ALARP, and broadly acceptable regions. The middle category can be further divided into subcategories where certain actions are required, such as cost-benefit analysis for lower risks and required risk reduction for higher risks as illustrated in Figure 9.10.

Chapter 10

1. Define the terms *risk treatment* and *risk control*. List and describe the seven risk treatment options.

   A. Risk treatment is defined as the "process to modify risk" (ISO Guide 73/ANSI/ASSP Z690.1, 2011) and may include different or multiple strategies. The term "risk control" is often used in the insurance industry and occupational safety and health (OSH) profession. "Control" is defined by ISO 31000 as a "measure that maintains and/or modifies risk." "Avoid" means deciding not to engage in an activity. "Pursue" means deciding to engage in an opportunity. "Eliminate" means to remove existing risk. "Reduce" means to take actions that will lessen the likelihood or severity of a risk. "Transfer" means taking steps to remove potential effects of a risk through insurance or contractual agreements. "Share" means to divide the risk among parties. "Retain" means to accept the risk and/or self-fund any insurance.

2. Identify and describe four different terms used in risk reduction.

   A. Prevention is the act of keeping something from occurring that would otherwise cause risk or harm (reducing the likelihood of occurrence). Mitigation is the act of reducing the severity of something, thus making a condition or consequence less severe (reducing the severity of consequences). Protection is the act of shielding, covering, or keeping an asset from harm. Control is the act of managing risk by reducing the likelihood of its occurrence and the severity of its impact.

3. Identify and describe the options used in risk transfer.

    A. Unacceptable risks that cannot be avoided, eliminated, or reduced through risk control measures may be transferred to third parties through insurance, noninsurance contracts, or hedging. Insurance is a form of risk transfer that transfers the potential financial consequences of certain specified events from the covered (or insured) party to the insurer. Contractual risk transfer is an agreement between the risk owner and a third party to transfer financial or legal responsibilities associated with specified activities, events, injuries, or damages. Hedging is often used to reduce the risk of adverse price variability of an investment and requires making a second investment that offsets the potential consequences or losses of the original investment.

4. Explain how the hierarchy of risk treatment is used in selecting risk treatments. Identify and describe the three strategy groups in the hierarchy.

    A. The selection of risk treatments and controls should be made in accordance with the concept of the hierarchy of risk controls. The concept is based on the ranking of control strategies for risk reduction from the most effective and reliable to the least. The hierarchy of risk control models includes three areas: design-level controls, engineering controls, and administrative controls. Design/redesign-level risk control strategies are the only risk treatments that are long-lasting and typically do not degrade over time. When hazards are avoided, eliminated, or replaced with less hazardous elements through design, the risk level will not change unless the design feature is changed. Engineering controls are less resilient and can be circumvented. Such controls can degrade, wear out, or lose effectiveness or reliability over time due to lack of maintenance or damage. These types of controls also require ongoing inspection, testing, maintenance, and repair. Administrative controls are the least effective and least reliable, since they degrade more quickly due to variations in the quality of training, application, and management, as well as organizational influences and human fallibility. Administrative controls, including procedural, training, and personal protective equipment, are considered the last resort in the hierarchy.

5. Describe what a risk treatment plan is and why is it important.

    A. As a result of the risk assessment, plans are made for treating the risk. Such plans can involve a single treatment or control; however, it is more likely that multiple risk treatment measures will be required to manage risk and reduce it to an acceptable level. The plan should also specify the sequence and order in which various risk treatments are to be integrated and implemented. As outlined in ISO 31000, risk treatment plans should include information regarding proposed actions and their timeline for implementation, the rationale and justification for risk treatment selections, benefits to stakeholders, responsibilities and accountabilities for their implementation, performance metrics, and procedures for monitoring and communicating results.

6. Describe the concept of residual risk. Identify and describe the various stages of risk in the risk continuum.

   A. Residual risk is the risk remaining after risk treatment. It is also known as retained risk (ISO Guide 73, 2009) and can contain unidentified or unknown risks as well. The concept of residual or remaining risk is important to understand when managing risks both internally and externally. New risks are created from new risk sources introduced into the system and can also develop and emerge from new technologies, activities, or expansions into different areas that require scanning, detecting, and monitoring. Inherent risk is described "as the risk to an entity apart from any action to alter either the likelihood or impact of the risk." Initial risk is defined as "the first assessment of the potential risk of an identified hazard. Initial risk establishes a fixed baseline for the hazard." Residual risk is the risk level that remains after applying the selected risk treatments from the initial risk assessment. A secondary risk is a risk that arises as the result of implementing a risk treatment or control measure. Future state risk is the estimated risk level expected from the application of prescribed risk controls.

7. Identify and describe four methods used to select risk treatment.

   A. Hierarchy of controls: In hierarchy of controls, control strategies are stratified according to their effectiveness and reliability in a top-down fashion. This is commonly represented in a table or pyramid graphic. Cost/benefit analysis: A cost-benefit analysis weighs the total expected costs of options in monetary terms against their total expected benefits in order to choose the most effective or the most profitable option. It can be qualitative or quantitative or may involve a combination of quantitative and qualitative elements, and it can be applied at any level of an organization. Multi-criteria analysis (MCA): MCA uses a range of criteria to transparently evaluate and compare the overall performance of a set of options. In general, the goal is to produce an order of preference for a set of options. Business impact analysis (BIA): This is a systematic method used to determine and evaluate potential effects of an interruption to critical business operations as a result of a disaster, emergency, or serious incident. See Table 10.1

Chapter 11

1. Identify the three process steps that follow risk treatment in the ISO 31000 risk management process. Briefly describe each of these three steps.

    A. In the ISO 31000 risk management process (shown in Figure 11.1), there are three components that surround the risk assessment and treatment process: (1) monitoring and review, (2) recording and reporting, and (3) communication and consultation. These components are the "check points" in the Plan-Do-Check-Act continual improvement model, and the key input to "communication and consultation" in the risk management process. The purpose of monitoring and review is to assure and improve the quality and effectiveness of process design, implementation, and outcomes. ISO 31000 indicates that recording and reporting should communicate related actions and outcomes across the organization and provide appropriate information to decision makers. Communicating and consulting should occur throughout the risk management process.

2. Compare the similarities of the risk management process to the Plan-Do-Check-Act continual improvement process cycle.

    A. One of the guiding principles of risk management found in ISO 31000 is continual improvement. Continual improvement is achieved through learning and experience using a Plan-Do-Check-Act (PDCA) cycle approach. Management systems, such as ISO 45001 and ANSI Z10, are also built upon a PDCA cycle as shown in Figure 11.2. The checking and communicating function of PDCA should be applied throughout the risk management process and used to validate and verify outcomes; identify deviations, changes, or gaps; and track and measure performance.

3. Explain the differences between monitoring and reviewing.

    A. Monitoring is defined by ANSI/ASIS/RIMS RA.1 as "ongoing scrutiny, oversight, evaluation of situational awareness, for determining the current status and to identify changes in the internal and external environment as well as performance." In ISO Guide 73, it is defined as "continual checking, supervising, critically observing or determining the status in order to identify change from the performance level required or expected"

(ISO Guide 73/ANSI/ASSP Z690.1, 2011). It is an active process used to understand the current performance or output of a system. Risk review is defined by ANSI RA.1 as an "activity undertaken to determine the suitability, adequacy and effectiveness of the management system and its component elements to achieve established objectives." It is also defined by ISO Guide 73 as an "activity undertaken to determine the suitability, adequacy and effectiveness of the subject matter to achieve established objectives" (ISO Guide 73/ANSI/ASSP Z690.1, 2011). Like risk evaluation, the process of risk review is used to determine if the current performance is acceptable in terms of the context and the objectives.

4. Describe what is meant by a key performance indicator (KPI). Provide five examples of KPI.

    A. Key performance measures or key performance indicators (KPI) are a set of specific, quantifiable measures that an organization tracks to gauge performance over time. Such metrics are used to determine progress in achieving strategic and operational goals and to benchmark an organization's position or performance in comparison to baselines, internally or externally. Qualitative or subjective measures include items such as signal words and descriptions. Quantitative or objective measures include items such as percentages, numbers, and ratios. Often qualitative and quantitative indicators are used together to provide a more holistic picture of performance. Input-based or action measures that are designed to achieve a desired outcome are sometimes called leading indicators. Input-based measures are activity-oriented measures that signal a change in performance. Input-based measures indicate improvement in the process and detect changes that require adjustment. Examples of input or action based KPIs include quarterly evaluation of the assessment process, the number of process improvements completed per month, the number of stakeholders trained in risk assessment (trained risk assessors) per quarter, or the number of emerging risks identified prior to any incidents in a year. Output-based or result measures that produce numbers indicating the level of success are sometimes referred to as lagging indicators. Out-based measures are used to analyze events (successes or failures) and results or trends to determine if the process is effective. Examples of result KPIs include the number of near-miss incidents per quarter, the number of corrective actions successfully completed, the average number of days to complete corrective actions, and incident rate numbers. Process measures are used in measuring and evaluating a process's efficiency or productivity.

5. Describe what is meant by a key risk indicator (KRI). Provide examples of KRIs.

    A. KRIs are risk measures that provide indications of the detection and identification of new emerging or developing risks. Performance indicators provide insights into known risks, while key risk indicators (KRIs) provide an early warning of emerging risks that have reached a threshold of concern. KRIs are used to develop strategies to identify and manage new risks and can be identified through analyses methods such as root cause analysis and causal factors analysis of previous incidents. In addition, outside sources such as industry trends or developments, technology and research, economic indicators, and competitor actions can be helpful in developing KRIs. Examples might include: time between failures; recovery time after failure; detection and warning level of failure; percentage of system affected by failure; percentage of population exposed.

6. Explain the differences between verifying and validating.

    A. Verification involves checking that the analysis was done correctly. Validation involves checking that the right analysis was done to achieve the required objectives.

7. Identify several key factors to consider when designing risk reporting systems.

    A. In the design of risk reporting systems, several key factors should be considered. First, it is critical to define the audience and their needs. Internal decision makers and stakeholders will require specific risk-based information presented in a way that is useful to them. Dashboards, risk matrices, heat maps, and key performance metrics are helpful in communicating risk performance at a glance and may be most useful to the organization's senior management and decision makers. Striped bow tie diagrams can be useful in presenting more complex risk scenarios.

8. List and briefly describe five methods used to monitor and report risk.

    A. Risk matrix: A risk matrix compares individual risks by selecting a consequence likelihood pair and displaying them on a matrix with the consequence on one axis and the likelihood on the other. Risk register: This is a means of recording information about risks and tracking actions. S curve: This is a means of displaying the relationship between consequences and their likelihood plotted as a cumulative distribution function (S curve). Key performance indicators (KPIs): KPIs are considered business metrics used to assess critical performance aspects that help an organization assess progress towards declared goals. Key risk indicators (KRIs): KRIs are measures that tend to predict changes in risks or the development of new emerging risks. See Table 11.1.

Chapter 12

1. Describe why communication and consultation are important in the management of risk.

    A. Without effective communication, risk assessment does not enable an organization to achieve its objectives successfully. Risk communication and consultation are required to understand and reduce uncertainty and ultimately manage risks. Through consistent and effective risk communications, decision makers are kept better informed and will be more confident when they make decisions.

2. Identify key design criteria for effective communication systems.

    A. Key design criteria for communication systems include the following: clearly define responsibilities and accountabilities; determine and establish internal and external contexts; identify and capture relevant data; verity the accuracy of the data; refine data and provide appropriate and meaningful information; deliver needed information on a timely basis; maintain appropriate confidentiality; ensure exchange of information through stakeholder feedback; and monitor feedback and remove communication barriers. See Figure 12.2.

3. Identify and describe the four risk information categories.

    A. (1) Nature of risk: This provides an understanding of the risk. (2) Uncertainties: This provides information concerning known unknowns and unpredictable elements, (3) Risk management options: The choices within the risk management framework are identified. (4) Benefits: The potential or expected benefits and their costs are identified. See Figure 12.3.

4. For each risk information category, list and describe five examples of each.

    A. (1) Nature of risk: Items to consider include characteristics, consequences, and likelihood of the risks; whether they are increasing or decreasing; their distribution; and the risk of exposure, (2) Uncertainties; Items to consider include methods, type of uncertainty, criticality, weaknesses of data, assumptions, and sensitivities. (3) Risk management options: Topics to cover include treatments, justification, effectiveness, benefits, costs, and remaining risk. (4) Benefits: These may include actuarial or expected, financial, nonfinancial, who benefits, magnitude, total benefits. See Figure 12.3.

Index

Note: In this index, the letter "t" at the end of a page number indicates that the topic is presented in a table, and the letter "f" indicates that it is presented in a figure.

A

absolute risk *see* pure risk
acceptable risk 26
    ALARP and 183
    defined 74
    dynamic nature of 183
    organization and 184
    risk assessment methods and 75–76
    risk assessment planning and 74–75
    risk criteria selection and 77–78
Age of Exploration (and insurance) 30–31
ALARP (as low as reasonably practicable) 64, 74–75, 247, 248
    defined 74
    example 76f
    model 163f
    risk evaluation and 155, 157, 159t, 162–64, 247f
    risk treatment 181, 182f, 183–84

ANSI/ASIS/RIMS RA.1, *Risk Assessment* 48
    risk identification 116–17
ANSI/ASSP/ISO 45001-2018 13
ANSI/ASSP Z590.3, *Prevention through Design* 48 *see also* prevention through design
    hazard/risk identification 117
    life cycle focus 117
ANSI/ASSP Z690.1-2011 3, 38
ASSP TR-31010 *Risk Management—Techniques for Safety Practitioners* 48
    risk continuum 116
Arnauld 32

B

Bernoulli, Jacob 32
Bernstein, Peter 30, 33
black swan events 20
bow tie analysis 90t, 93t, 96t, 136t, 182, 208t

C

Cardano, Gerolamo 32
case studies
    auto supply company 257–61
    chemical release 239–51
    drilling rig site forklift 232–38
    metal dust explosion 255–56
    petroleum tank fires 254
cascading events 20
central limit theorem 33
chance (concept of) 31
checklists 128
    limitations of 128
Columbia (space shuttle) 212–13
consequence 24
context 59–61
    risk assessment 61–63
    risk management 61
control (of risk) 25
    definition 168
CSB *see* U.S. Chemical Safety and Hazard Investigation Board
cumulative risk 20

D

data analysis 102–3
    critical elements 102
    information management and 102
decision models 101–11
    definition 103
    development steps 103–4
    influence diagram 104f
    influence factors 104
    information management and 103–4
    Pareto analysis 105, 108–10
    scenario analysis 105, 108
    sensitivity analysis 105, 106–7
    software models 106
    testing and validating 104–6

Deming, W. Edwards 13, 196
Dionne, Georges 33
diversification 31, 33
dust explosion pentagon 256f

E

emerging risk 7–8, 186
    decisions 119f
    defined 118
    risk identification and 118
enterprise risk management (ERM) 4, 12, 13, 33–34, 57, 114 *see also* risk management
    iterative method 13
    standards and 13
Environmental Protection Agency 137–38
event 24
existing controls 122–23
    multiple controls 123
    verification during risk analysis 123

F

failure modes 55, 123–24
    definition 123
    example 123–24
fatal and serious incidents 231–32
    example 232–40
    numbers of 234f
Fermat, Pierre de 32
Fibonacci *see* Pisano, Leonardo
financial risk 4 *see also* risk quadrant
fire triangle 256f
Franklin, Benjamin (fire insurance) 32
future state risk 10, 11, 188, 197

G

Great Fire of London (1666) 32

H

Hamilton, Gustav 33
hazard 29, 67
    analysis 131, 134–35, 238 *see also* process hazard analysis
    analysis methods 135, 136–37t
    converting hazard analysis to risk assessment 147–48
    definition 134
    list of 120–21t
    origin of term 29
    relationship to risk 134f
hazard risk 4, 252 *see also* risk quadrant
Health and Safety Executive (UK) 38
hierarchy of controls 26
hierarchy of risk treatment 26
Hindu-Arabic numerals (introduction of) 31

I

information management 101–11
    data analysis 102–3
    data sources 102
    data gathering methods 102
    decision models 103–4
    determining required information 101
inherent risk 7, 8–9, 186
initial risk 9, 186
insurance 33, 172–73
    origin of 30–31
ISO 31000 2, 38
    communication 212
    continual improvement 40, 194
    control 168
    core purpose or risk management 39
    definition of risk 4
    design 45–46
    framework 43–44
    integration 44–45
    iterative process of risk management 40
    leadership (and commitment) 43–44
    practice 168
    policy 168
    principles 40–42
    process 46, 168
    relationship between parts 41f
    revision in 2018 38–39
    risk analysis 132
    risk assessment context 60f
    risk assessment methods and 83–84
    risk assessment planning 59, 66
    risk evaluation 153
    risk evaluation methods 157
    risk identification 113, 114–15, 125f,
    risk management 37, 39, 42f, 194f
    risk management standards 38–40
    risk monitoring 193
    SWIFT analysis 242
ISO 31010 38 *see also* ASSP TR-31010
    core purpose of risk management 39
    principles of risk management 39
    severity of consequences and 145
    risk assessment techniques 92t,
    risk identification 115–16

K

knowable unknowns 18–19

L

Laplace, Pierre-Simon 32
law of large numbers 32
layers of control analysis 252–53
    case study 254–57

chemical processing 252
definition 252
model 253f
Lloyd's of London 30, 32
Lowrance, William W. 183

M
Markowitz, Harry 33
Monte de Paschi (bank) 31

O
occupational health and safety (OHS) 14–15
    differing views on risk 15
    standards 14
Occupational Safety and Health Administration (OSHA) 137–38
    RAGAGEP and 184
operational risk 4, 5, 7, 221, 52 *see also* risk quadrant
opportunity risk *see* speculative risk

P
Pareto, Vilfredo 108
Pareto analysis 105, 257
    as bottom-up approach 108
    development steps 109–10
    examples 109t, 110f, 111t, 112f, 224f
    graphical representation 109
    possible limitations 105
    steps in 223–24
Pascal, Blaise 31
Pisano, Leonardo 31
plan-do-check-act (PDCA) process 13, 14f, 193–96
    model 195f
Poisson, S. D. 32
practical applications of risk management 221–65
    case study 232–38, 239–51, 257–61
    CSB 239–40
    EMR (experience modifier rate) 261
    radar/spider charts 225–26
    risk analysis 238–46
    risk evaluation 246–48
    risk identification 230–37
    risk management process 222f
    risk monitoring 257–62
    risk reporting 262–64
    risk treatment 248–57
    sensitivity analysis 257–61
    SWIFRA model 246, 248
    SWOT analysis 226–30
    what-if analysis 241–42
prevention through design (PtD) 49–57, 253
    acceptable risk level 51
    alignment with ISO 31000 54f
    analysis parameters 55
    assessment methods 57
    components of 51
    design reviews 52–53
    documentation 56
    failure modes 55
    follow up 56
    hazard analysis 53, 55
    hierarchy of controls 50f
    initial risk 56
    integration into management 50–51
    management role in 53–54
    operational stage 50
    post-incident stage 50
    post-operational stage 50
    pre-operational stage 50
    primary goals 49
    probability analysis 55

residual risk 56
risk acceptance 56
risk assessment matrix 54
risk identification 117–18
risk reduction 56
severity analysis 55
stakeholder input 51
standards 25, 48
supplier relationship 42
probability theory (development) 31–32
process hazard analysis 137
    applicable areas 138
    EPA and 138
    OSHA requirements 137–38
    success factors
Prouty, Richard 175
Prouty approach (risk treatment) 175–76
    model 175f
pure risk 3, 8, 24, 114, 119, 134, 169, 170, 174, 176, 184, 267

Q

qualitative/semi-quantitative risk assessment 243–45
    example 243f, 245f
    scoring action example 244t
    severity descriptions 244t
quantitative risk assessment 243t

R

RACI (responsible, accountable, consulted, informed) 205–8
    assignment matrix 207f
    chart 206f
    example 206f, 207f
radar/spider charts 225–26
    anatomy of 226f
    example 226f

RAGAGEP (recognized and generally accepted good engineering practice) 184–85
Reason, James 253 *see also* Swiss cheese model
residual risk 9–10, 26, 185–86, 187, 219
risk 29 *see also* pure risk, speculative risk
    cascading effect 5, 6f
    components of 154f
    definition 1, 2–3, 134
    development 9f
    dynamic nature 7, 10
    earliest mathematical definition 32
    effects on organization 1
    interdependency 12
    origin of term 29–30
    positive returns from 33
    relation to uncertainty and objectives 18f
    synergistic effects 12
    terminology 22–23
    timeline 34f
risk analysis 25, 131–51, 238–46
    cascading effect of consequences 145f
    compared to hazard analysis/risk assessment 239f
    definition 132–32, 135
    elements of 133f
    example 144
    fundamental terms 133–34
    hazard analysis in 135
    interactions and dependencies 147
    likelihood 147
    methods 142–44t
    multiple consequences 146
    percentages 147
    purpose of 132
    qualitative descriptors 147

risk identification and 132
risk management process and 132f
structured what-if analysis 242
understanding consequences 144
what-if analysis 241–42
whole-system risk 150
risk assessment 25, 46–48, 238
    codes 70
    communication and 211
    compared to hazard and risk analysis 53
    definition 135
    example 71t
    improved decision making 19
    legal requirement in UK 137
    steps 46
risk assessment methods 83–98
    risk identification 230–37
    selection criteria 83–84
    selection process steps 84–86
    stakeholders and 84
    trending analysis tool 231–32
    modified what-if 256
risk assessment planning 59–80
    acceptable level of risk 74–79
    context 59–61, 63, 222–30
    example 64–65
    external context 66
    human factors 67
    internal context 66–67
    need for information 64
    mission 65
    objectives 63–66
    organizational factors 67
    purpose 63–66
    risk matrices 79
    risk scoring systems 69–74
    scope 63–66
    selecting methods 75–76
    SMART information 64
    social factors 67
    SWOT analysis 226–30
risk avoidance 25
risk-based auditing 198
    risk continuum model 196f
risk-based decision-making (RBDM) 15–17, 61–63, 153
    context 62f
    definition 156
    model 156f, 157
    process steps 16f, 16–17, 62–63, 156
risk characterization 69–70
    qualitative models 69–70
    risk scoring systems and 69–70
    semi-qualitative models 70
risk communication 211–20, 264–66
    annual and quarterly reports 266
    benefits of treating risk 219
    dangers of inadequate 266
    definition 212, 264
    disasters 264–65
    examples of breakdown 213–14
    improving 214–15
    information categories 215
    key practices 265t
    methods 266t
    nature of risk 216–17
    need for 211, 212–13
    process 214
    purpose 212, 215
    risk management process 213f
    risk management options 218–19
    standards 214
    system design criteria 215f
    uncertainties 217–18
risk continuum 6, 8f, 187f
risk criteria 77, 96t
    action guidelines 74
    determining 68

definition 67
list of 68
organizational values and 68
risk factor levels 72–73
risk levels 74
risk scoring mechanism 73
risk scoring tools 74
selection process 77
risk drivers 3
    definition 24, 122
    example 122
risk exposure 24
    defined 122
risk evaluation 25, 153–66
    heat maps 159–62
    factors for 155
    in risk management process 158f
    methods *see* risk evaluation methods
    prioritizing risk, 155–56
    purpose of 153, 154
    risk analysis as input 153
    risk levels and 155, 247–48
    risk matrix 159–62
    significance of risk 154–55
    stakeholders' role 157
    unacceptable risk levels 247–48
risk evaluation methods 157, 158–59t
    see also risk indices
    ALARP 162–64
    opportunity threat matrix, 162f
    risk frontier graph 162, 163f
    SFAIRP 162–64
    value at risk 164
risk factors 67, 78
    listed 71–72
    risk scoring systems and 70–72
    time duration 72
risk heat map 75f, 160–62
    example 161f

risk identification 25, 113–29
    as part of risk assessment process 113
    causes or triggers 124
    conducting 128–29
    definition 113
    emerging risks 118
    existing controls 122–23
    methods 125–28
    range of consequences 124–25
    risk exposure 122
    risk management standards and 114–18
    risk sources 119–21
    scope of 113–14, 118–19
    steps of 128–29
risk indices 164
    example 164, 165t
risk management 24–25
    as dividing line between ancient and modern worlds 33
    balance 4
    circle 33
    communication and consultation 40
    components of 37
    definition 61
    framework in organization 39
    integration of 12–13
    monitoring and review 40
    objectives 37, 38f
    organizational commitment 37
    practical applications *see* practical applications of risk management
    process 47f, 222f
    purpose of 1
    standards 14–15, 38–40
    strategic goals 4

risk management methods 86–91
    applicability of 92–97t
    checklist method 87
    combining 98
    comparison of 88–91t
    customizing 98
    need for multiple methods 91
    risk assessment matrix 87
    selection criteria 92, 97t
    what-if analysis 87
risk matrix 159–62
    construction 159
    example 160f
    probability levels 161f
    severity categories 160f
risk monitoring 193–209 *see also* RACI
    continual feedback 193
    definition 197
    documentation 203–4
    example 200
    emerging risks 196–97
    future state risks 197
    key performance indicators 198–99
    key risk indicators 201
    methods 208t
    process 198
    risk hierarchy 205f
    risk performance measurement 200–201, 202f
    risk profile 203–4
    risk register 203, 204f
    risk reporting 204
    sparkline charts 199–200
    verification 202–3
risk pathway 3f, 24
risk quadrant 4, 5f, 267
risk reduction percentage (RR%) 10
    definition 11
risk reporting *see* risk communication

risk review 197–98 *see also* risk monitoring
risk scoring systems 69–74, 78
    characteristics 69
    formulas for 73
    purpose 69
    risk characterization 69
    risk factors 70–72
risk source 2–3, 23–24
    definition 114, 119
    hazards and 119
risk summation 150–51
risk treatment 10–11, 25 167–90 *see also* risk management
    administrative controls 176, 180
    additional controls 250f
    as primary purpose of risk assessment 167
    avoiding risk 168–69
    barrier analysis 182
    combinations 175f
    contracts 173
    continuum of 186
    cost-benefit analysis 169
    decision tree 181f
    definition 167, 168
    design-level controls 176–78
    eliminating risk 170
    engineering controls 176, 178–79
    escalation factor 172
    examples of 169, 170, 173, 177, 178, 179
    hedging 173
    hierarchy model 177f, 249f
    hierarchy of controls 180, 248, 249f
    inherently safer design 184
    insurance 172–73
    layering treatments 181–83, 184
    layers of protection analysis (LOPA) 182

options 168f
plans 18485
purpose of 167
pursuing risk 169
reducing risk 170, 171f
risk control 171
risk elimination 177
risk minimization 178
risk management process and 188
risk mitigation 171
risk prevention 170–71
risk protection 171
risk sharing 173–74
risk simplification 178
risk substitution 177
risk transfer 172–73
selection methods 189–90t
unwanted consequences 11
warnings and awareness controls 179
risk trigger 24

S
safety through design *see* prevention through design
scenario analysis 23t, 105
    developing 108
    requirements for 108
secondary risk 11, 187–88
sensitivity analysis 106–8,
    applicable areas 106
    branching analysis 259f
    cost projection 258t
    example 107–8, 257–61
    financial 106
    "what-if" question 106
SFAIRP (so far as is reasonably practicable) 162–64 *see also* ALARP
Shewart, Walter 13

SMART information (specific, measurable, attainable, relevant, and time-sensitive) in risk assessment planning 64
speculative risk 3, 4, 5f, 7, 114, 134, 186, 267
strategic risk 4, 5 *see also* risk quadrant
striped bow tie analysis 144t, 146, 204
    example 145f
    SWIFRA (structured what-if risk assessment) 147–50
    example 148, 150, 250f
    questioning process 148
    similarity to 5 why model
    steps in 246
    worksheet example 149f
SWIFT (structured what-if technique) 242
Swiss cheese model 253, 254f
SWOT (strengths, weaknesses, opportunities, threats) analysis 226–30
    applications 227–28
    category ratings 228f
    example 228–29, 230f
    matrix 228f
    opportunities 227
    presentation 228
    radar chart 230f
    strengths 226
    threats 227
    weaknesses 226–7

T
Taleb, Nassem Nicholas 20 *see also* black swan events
The Institutes (American Institutes for Chartered Property Casualty Underwriters) 4 *see also* risk quadrant

trending analysis tool 231–32
    barrier analysis 234
    causal factor tree diagram 236–37
    change analysis 235–36
    case study 232–38
    example 231f
    5 why analysis 236
    incident map 233–34

U

uncertainty 17–18, 26 *see also* knowable unknowns, unknowable unknowns
    aleatoric 17, 19
    decision 17
    epistemic 17, 18
    factor in risk analysis 21–22
    increasing level of 19
    linguistic 17
    quality of information 18
    strategies for reducing 21t, 22, 23t
underwriting 30–31

unknowable unknowns 19
U.S. Chemical Safety and Hazard Investigation Board (CSB) 239–40, 254, 255

V

verification 202

W

what-if analysis 139
    communication and documentation 141
    context in 140
    cross-functional teams 139, 140
    example 141f
    information gathering 140
    process steps 139–41
    question generation
    risk assessment 141
    variants 139

CONNECTING GREAT RESOURCES AND GREAT PEOPLE

Our exclusive online member community connects you with great resources and great people to help you grow professionally and engage with colleagues on a global scale.

Benefits of the online ASSP Community

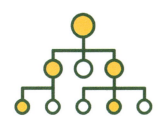

Connect and network with a vibrant **community of 39,000 OSH professionals**

Establish yourself as a **digital thought leader**

Use the community to solve problems and **exchange technical expertise**

Visit **community.assp.org** to connect today!

AMERICAN SOCIETY OF
SAFETY PROFESSIONALS

COMMUNITY